CW00547783

Reyes Calderón's
Lola MacHor Series

"No me olvides que, en los asuntos humanos, también los otros pueden tener razón: ven la misma cuestión que tú, pero desde distinto punto de vista, con otra luz, con otra sombra, con otro contorno."

Josemaría Escrivá de Balaguer

"Mírame dentro y comprender / que tus ojos son mis ojos / que tu piel es mi piel / en tu oído me alborozo / en tu sonrisa me baño / y soy parte de tu ser / que no vale la pena andar por andar / es mejor caminar pa' ir creciendo."

Chambao, "Pokito a Poko"

Reyes Calderón's Lola MacHor Series

A Conservative Feminist Approach to Modern Spain

Jeffrey Oxford

SUSSEX
ACADEMIC
PRESS
Brighton • Chicago • Toronto

2 4 6 8 10 9 7 5 3 1

First published in 2015 by
SUSSEX ACADEMIC PRESS
PO Box 139
Eastbourne BN24 9BP

and in the United States of America by
SUSSEX ACADEMIC PRESS
Independent Publishers Group
814 N. Franklin Street, Chicago, IL 60610

and in Canada by
SUSSEX ACADEMIC PRESS (CANADA)
24 Ranee Avenue, Toronto, Ontario M6A 1M6

British Library Cataloguing in Publication Data
A CIP catalogue record for this book is available from the British Library.

Library of Congress Cataloging-in-Publication Data
Oxford, Jeffrey Thomas, 1966–
Reyes Calderón's Lola Machor series : a conservative feminist approach to modern Spain / Jeffrey Oxford.
pages cm
Includes bibliographical references and index.
ISBN 978-1-84519-646-2 (hb : acid-free paper)
1. Calderón Cuadrado, Reyes—Criticism and interpretation.
2. Feminism and literature—Spain. I. Title.
PQ6703.A3954Z79 2015
863′.7—dc23

2014040631

Typeset and designed by Sussex Academic Press, Brighton & Eastbourne.
Printed by TJ International, Padstow, Cornwall.
This book is printed on acid-free paper.

Contents

Acknowledgments

I would like to express my deepest gratitude to Reyes Calderón for her willingness to accede to an interview regarding her writings, her consent in permitting me to record that interview, facilitating reprint permission of quotes from the novels, and the many special efforts she made in assuring that my visit to the Universidad de Navarra and Pamplona in 2012 would be most enjoyable. I am deeply appreciative of Isabel Méndez-Santalla's assistance in transcribing said interview with the novelist. Thanks to the many students, colleagues and friends around the world who have helped me further develop my research and thoughts both in one-on-one conversations and at conference venues in various locations. And a special note of appreciation to my wife, Raquel, for her reading of a draft of this book, her commentary and criticism . . . and her unwavering support through the years. Obviously, any errors that remain in the text are my own, and for such I apologize beforehand.

I am grateful to Editorial Difácil for granting reprint permission of several quotes from *Lágrimas de Hemingway*.

Additionally, I am extremely grateful to Antonia Kerrigan Agencia Literaria for conceding rights to reproduce several extracts of the novels in the present work.

Finally, I would like to mention my appreciation of the cover illustration of Lady Justice, courtesy of Klinko <www.klinko.com.ar>.

Reyes Calderón's Lola MacHor Series

A Conservative Feminist Approach to Modern Spain

CHAPTER ONE

Introduction: Setting the Scene

In various interviews Reyes Calderón has attempted to distance herself somewhat from the majority of the authors of the *novela negra* saying, for example in September of 2010, that "a mí no me interesa la violencia por la violencia. Me interesa comprender la condición humana, al chaval que graba la muerte de una mendiga" (Stegmeier). In another interview from the same year, she rejects the idea that her novels are "novela negra," emphasizing the importance of character development over plot: "Siempre he dicho que mis libros no son novela negra. No importa tanto quién [sic] mata o quien muere, como la vida de estos personajes" (Rubio 60). While perhaps the author is somewhat successful in distancing herself from the "ambientes marginales con dosis de crimen, sexo y violencia" (Cercas) of the traditional *novela negra*, it should be pointed out—as do various critics such as Kalen Oswald, Patricia Hart, José Colmeiro, René Craig Odders, and Joan Ramón Resina—that in many of the detective novels of contemporary Spain what stands out more than the investigation, and even more than the mystery itself, is the social commentary "expressed by the words and actions of the characters" (Oswald 11).

Malgorzata Janerka posits that "Los detectives protagonistas de las novelas policiacas muestran una desconfianza profunda respecto a la cultura, el saber y la religion, los dominios tradicionales del abuso de poder por parte de la autoridad" (116) and that "[e]n la literatura crítica, la novela policiaca suele asociarse con una denuncia social" (127). The social criticism of Reyes Calderón, however, very frequently appears so subtly in the narrative that it gives the impression of being a tacit moral to the story—something that the author has denied on several occasions. It is my argument in this book, however, that one of the principal themes of all the novels in her MacHor series is her desire that humans understand each other better and that they have more compassion one for the other. In 2010, when *El último paciente del Doctor Wilson* was published, the novelist commented to the Agencia EFE that "Estamos tan concentrados en nuestro consumo y en nuestro éxito que el de al lado es invisible. Lo vemos como instrumento y la muerte del otro cada vez nos importa menos." In and of itself, perhaps this comment would not mean much; however, in combination with what one reads in the novels, her statement takes on a more nuanced meaning. In the first novel of the series, *Las lágrimas de Hemingway*, for example, Lola previews the letter that ends up tarnishing her mentor's reputation by saying that "Sé que todos creemos tener derecho a juzgar a los demás, especialmente cuando se equivocan. Pero en realidad no somos quién para juzgar a nadie" (293). In *Los crímenes del número primo*, thinking once again of the repulsiveness of what she had seen/learned in Brothers, the gay bar, Lola admits that

> Me afectó . . . No consigo despegarme de esas imágenes, de esos recuerdos . . . Yo no soy mejor que ellos, ¿sabes? [. . .] A veces, cuando recuerdo aquellas imágenes, pienso que he tenido suerte al caer en este ambiente, contigo y los niños . . . ¿Qué hubiera sido de mí si el destino hubiera sido otro? (486)

The last words of *El Expediente Canaima* are: "el culpable lleva nombre de detergente y de político y de VIP. Y de este mundo desleal y miope que encumba a Jimenas y abandona a Marías. [. . .] ¿cuántas Marías, cuántos Parada, cuántos Herrera-Smith han de caer por cada Jimena?" (420). And in *El último paciente del Doctor Wilson*, Lola suffers a miscarriage and the subsequent psychological trama, during which she plans and almost carries out her own suicide; once cured, Lola philosophizes that "Fue una mala época . . . Y, no obstante, agradezco haber dormido en esa cueva. De no haberlo hecho, nunca habría comprendido al doctor Wilson, ni al cuerdo asesino llamado Rodrigo" (*Dr. Wilson* 352). Later, in the book's "Epitaph" the narrator states that "Hablo de ti, que crees dominar tu juicio, que te tienes por un tipo racional y razonable. [. . .] Desconoces que hay muchos yos dentro de ti [. . .] Es tu vida: la vives, la sientes, la disfrutas, la sufres. Es tuya, pero estás lejos de controlarla. No la dominas del todo. A veces, ni siquiera puedes entenderla" (481). That is, in the final analysis, all this leads the reader to the conclusion that Calderón creates books that are more than mere entertainment; as she herself indicated in an interview in October 2011: "Los libros enseñan con profunda humildad, algo muy necesario en una cultura de éxito arrogante como la nuestra. Los libros, si son buenos, te hacen mejores" (LESEG).

Be that as it may, the principal character of the novels, the judge ("examining magistrate") Lola MacHor[1] is, in certain respects a common person—if not a common Spaniard—fighting the same daily battles as millions of other Spanish women, mothers, housewives, and professional women of the 21st century. The criminal Rodrigo reprimands her for being so ordinary, telling her that "ningún juez de provecho bebe cerveza con limón" (*Dr. Wilson* 480). Moreover, even Reyes Calderón herself comments that "[y]o creo que al lector lo que le gusta es ir poniéndose en la piel de una persona normal, alguien que es juez pero que tiene que comprar leche, o ir a levantar un cadáver pensando que tiene que recoger al niño de un cumpleaños" (Stegmeier).

On the other hand, Lola MacHor is very much a woman who has broken through the glass ceiling even though she is not a typical detective of the traditional detective novel. It is abundantly clear that the author has in mind something other than a female protagonist who blindly supports or rebels against traditional masculine patriarchy or who exemplifies the feminist subversion of such. That is, I argue that Calderón's works go much beyond the easily defined ideologies of patriarchy, feminism, post-feminism, conservatism, and liberalism in an attempt to present a professional woman with a career who is much more complex than that exemplified by the *ángel del hogar/femme fatale* or the patriarchal/feminist dichotomies. The author converts the principal female character from the traditional background role—or the inverse, the fighting antagonist—into one who enters the traditional masculine arena of detective work as something more than simply just another female detective; she is an examining magistrate. But at the same time the development of Lola MacHor parallels the typical Spanish female woman of her age who has been influenced by vestiges of traditional stereotypes very much in play in Spain during the middle to later years of the 20th century.

Since it is my thesis that Lola transcends traditional patriarchal, feminist, post-feminist, conservative, and liberal values, it should be pointed out from the beginning the manner in which I am using each of these terms. "Traditional patriarchy" means an acceptance or promotion of the patriarchal hegemony in which the feminine character is relegated to some second-level, inferior plane, in which she is completely silenced, or she is merely an object of sexual desire. "Feminist" means, as Fernández Rodríguez explains, "un intento de desbaratar el sistema patriarcal y [. . .] de erigirse como signos de discontinuidad con la tradición" (124). "Post-feminist" is another type of critical framework which rejects as too restrictive the masculine-as-oppressor patriarchy and the woman-as-fighter feminism. Various critics name several basic characteristics of post-feminist ideology: nesting (the woman takes pride in her well cared for house), consumerism (the woman has a career and economic power), individualism (the woman fights for herself as an individual and not as a representative of her gender), the breakdown in dichotomy between private and public space (women bring work home from the office), and maternal violence (in particular emotional manipulation), to name only a few.

Some traces of conservatism that are apparent in the Lola MacHor series are the sacrificing love and affection that Lola has toward her husband, her acceptance and labor as a housewife, the large number of children she has, the accepted, stereotyped views of the woman's role in society, and a strong anti-abortionist belief. At the same time, Lola demonstrates a more liberal, if not anti-patriarchal, side as well: she is a judge (one of the first females to serve in the various professional roles she has throughout the novels); she works outside of the house; she is a doubting-believer or a believing-doubter (she cannot decide which); she has problems with the Church and the clergy who allow themselves special favors, and she never takes on or accepts as her own her husband's last name. Additionally, she believes in the rights of the criminals and the accused, but she laments that there is no justice for the average person. Those psychological conflicts of Lola are also seen in the opinion of the Spanish population: According to the 2009 Eurobarometer survey, only 40% of Spaniards have confidence in the judicial system and only 2% name religion as one of the most important values of their life (European Commission 150).

In spite of possessing a well-developed personality, demonstrating a variety of emotions, and representing in various ways a verisimilar person, Lola remains quite static chronologically.[2] Her age does not correspond to the years that transpire in the novels; that is, throughout the five novels she ages only nine years while those represented in the works are at least twenty.[3] In *El último paciente del Doctor Wilson*, for example, Lola says that "Cuando conocí a Juan Iturri, de eso hace más de diez años" (178). The exact year of this initial encounter is not known with precision, but those "hace más de diez años" when they met are detailed in the first novel of the series, *Las lágrimas de Hemingway*, when Lola is forty-one years old. In the fourth novel, *El último paciente del Doctor Wilson*, Lola says that she is "más cerca de los cincuenta que de los cuarenta" (14), while her gynecologist—and the doctor being a male reiterates the lack of only an overt feminist agenda in the novel—says that she is "cuarenta y siete años cumplidos (si mis datos son correctos)" (35), and the events of the fifth novel, *La venganza*, occur two years following.

It is evident, then, that these dates and years in the five novels are not completely veridical. In the restaurant in the Pamplona hotel, Lola learns something about Lentejillo, the toreador, who "se había confirmado en Las Ventas en el año 1999" (*Hemingway* 133), thereby confirming through the use of the past perfect verb tense that the events of the novel had already occurred after the year mentioned. Later, Lola tells the reader that she is going to detail more regarding the investigation into Alejandro's death and "aquellos hechos que fingieron empezar un 12 de julio, domingo, a las 8 de la mañana" (165). A calendar analysis of all the years since 1999 indicates that the year 2009 is the only one in which July 12 fell on a Sunday; thus, it is completely impossible, according to the Western calendar, that the events of the first novel (2009) and those of the fourth be separated by either five or ten years.[4] This obvious discrepancy in day and years, especially when considering the normally verisimilar description of Lola's thoughts and actions, obviously cannot be merely an unconscious slip on the part of the author, her assistants, and her editors, all of whom she thanks in the various books for help in editing, revising, investigating and verifying the information in the manuscripts. In fact, I would argue that the author's stated purpose of always presenting Lola as a "mujer de mediana edad" (*Hemingway* 79) in her fourth decade of life with a minimum of aging offers more credibility to Calderón's interpretation of a generation of Spanish women born during the so-called "Spanish Miracle" of the 1960s who today are more or less the same age as Lola and who may be suffering the same "crisis de la mediana edad" (Lemmo).

Lola's physical appearance owes itself to the "fruto de sus genes irlandeses" (*Canaima* 36); she has green eyes, freckles, and "rojizos cabellos alborotados" (*Hemingway* 79). She is frequently preoccupied by the appearance of her hair; in *Los crímenes del número primo*, for example, she combs her hair before undertaking the interrogation of Father Lucas at the scene of the crime: "Instintivamente, ensayé domesticar mis rizos, tras las orejas. Sabía que si el sacerdote se topaba con la mata pelirroja con la que me adornó el destino y los genes irlandeses de mi familia, no me tomaría en serio" (204). At the same time, on more than one occasion she is portrayed as on her way to the beauty salon, and it bothers her that the changes in weather affect her coiffure: "Los treinta euros y la hora y media en la peluquería serían gasto inútil si las nubes descargaban cuando me hallara en medio de aquel bosque" (*Número primo* 253). This preoccupation about her personal appearance carries over into other aspects of her life as well; she is more than merely a "juez de instrucción," mother, or object of sexual desire—although she does not intend to disregard this aspect of her life either. At times she even subverts the traditional, patriarchal "masculine gaze" and makes it an instrument of her own; in fact, one of the first descriptions of her in the series is when Jaime awakens her in "La Perla," comes out of the shower, and "a Lola le encantaba contemplar el cuerpo desnudo de su marido" (81). "'¿Qué miras, fisgona?' oyó decir a Jaime [. . .] 'Mis posesiones' replicó ella. 'Tengo que proteger mi inversión'" (83).

The third novel of the series, *El Expediente Canaima*, is where it seems that Lola is most suffering from a middle-age crisis. When she invites Juan Iturri to dinner with her family, she feels romantic emotions toward him at the same time as she sees herself aging:

> Lo decían sus arrugas, sus pechos colgantes y su estómago abultado por los embarazos y la falta de ejercicio. [. . .] Empezaba a necesitar ser admirada por algo más que su inteligencia. Porque aquel cuerpo daba sus últimos coletazos. Estaba en la antesala de la invisibilidad, de la vejez. Se arrugaba y se marchitaba, sin remedio. [. . .]
>
> Juan Iturri representaba el feliz pasado. Un momento en que ella había sido de nuevo deseada, en que se sintió hermosa. Un momento que, si ella quisiera, podría volver. (277)

Later, when her husband Jaime travels to Barcelona without first advising her, Lola becomes angry and "Volvió a pensar en Iturri y en su ofrecimiento. Era tentador: charlar sin prisas, reír, ser escuchada, sentirse apreciada" (*Canaima* 300). But, as is the case in all the novels, she fulfills her marriage vows and remains faithful to her values; if one is desirous of seeing an eroticized and libertine main character, this is not the series to read.

Also corresponding to traditional conservative values, the most important thing to Lola is her family. She is very much in love with her family, and more than anything else what she wants "era a ser feliz. Y Jaime, su marido, formaba parte de esa felicidad" (*Canaima* 97). When Jaime is offered a job in Madrid, she is not willing to deny him the promotion or to remain in Pamplona working by herself (*Canaima* 97); therefore, she immediately finalizes her plans to request a position on the Audiencia Nacional. At the beginning of the fourth novel, *El último paciente del Doctor Wilson*, Lola is pregnant, and she and Jaime are resolved that in spite of everything "no lo vamos a tirar a la basura" (*Dr. Wilson* 227). In *El expediente Canaima*, believing herself incapable of bringing to justice those guilty of extortion, she puts what she believes to be the original archives of the matter into the designated trashcan in an intent to save the life of her son Javier, knowing that this puts even her own career into jeopardy. When she subsequently learns that Iturri and Kalif have switched the contents of the envelope, "se lanzó sobre Juan Iturri. '¡Me has vendido, no puedo creerlo! ¡Nos has traicionado tú' [. . .] Lola lloraba mientras con los puños golpeaba a Iturri en el pecho" (382). And she tells Kalif, the FBI agent: "'¡Es usted un canalla, Über! Nunca le hemos importado. Sólo quiere vengarse de los que atentaron contra un compatriota. ¡El FBI, son todos unos matones!'" (382).

Lola also desires a change in career since "los días que pasaba en los tribunales se habían convertido en una colección de rutinas" (*Canaima* 47). Perhaps more importantly, the source of her frustrations seem to be that she "estaba harta de gente imposible de recuperar" (*Canaima* 47) and "ofendida por el hecho de que la gente se refiere al lugar de su empleo como el Palacio de Justicia" (*Canaima* 92) while she believes that justice is not meted out equally to all citizens. In fact, she is bothered by the knowledge that some criminals, in particular the drug trafficker responsible for the death of María Bravo (*Canaima* 114–15), are never brought to justice and she is incapable of effecting change due to the legal constraints placed upon her by the rules governing the judicial system itself. She is also fed up with politicians (*Canaima* 92–93) and journalists who "[p]resumían de ser los voceros morales de la sociedad, la conciencia del pueblo" (*Canaima* 34); she calls them "vultures" (*Canaima* 125). Once again the reader sees in Lola's anguishes a reflection of the Spanish mentality; the aforementioned 2009 Eurobarometer, for example, reports that confidence in the "media" in Spain is at only 44%. In regards to politics, only 20% of Spaniards trust the national government, 21% the Spanish parliament, and only 36% the regional or local authorities (European Commission). Confidence in the judicial system is rated at only 2.73 (on a scale of 0 to 5) according to a 2009 study by Gómez Fortes and Palacios Brihuega. And confidence in the Church is rated at 2.9 (on a scale of 0 to 10 points), somewhat similar to Lola's beliefs, who calls herself a "creyente dudosa, o dudosa creyente" (*Canaima* 131). A more in-depth analysis of social issues and social commentary is the focus of Chapter 5.

While Lola is not a person who employs violence or mistreats suspects/criminals, she is very capable of utilizing trickery and "white lies" to throw off other people. In *Los crímenes del número primo*, she leaves the church where the cadavers have been found and goes to where Father Lucas is, telling him that "ninguna de las preguntas que le formulo está destinada a inculparle. Sólo quiero aclarar las cosas, únicamente. [. . .] yo no creo que usted tenga nada que ver con estos hechos—mentí" (213). Before María Bravo's funeral, in *El Expediente Canaima*, she tells her secretary that she has not yet decided if she is going to attend the funeral mass or not, although both of them know full well that she will do so (129). And in *El último paciente del Doctor Wilson*, it is Lola who has the idea of feigning to be a journalist in order to be able to interview the various psychiatrists at the conference in an attempt to discover who the real Doctor Wilson is (260). That is not to say, however, that she is a pathological liar. In fact, she refuses to reveal to the reader the causes and nature of the problems that her bodyguard Agapito suffers, twice using the letters XXX instead of the name of the judge with whom she spoke in order to remedy Agapito's problems: "Me produciría un intenso placer reveler los detalles, pero le prometí que no lo haría y mantendré mi promesa" (276).

Another place where the reader sees the two sides of Lola—that is, something more than simply a static personality, a caricature that does not experience conflictive emotions as do other humans—is "[e]n lo relativo a las cuestiones formales, MacHor era muy estricta. A diferencia de algún colega [. . .] MacHor creía que la corrección en el habla y en el vestir contribuía a sostener el procedimiento jurídico. Sus detractores la consideraban anticuada y elitista" (*Canaima* 35). She is, without a doubt, a cold person when she needs to be, but at times she lets herself be carried away by her emotions: for example, when she screams at Susana ordering her to file the documents that concern María Bravo without waiting for an explanation. Even before María's death, Lola is anguished by the girl's situation, in large part because she herself has been unable to remedy the youth's situation: "Sus finas cejas pelirrojas se contrajeron en un angustiado espasmo. Las lágrimas comenzaron a brotar por María" (*Canaima* 65). "Algún tipo de delito, sobre todo los de naturaleza sexual, o los relacionados con el género, despertaba a la MacHor combativa, fiera y, al mismo tiempo, casi miedosa" (*Canaima* 133). This comes from an event in the personal childhood of the judge, when she was six years old and was assaulted when she went for *buñuelos* only a few yards from her home—something that she recounts to Jaime when he discovers her locked up in her bedroom, attempting to control her tears, with a butcher's knife in the bed beside her (*Canaima* 143–57) due to the threatening note that María's molester has left on the windshield of Lola's car. In an attempt to calm her, Jaime advances his wife's trip to Singapore, but she does not relax until she has walked up and down the plane's aisle, assuring herself that Ariel has not boarded the craft.

In spite of this paralyzing crisis that she suffers in certain grave moments, MacHor can be quite combative when she perceives personal slights. Upon discovering that the police have entered her room in the Singapore hotel, she vociferously scolds them, denying that Ng is her lawyer, (*Canaima* 208), insisting that they call her "señoría" ("Your Honor") instead of "señora" ("Mrs.") (*Canaima* 211), she threatens them with an official complaint (*Canaima* 209), and tells the ambassador that she wants in writing an apology from the lawyer

(*Canaima* 216). When she learns that the black car that she has seen following her several times belongs to the FBI, she calls Kalif, reprimanding him, blaming him for all the assassinations and for attempting to take her life as well, demanding that he take out all the hidden microphones in her house (*Canaima* 332). When she learns that the envelope that she has placed in the trashcan does not contain what she thought, she realizes the potential danger, and "Lola lloraba mientras con los puños golpeaba a Iturri en el pecho" (*Canaima* 382), calling Kalif a "canalla" (382) who "[s]ólo quiere vengarse de los que atentaron contra un compatriota. ¡El FBI, son todos unos matones!" (*Canaima* 382).

In Chapter Two, "Lola MacHor: The Principal Character," it is my goal to demonstrate that while it is true that there are certain vestiges of patriarchal, feminist and post-feminist ideologies in the five novels of the series, a careful analysis reveals that Calderón rejects all of them as her only aesthetic and creates a new, non-sexist, paradigmatic structure that contains an important element of social justice. That is, Calderón rejects patriarchy's emphasis on man-as-oppressor, feminism's proponent of the warrior-woman, and post-feminism's consumerism, individualistic woman and maternal violence. Relationships between the genders, as seen in these novels, demonstrate the utilization on the part of Calderón of an almost gender-neutral (although certainly not libido-absent) narrative. The result, then, is a dynamic character who better reflects the various ideas, thoughts, fights, daily battles, and emotions of human beings, in this case in particular, a female, middle-aged Spaniard who has seen and lived quite a bit in her almost fifty years; as the author herself has expressed it: "la situación actual de la mujer presenta bastantes luces, pero también, sombras" (School of Humanities and Social Sciences).

Chapter Three is an examination of the narrative structures as well as traditional and progressive ideologies that Calderón includes in her novels. I begin the analysis with an examination of the age-old debate of heredity vs. environment vs. free will. As I demonstrate more clearly in my analysis, the conflict inherent in Lola herself is also portrayed in the narrative structures and styles that the author employs, and these range from the pathetic fallacy to Naturalism's determinism and dehumanization, to more modern techniques of the braided narrative. Because content and style are so closely intertwined in the series, I also include in the chapter a discussion of sexism and both masculine and feminine stereotypes.

Given that the series is detective fiction,[5] and a large part of the novels present a conflict between tradition and progressivism, Chapter Four is an examination of how such plays out in the view of criminality itself, both historically and within the series. I end the chapter with the conclusion that in the novels, just as in society at large, there is no definitive conclusion given to why a person turns to malevolence. Reyes Calderón merely presents the different reasons and urges compassion since all of us are only one chemical imbalance away from the psychological ward ourselves. Chapter Five represents a similar train of thought, detailing the various ideas, ways and methods in which the author includes both overt and covert social criticism with the novels. Chapter Six is an examination of the author's portrayal of cultural and societal norms and traditions through the use of food and drink in the novels. As might be expected by an author attempting to establish maximum verisimilitude, there is a close correspondence between specific uses of food and drink and the plot, cultural setting, and the level of society to which the individual characters belong. I conclude the study with the transcript of a personal interview that I had with the author in May 2012.

In sum, until very recently—if we exclude those rare exceptions of the Second Republic (1931–1939)—adult women in Spain generally have not enjoyed many liberties, being relegated instead almost always to the more traditional roles of wife, mother, or prostitute. The cultural and social transition accelerated after the death of Franco in 1975, however, and Spanish women have been adopting less traditionally sexist roles in society, assuming and showing off more "masculine" characteristics and taking on jobs in professions accessible formerly only to men. Due to, perhaps, her own experiences in breaking the glass ceiling—the author was the first female Dean of the Facultad de Ciencias Económicas y Empresariales en la Universidad de Navarra—Reyes Calderón is better prepared and more capable of presenting in a convincing manner a judge who performs a myriad of aspects of a "more human," more verisimilar, woman with a "normal" career climbing through the various professional levels of university professor (*Las lágrimas de Hemingway*) to President of the Sala Penal de la Audiencia Penal in Madrid (*El último paciente del Doctor Wilson*). Lola MacHor is not portrayed as a stereotypical feminist ideologue (oppressed or rebellious), a post-feminist, a static character or other type of caricature. She is a working mother growing old with several children, feeling herself pulled by family and professional responsibilities, by her own personal history, and by a desire to be loved and to escape the devastations of growing old. When all is said and done, Lola is—in the Spain of today where there are a plethora of ideas thought, expressed, and promoted—an opportune model for Spanish women in a rapidly changing culture at the beginning of the third millennium.

Notes to the reader

For purposes of this study, the novel titles will most often be shortened as follows throughout the remainder of this book:

Las lágrimas de Hemingway	*Hemingway*
Los crímenes del número primo	*Número primo*
El Expediente Canaima	*Canaima*
El último paciente del Dr. Wilson	*Dr. Wilson*
La venganza del asesino par	*Venganza*

Please see Appendix A for a list of the main characters in each novel as well as Appendix B for a basic plot summary which will aid in the understanding of the following analyses.

Notes

1 It should be noted that the author rejects the neologism "jueza" (see my interview with Calderón in Chapter Eight).

2 Lola MacHor's "official website" states that, among other "Datos personales," her "Edad: 48 años."

3 It should be noted, as well, that the 1979 law establishing the duties of the Spanish Supreme Court, as well as the qualifications of those judges, requires a minimum of 15 years experience in the field in order to be named to the that bench (*Ley Orgánica*). Obviously, then, this introduces yet another element in firmly establishing Lola's age—something one would never do in polite society.

4 It should also be noted that the novel was originally published in 2005 and the next occurrence of July 12 on a Sunday is in 2015.

5 While in this study I do not go in-depth into an examination of the Spanish "thriller," it should be noted that in addition to being simply detective fiction, these novels show various characteristics of the "thriller" subgenre and the novelist herself called them such in my interview with her (see Chapter Eight). In particular, future work remains to be conducted on detailing how *Hemingway* is an "academic thriller," *Número primo* is a "religious thriller," *Canaima* is an political thriller, and *Dr. Wilson* and *Venganza* are psychological thrillers.

CHAPTER TWO

Lola MacHor: The Principal Character

I Introduction

As a female Catholic who has broken the glass ceiling of post-Franco Spain, Lola MacHor is not the typical detective found in traditional detective fiction. The mere fact that the woman in Calderon's work is the main character and detective, instead of a prostitute, a *femme fatale*, or the girlfriend of the male detective, is a profound break from the traditional Hispanic variant of the genre. Even with the societal changes that have been occurring in Spain since the death of Franco, only slowly has the fictional female protagonist been able to move out of the domestic realm into the more public arena.[1] Landeira perhaps best describes this extended evolution when he notes that "A lo largo del desarrollo de la narrativa policiaca, la mujer empezó siendo la víctima ineludible, pasó luego a cómplice, después a culpable, y por fin culminó su papel en el de detective femenino" (18). However, even when she finally is able to asume a public role, "lo más probable es que sea vieja, solterona o asexuada" (Landeira 17). Salvador Oropesa argues along the same lines, stating that "Las mujeres detectives son mujeres independientes que vienen de malos divorcios, que son menospreciadas por superiores, que tienen que batallar con inferiores, que usan la violencia y la reciben, que tienen que recorrer la ciudad y conocer sus mapas reales e imaginarios" (9). Lola breaks that mold; she is neither victim nor victor, old, single or sexless, nor does she come from a bad divorce.

More recently, however, focus has begun to shift, in the critical world, from the female *detective* (most commonly, but not exclusively, created by a female author) to the female *author* who employs a female detective. Genaro Pérez has noted, in fact, that: "hasta cierto punto las escritoras en cuestión cambian y subvierten un género tradicionalmente masculino, reflejo patente de los tradicionales valores machistas y falocéntricos" (38). And Godsland argues that: "Crime fiction provides an ideal literary medium for the articulation of the shift from a feminist consciousness to a postfeminist economy for a number of reasons, foremost among which is the portrayal of the female detective or criminal herself" (85). That is, detective fiction is fertile territory for an examination of changing societal and cultural norms, and the role of women.[2]

A study of the five novels of Reyes Calderón's Lola MacHor series represents an analysis of the double-breaking of tradition: both the main character and the author are female. Additionally, however, Lola MacHor poses yet a third break from literary tradition in that Lola is neither a police investigator nor a private detective; she is a "juez de instrucción." And, as such, she is breaking professional and gender roles when she personally conducts the investigation itself instead of handing off such to the police detectives or a *fiscal*, as would be the usual pattern in "real life."

It is apparent, through an examination of the novels, that Reyes Calderón Cuadrado's characterization and development of Lola MacHor demonstrates that the author clearly has in mind something other than a main character either blindly supporting or rabidly rebelling against either a traditional patriarchy or a feminist subversion of such. That is, I argue that Calderón's works go beyond merely easily defined ideologies of stereotypical and atypical patriarchy and (post)feminism, conservative and liberal, or traditional and nonconformist, to present a career woman with a personality much more complex than those of the *ángel del hogar/femme fatale* dichotomy. This author takes the principal female character from being merely in the background and as support cast, or, conversely, as an antagonistic subversive feminist fighter, to one who enters the traditionally masculine arena of detective work on her own terms—as a "juez de instrucción." The portrayal of this female "detective," while displaying certain elements of traditional stereotypes, ultimately transcends those traditional gender-specific characteristics and appropriates other characteristics traditionally valued as negative into positive elements.

The remainder of the chapter, then, will be an examination of Lola in light of the major characteristics of traditionally patriarchal, feminist, and postfeminist ideologies. Ultimately, I will show that Calderón's aesthetics and portrayal of Lola MacHor detail a variety of the manners in which traditional feminine roles and attitudes are changing on the Iberian Peninsula and that Lola is an apt model for Spanish women in the rapidly changing culture of Spain at the turn of the third millennium.

II Stereotypical, Traditional, Patriarchal Values

"Stereotypical, traditional, patriarchal values" is not merely one set of values which is necessarily stereotypical, traditional and patriarchal in nature; they may be simply opinions, prejudices, or manners of comportment (overt or by insinuation, consciously acted upon or unknowingly carried out) which are governed or influenced by stereotypical, traditional and/or patriarchal values or institutional guidelines. My usage of this term therefore relates to more than only an active promotion of those values; it also encompasses a conscious or unconscious, active or passive, acceptance and/or promotion of patriarchal hegemony in which the female character is relegated to some "inferior" position. Most frequently in this paradigm, the female is at most a secondary character. Often, however, although she may serve as an "assistant" to the male, she is silenced completely and exists most notably as an object of male sexual desire. It is the male who characterizes and personifies the primary actions, voices, and empowered members of society. Additionally, most stereotypical, traditional, patriarchal views of women and their role in society generally correspond to a masculine hegemony usually expressed in some form of the "male gaze" (Mulvey).

Obviously Lola is not a second-tier character in the novels; she is, other than in *Las lágrimas de Hemingway*—the first novel of the series—the "juez de instrucción" who is in charge of the various investigations or, as is the case in the fifth novel, *La venganza del asesino par*, a recently-appointed member of the Spanish Supreme Court who serves as the key to solving the convict's continuing crimes. Even in the first novel, however, she is a principal character and is the person who receives and finds the hidden message which both exonerates her and implicates her colleague. That is, Lola's normal activities in the series reflect the one in charge, the one who determines if there is sufficient reason for a criminal prosecution to go forward, and the one who wields power over the masculine-dominated world of the criminals. As is customary in traditional detective fiction, then, the principal character's main goal is that of setting evils right in the world.

Admittedly, Lola presents a well-developed personality, range of emotions, and verisimilar portrayal of an advancing, post-Franco, female, adult Spanish professional; in spite of such, she remains true to many patriarchal expectations and traditional stereotypes. As noted more fully in this book's introduction, she is fairly static in representing a certain decade of life, and her age does not correspond to the time that transpires in the novels; that is, over the events of the five novels she matures only some nine years while the chronological passage of time is at least twenty years. Lola is of Irish descent and "su aspecto [es] fruto de sus genes irlandeses" (*Canaima* 36), a stereotype propagated by many others besides just Calderón (Hackney Blackwell and Hackney 14): Lola has green eyes, freckles, and "rojizos cabellos alborotados" (*Hemingway* 79). Stereotypically, as a woman she is often quite concerned with her appearance, in particular her hair; in *Los crímenes del número primo*, she attempts to transform herself in order to display an air of authority by taming her curls before questioning Father Lucas at the crime scene: "Instintivamente, ensayé domesticar mis rizos, tras las orejas. Sabía que si el sacerdote se topaba con la mata pelirroja con la que me adornó el destino y los genes irlandeses de mi familia, no me tomaría en serio" (204). At the same time, her obsession with her personal appearance is apparent through her frequent visits to beauty salons—most notably in *Número primo* and *Dr. Wilson*—and she worries when weather changes might alter her coiffure: "Los treinta euros y la hora y media en la peluquería serían gasto inútil si las nubes descargaban cuando me hallara en medio de aquel bosque" (*Número primo* 253). This fear is, in fact, realized when a downpour occurs while she and the monk Chocarro are talking in the monastery garden: "me mojé completamente. Lo recuerdo bien, no solo porque hube de volver al día siguiente a la peluquería" (*Número primo* 330–31). By the time of the fourth novel, however, Lola notes that although "sigo siendo pelirroja [. . .] ahora es una tintura vegetal la que mantiene el color" (*Dr. Wilson* 14). And by the fifth novel, when she is appointed a Magistrate to the Spanish Supreme Court, she decides it is time for a complete makeover; she cuts her hair, and thereby submits to the societal pressure of a woman needing to maintain a more youthful appearance.

Although Lola ages very little in the novels, she evidently accepts as her own the patriarchal dictates regarding the woman maintaining a youthful look. In fact, such is her worrying preoccupation for appearing to be aging that, in *Venganza*, she does not want to let her investigative partner Juan Iturri know that she now has to don reading glasses in order to make out the words in the newspaper: "Sé que me ha pasado el arroz. Y el pollo. Y todo lo demás. [. . .] Me gusta verme bien. Y las gafas me sientan fatal" (79–80). After preparing dinner, in *Canaima*, she comforts herself in the shower, feeling herself old:

> Lo decían sus arrugas, sus pechos colgantes y su estómago abultado por los embarazos y la falta de ejercicio. [. . .] Empezaba a necesitar ser admirada por algo más que su inteligencia. Porque aquel cuerpo daba sus últimos coletazos. Estaba en la antesala de la invisibilidad, de la vejez. Se arrugaba y se marchitaba, sin remedio. [. . .]

> Se resistía.
> Juan Iturri representaba el feliz pasado. Un momento en que ella había sido de nuevo deseada, en que se sintió hermosa. Un momento que, si ella quisiera, podría volver. (*Canaima* 277)

This third novel of the series, *El Expediente Canaima*, is where Lola seems to be suffering the most from an attempt to maintain her commitment to traditional, patriarchal values, here portrayed through her obsession with her physical appearance, her battle against weight-gain, and her sex appeal. When the local café owner doña Emilia offers her *buñuelos*, Lola refuses, saying that "Ya sabe que tengo que vigilar el peso" (122), and she requests coffee without cream instead. Lola's sentiments toward the detective Juan Iturri go beyond simple gratitude for his exonerating her of murder in the first novel, *Las lágrimas de Hemingway*; she clearly has romantic feelings for him, even after his drug-induced attempt to force himself on her in the second novel, *Los crímenes del número primo*. While she also has feelings of lust for him, she realizes that "[s]i me acuesto contigo, sólo te utilizaré" (451), and she rejects his advances. In the subsequent novel, *El Expediente Canaima*, she blushes when her mentor Uranga says that she should consult with Iturri concerning the international extortion case which has unexpectedly fallen in her lap and "Lo que ocurrió en el pasado, pasado y olvidado está" (*Canaima* 258). When Lola finally does call Iturri for assistance, she first breathes deeply a couple of times to get her composure (*Canaima* 271). Realizing that her feelings toward Iturri are not dead, she refuses to meet him alone, and instead invites him to dinner with her family, proposing that after the meal she, Iturri, and her husband discuss the case. In preparation for his arrival, however, she spends so much time preparing exquisite dishes that her young son Pedro asks: "¿por qué tanto jaleo? ¡Iturri es como de la familia! Y no creo que venga por tus cualidades culinarias" (*Canaima* 276).

Shortly after Iturri's visit, Jaime unexpectedly goes to Barcelona on a business trip without first informing Lola. She becomes upset, and "[v]olvió a pensar en Iturri y en su ofrecimiento. Era tentador: charlar sin prisas, reír, ser escuchada, sentirse apreciada" (*Canaima* 300). Lola's command over the police officers is well established, with the exception of Iturri: "lejos de molestarla, la indisciplina y la insociabilidad de Juan Iturri le parecían deliciosas" (*Canaima* 283). Once again in the fifth novel, *La venganza del asesino par*, Lola finds herself being tempted by the excitement of a youthful dalliance with Juan. These feelings are, however, only recurrences of previously felt emotions when she had felt school-girlish giddy upon unexpectedly seeing Iturri at the archbishopric in *Los crímenes del número primo* (284) and hugs him in private, remarking on how good he looks, knowing that doing such in public would demonstrate a profound lack of professional decorum (286). While a tryst with Iturri would parallel the woman's role in much of traditional detective fiction, Lola's commitment to traditional values goes much deeper. Her commitment reflects an adherence to conservative, religious norms promulgated by her Catholic, Hispanic, and machista upbringing. The male can, and many times is expected to, have non-monogamous affairs, but a woman who does such immediately loses all respect, honor, and credibility. Lola, then, maintains her marriage vows, professionalism and conservative values by decidedly rejecting the advances, as well as her own carnal desires, knowing that a break with the traditional vows of a monogamous, heterosexual marriage will change her into someone she does not desire to be. She tells Iturri, in *Venganza*, in no uncertain terms that: "hace años que vengo nadando entre dos aguas; quería a Jaime, pero sabía también que tú siempre estabas allí. [. . .] No podemos seguir así. [. . .] Porque, en otro caso, un día como ayer, o como hoy, terminaríamos en la cama . . . Y yo perdería a Jaime, y tú no ganarías nada" (125).

Obviously, Lola is very much in love with her family, even to the point of adherence to a paradigm which denies her immediate pleasures. More than anything what she wants "era a ser feliz. Y Jaime, su marido, formaba parte de esa felicidad" (*Canaima* 97). When Jaime receives a job opportunity in Madrid, Lola is not willing to deny him the promotion or to continue her career alone, in Pamplona, with Jaime moving to Madrid (*Canaima* 97). In order to resolve this problem, and to maintain the unity of the family, she immediately finalizes her plan to solicit a position as judge at the Audiencia Nacional.

The maternal instinct in Lola is also quite evident, and motherhood is woven in the fabric of who she is personally and professionally. In fact, Lola believes that her car being strewn with children's items, and the subsequent perception by her kidnapper of her as a mother, is what deters him from killing her in *Los crímenes del número primo*: "Ya sabes cómo suelo llevar el coche: un juguete olvidado, un almuerzo en el suelo, un chupete . . . De algún modo, me vio como una madre, no como una jueza" (551). And in *Venganza*, after being sworn is as a judge on the Tribunal Supremo, Lola greets her daughter María and notes that "[n]o había nadie como ella en aquel burladero plagado de celebridades. Era lo más importante del mundo, una razón ineludible para tirar hacia adelante" (47).

When the reader is first introduced to Lola, we learn that she has four children. Slowly, over the course of the five novels the reader learns more and more about the family. One of her sons suffered an unnamed childhood disease which left him paralyzed for four years, but from which he apparently has now recovered and "Ahora vive una vida normal" (*Hemingway* 223). When her husband Jaime goes with the children to the pastry shop, Lola's daughters save her a *napolitana* (*Número primo* 301), and on another occasion one of them, María, is especially upset when the clergy come to the house and eat all the canned olives. When the nuncio reappears at the house the second time, María comments that "es de los que se comen las aceitunas" (*Número primo* 534), and to Lola's offer to prepare some sandwiches for him, the child instantly comments: "'Ya no quedan aceitunas' se oyó machaconamente a lo lejos" (*Número primo* 535). Afraid that someone has invaded her home, Lola's defense of her home and family results in her son Javier receiving a blow from the candelabra-turned-weapon and suffering a head wound that requires "cinco puntos y muchas explicaciones" since "el médico de guardia dedujo que estaba ante un caso de malos tratos" (*Canaima* 354).

The fifth child, a daughter born between *Las lágrimas de Hemingway* and *Los crímenes del número primo*, is the result of an unexpected pregnancy: "Tengo 46 años y una barriga de seis meses. No pensé que a estas edades se tuviesen hijos. Al menos la gente normal" (*Hemingway* 164). The child is "nacida a destiempo. La deformidad de su cuerpo no hizo sino aumentar su encanto" (*Número primo* 149). Apparently, however, this deformity does not manifest itself further in her childhood as the reader never hears anything else concerning such. At the beginning of the fourth novel, Lola herself is once again unexpectedly pregnant, a pregnancy that she is determined to see through to the end, but it ends in a miscarriage. While her views of abortion as an ethical/moral issue are never specifically detailed, her conservative opinions concerning such are repeated several times: "[E]s mi hijo. No lo puedo matar como si fuera una cosa sin vida" (*Dr. Wilson* 35). Later, she tells Iturri: "Lo noto dentro, ¿sabes?, como al resto de mis hijos. Descubro su presencia, como una sombra. Está vivo . . . No puedo hacer daño a otro ser humano, sea quien sea, o sea cual sea su número de cromosomas" (*Dr. Wilson* 181). Indeed, it becomes abundantly clear that she holds a fairly strong version of the traditional anti-abortion conservative view; both she and Jaime agree that "no lo vamos a tirar a la basura" (*Dr. Wilson* 227).

While family is very *important* to Lola, she half-heartedly insists that "No soy excesivamente sentimental" (*Dr. Wilson* 94), protesting when her daughter María places photos of the children in her purse (94). However, her actions do not always ring true to her words since she loves her children dearly and is extremely protective of them. In fact, in *Canaima*, when she is unable to prove who is behind the extortion ring and who committed the murders under investigation, she agrees to the demands made by the anonymous extortioner in his phone call to her home and places what she believes to be the original file of the case in a trash can on the street for him to retrieve in order to save the life of her young son Javier. She willingly obliges her strong maternal instinct, attempting to fulfill her private domestic role, knowing that such actions may even place in jeopardy her own public, professional career: "Sólo quiero proteger a los míos" (379). And she does such even after having told the head of the World Bank Office of Institutional Integrity, Herrera-Smith, "Nunca se debe negociar, David, nunca. Siento ser tan tajante, pero esa es mi norma. [. . .] no accedería jamás a pactar con un chantajista" (185). That her domestic side has overridden the public and professional becomes even more clear when she learns that the envelope has been replaced with another one by Interpol agent Iturri and FBI agent Kalif, and she has not, in fact, handed over the documents that the extortioner has demanded. At that point, "se lanzó sobre Juan Iturri. '¡Me has vendido, no puedo creerlo! ¡Nos has traicionado tú' [. . .] Lola lloraba mientras con los puños golpeaba a Iturri en el pecho" (382). And she tells Kalif: "¡Es usted un canalla, Über! Nunca le hemos importado. Sólo quiere vengarse de los que atentaron contra un compatriota. ¡El FBI, son todos unos matones!" (*Canaima* 382). Her utmost concern is her immediate family, even more so than herself, and she demonstrates such quite emotionally.

It is evident, however and in spite of her professional career, that Lola quite often follows the dictates of traditionally patriarchal values of the woman as the goddess of the domestic domain. She often completes household chores: "Anduve el resto de la mañana ejerciendo de ama de casa. Recogí juguetes desordenados, quité el polvo a los muebles, puse una lavadora de color y preparé albóndigas acompañadas de una gran ensalada de tomates" (*Número primo* 482). When the nuncio appears at her house, she insists on making sandwiches for him even though he says that such is not necessary (*Número primo* 535). She loves her home: "Estaba en casa; ese sitio único al que siempre, ocurriera lo que ocurriera, podía volver. Mi sitio, mi cueva, mi caparazón" (*Número primo* 487–88). And she says that she is just an ordinary mother: "Como una madre cualquiera, como lo que soy, me levanté de inmediato, desayuné tocando a rebato, corrí para dejar a los niños en el colegio a tiempo y aguardé turno en la consulta del médico hasta que la enfermera se dignó recibirme" (*Número primo* 488).

Stereotypically, Lola, as a woman in a man's world, is not strong in mathematics; in fact, any type of mathematical calculations confuse her (*Canaima* 311). Judge Uranga, a male and former law-school classmate, teases her about such and how much studying was required "para aprobar la asignatura de economía" (*Canaima* 253). The male tax auditor Castaña wants to talk to Lola's husband Jaime since the possible crime involves a complicated financial accounting manipulation, and he tells Lola: "Se me ha ocurrido que yo podría explicárselo a su marido, y que luego él se lo tradujera" (*Canaima* 311). In fact, Lola notes the "nube de inquietud que emerge cuando dudas sobre la exactitud de tu respuesta, la misma que invadía mi rostro cuando era niña y el profesor de matemáticas me sacaba a la pizarra a resolver una ecuación (sencilla, yo no pasé de las dos incógnitas)" (*Dr. Wilson* 162). When Lola is at the doctor's office, he comments that "la probabilidad es de una entre treinta," that the child will have Down's Syndrome, to which she responds" "Ha dicho una probabilidad entre treinta . . . Eso, ¿a qué porcentaje equivale?" (*Dr. Wilson* 36). And in more than one of the novels she consults Chocarro, who had been a mathematician before entering the priesthood, to clear up questions she has concerning numbers and probability.

Additionally, she fits the stereotype of the absentminded female, especially when involved in trying to resolve a crime, repeatedly misplacing her purse—"tengo la fea costumbre de guarder en el bolso todo lo que llevo en la mano" (*Dr. Wilson* 218)—umbrella, and cell phone—which she often forgets to charge—in various places. Her assistant Galbis, in *Canaima*, in fact, ignores Lola's phone call when her number appears on his cell phone screen, knowing that there is nothing pending that he has with her and that "No era un secreto que la juez MacHor tenía problemas con las nuevas tecnologías" (69). In *Número primo*, Lola's husband Jaime cannot get in contact with her for quite some time because she forgets to disconnect after calling her doctor, but she defends herself by stating "¡No me mires así, ya sé que soy un desastre con las líneas telefónicas!" (483). And when Ituri tells her that an easy way to return a call is "solo devuelve la llamada" without manually entering the numbers, "[n]unca supe si era ironía lo que escondían sus palabras o simplemente una lección gratuita" (*Número primo* 417). Obviously, however, her issues with the cell phone are not something that are going to improve; rather, the reader can intuit that they may become worse. In the fourth novel, for example, Lola cannot find her phone in her purse and finally discovers it when she hears it ringing in the bathroom; she is unable to finish the conversation, however, as "La batería del móvil se agotó. Suelo olvidarme de esos pequeños detalles. Debería haber nacido en el siglo XIX" (*Dr. Wilson* 202). And in *Venganza*, she admits to having once found her cell phone where she had left it, in the refrigerator (15).

Lola displays various other stereotypical aspects of the traditional female in a patriarchal society as a weaker, emotional being: She is scared of mice and climbs up on chairs to get away from them (*Canaima* 290). She is easily excited out of jealousy: "Impotente para impeder que los celos la embargaran" (*Dr. Wilson* 81). She confirms the stereotypical view of women as bad drivers. In fact, she tells the forensics doctor Ramiro Sega that "Ya sabes que me pierdo con facilidad" (*Número primo* 177). She hates driving (*Número primo* 178) and admits that she is a bad driver (*Número primo* 355) although she is among the select few who have never been found at fault in, or had, an accident (*Número primo* 231). In *Venganza* Iturri explains the decision for the three men to drive the car to the prison as due to reasons peculiar to both Lola and the fairer sex in general: "Decidimos ir turnándonos al volante. Los tres. A Lola la dejamos fuera. No por ser mujer, o quizá sí: con un mapa en la mano es un peligro manifiesto. Podíamos aparecer en México si nos descuidábamos. Como es consciente de su enemistad con las carreteras, no protestó" (392).

One of the most obvious patriarchal views of women, however, is strong, frequent, and emotional outbursts of fear and crying, and Lola follows that stereotype. In their study of gender stereotypes in Spain, López-Sáez, Morales, and Lisbona report crying as the trait with the highest stereotypical feminine quotient (613). In the first novel of the series, Lola, fearful that Jaime may become enamored of the seductress Clara, breaks out in tears (*Hemingway* 81) even though that fear has no basis at all. Later in the same work, she cries upon awakening at the hospital and realizing that her being accused of murder is not a dream (*Hemingway* 175). She then cries because the other hospital patients believe the accusation and are happy when she is moved to a different room (*Hemingway* 189). She additionally sobs because she cannot convince the police that she is innocent (*Hemingway* 190), when she learns that her mom and Eregui are trying to assist the investigation (*Hemingway* 196), when she learns about her former professor's death (*Hemingway* 205), when the detective Juan Iturri tells her that at the end of a recorded conversation Jaime says he loves her (*Hemingway* 236), when thinking of her future if Alberto's death remains unresolved (*Hemingway* 271), and when Iturri informs her that her former professor and mentor Niccola was a member of a secret sect (*Hemingway* 293). That is, in a novel of only fifteen chapters, Lola is recorded as crying nine times.

Lola's crying, in fact, is one of the more frequently seen characteristics of her personality. She says that "Yo lloro por amor, por miedo, por odio, por dolor, por injusticia, por emoción . . . Puedo hacerlo en un cine, por un mal final, pero no lloro por un despacho, por muy exclusivo que éste sea" (*Venganza* 30). In addition to the previous examples, in the second novel (*Número primo*), Lola is seen crying on three occurrences: after her boss, the judge Uranga, intuitively perceives that a conflict has arisen between Lola and Iturri (463), upon worrying about her children's future when told by her kidnapper that he is going to kill both her and Jaime (563), and upon awakening after being knocked unconscious by her kidnapper and remembering only that she had not kissed Jaime good-bye that morning (497). In *Canaima*, Lola cries six times: When she thinks of the difficulty of María's recovering from being assaulted, "Las lágrimas comenzaron a brotar for María" (*Canaima* 65). Later, Lola herself winds up being the target, and she goes to bed with a knife, fearing for her life, and finds it difficult to "dominar las lágrimas" (142). Totally frightened by Kalif on the plane to Singapore, "Se agachó y, hecha un ovillo, rompió a llorar" (*Canaima* 174). Enraged, she cries on reading Herrera-Smith's letter explaining the reason for his taking his own life (*Canaima* 228), and crying, she tells Jaime she loves him after hearing of her nemesis, Lorenzo's death (*Canaima* 408). In *Dr. Wilson*, tears are related to Lola some seven times and range from corresponding to feelings of personal failure (31, 178) to a sense of professional inadequacy (425), from crying while looking at the results of a pregnancy test (57) to anger at the doctor for suggesting that she consider an abortion (35), and from feeling guilty for the miscarriage (346) to Jaime's unconscious use of insensitive language (403). And in *Venganza*, Lola is recorded as crying repetitive times: in reference to Jaime's absence at her investiture (29, 30, 49), when remembering their separation day (60), and when she sees Kimio Shabata in the photo posing with Rodrigo's other victims (339). Clearly, Lola fulfills the patriarchal feminine role as a crier. There seems to be no common thematic causality other than her own emotions. That her emotions have a strong impact in her life, and a strong influence over her actions, cannot be denied. As a female in a patriarchal society, she is very much an emotional being.

And, in a final nod toward traditionally patriarchal values, Lola at various times throughout the series both demonstrates and acknowledges her dependence on Jaime and her deference, or submissiveness, to males. In *Canaima* she is worried about Telmo's disappearance but does not know exactly what to do, so she "decidió consultar el tema con su marido. '¿Puedes ayudarme, Jaime? No sé qué hacer'" (*Canaima* 87); she subsequently follows his advice to wait until after the weekend before taking the matter seriously. When she wakes up in her car after being pummeled by her kidnapper, in *Número primo*, the first thing she does is call Jaime, begging him to come get her. In order to keep her awake, he orders her to sing, something she continues to do until he arrives, at which point she again faints (499). When Lola and Iturri go to interview the priests at the Leyre Monastery, she begins the questions, but "interrumpió Iturri" (342) and "me cortó Iturri" (346), at which point the interview ends. Later, she agrees to go to Málaga with him to conduct further investigations, and while there visits a gay bar: "No sé por qué me dejé convencer, crucé aquella puerta, vestida de aquella manera, y conocí medio a escondidas un extraño lugar que algunos llamaban cielo" (*Número primo* 436). In *Venganza*, Lola remembers the forensics doctor Ramiro Sega who "[i]nsistía en que, para saber juzgar su trabajo, debía conocerlo. A fondo. [. . .] no cejó hasta que acepté entrar en sus dominios" (70), but it is the third autopsy before she can control the uncontrollable vomiting. In the same novel, Lola accepts Fernando as "mi padrino del [Tribunal] Supremo" (104), and when he tells her, "Pues súbete a la cinta y corre un rato" (*Venganza* 104) in order to get over the depression caused by Jaime's departure to the U.S., "Sin pensarlo mucho, abandoné el sofa y, tal como estaba, me subí a la cinta y corrí (más bien anduve a buen paso) durante media hora" (*Venganza* 104–5). Iturri goes to her house and tells her he is inviting her out to dinner; she does not hesitate in going with him (*Venganza* 105). Later, on the plane to Boston, Iturri tells her to get his briefcase out of the overhead bin, and "Hice lo que me pedía. Como siempre" (*Venganza* 132). In *Dr. Wilson*, Lola wants to know that Dr. Wilson actually has a reservation at the restaurant in Washington, D.C. before she, Iturri, and Jaime go there, and she asks Iturri: "'¿Llamarás a Wilson?,' insistí. Mi voz sonó con impronta de rubia tonta necesitada de apoyo masculino" (*Dr. Wilson* 327). While Lola is the one who ultimately is able to put all the clues together and figure out the assassin's story in *Número primo*, even she admits that "En realidad, fue el propio asesino el que me mostró el camino. Si él no me hubiera hablado del suicidio de su madre, me temo que nunca lo habría averiguado, aunque había dejado pistas significativas" (544–45).

In *Dr. Wilson*, on the other hand, it is Jaime who finally both puts all the clues together and realizes who the murderer is (472), confronting him with the evidence. In fact, although Lola is the *juez de instrucción*, she demures to males in spite of her abilities and professional status, alleging that she is not the one who solves the mysteries. She, in essence, acknowledges the feminine trait of a collaborative collective in problem solving, with her role being a passive one. The last paragraph of *Número primo* begins with Lola stating, "Ahora que todo ha terminado, calibro mi verdadera y casi nula contribución al esclarecimiento de los hechos" (569). And, in *Dr. Wilson*, Lola suggests that:

> En cierta manera, formamos un equipo. Los tres nos complementamos y espontáneamente, sin hacerlo explícito siquiera, nos hemos distribuido las competencias: yo me ocupo de buscar los líos o, más bien, de dejar que ellos me busquen a mí; la agudeza de Jaime suele permitirnos encontrar las claves de los problemas, y, con ellas, Iturri, siempre en acción, resuelve los enigmas. (234–35)

III Feminist Values

The extensive, previous criticism would seem to indicate that Lola is a traditionalist, quite happy with her role as a submissive, stereotypical female; such a description, however, would not be an accurate characterization of her. While at times Lola MacHor does follow the traditional patriarchy in regards to the woman's role in society, she more often than not breaks that mode even though she is operating in a man's world of criminal investigation and meting out of justice. Importantly, Lola is the first *presidenta* of the Tribunal Superior de Justicia de Navarra (*Canaima* 97) and the first woman judge on the Spanish Supreme Count (*Venganza* 25),[3] demonstrating her abilities to function in the masculine world. Additionally, while the self-assessment may not be entirely true, she herself does state that "Nunca he permitido que nadie me defendiera, soy demasiado orgullosa, demasiado feminista" (*Dr. Wilson* 180). While Lola may purport to be a feminist, and that "[d]e pequeña soñaba con cambiar el mundo" (*Venganza* 30), feminist critics such as Klein assert that in reality "the feminist detective winds up supporting the existing system which oppresses women when she re-establishes the ordered status quo. This contradiction between feminist ideals and detectives' behavior is more apparent when the private eyes turn their criminals over to the law" (201). That is, the woman detective, even though she may appear and demonstrate feminist qualities in many areas, by merely surrendering her charge (i.e., the criminal) to the police (i.e., the establishment) tacitly supports and reaffirms the traditional order based on patriarchal hegemony. I would argue, however, that in the present detective series under study, a more mature version of detective fiction than the arguably formulaic *novela negra* or police procedural, the mere fact that the main character is a woman exercising authority in the judicial branch of government converts the narrative into something other than merely a promotion of traditionally patriarchal values since that ethos does not have, in Spain, a long history of supporting a female who works in the public arena as the dispenser of justice with masculine subordinates.[4] At the same time, it is worth noting that just because a novel has a female main character does not, in and of itself, mean that either the character herself, or the work itself, is either patriarchal or feminist in nature. Reddy observes that true "Feminist crime novels, far from being mere escapist literature or isolated, peculiar experiments in an essentially masculine preserve, participate in the larger feminist project of redefining and redistributing power, joining a long and valuable tradition of women's fiction" (149). In that sense, all but the first of the Lola MacHor series of novels can be classified, at least in part, as feminist works since the main character advances from judge on the Tribunal Superior de Justicia de Navarra, to the Presidency of the same (*Canaima* 33), to judge on the Audiencia Nacional in Madrid (*Canaima* 54), to Presidenta de la Sala Penal de la Audiencia Nacional [in Madrid] (*Dr. Wilson* 13–14), and to being a member of the Spanish Tribunal Supremo in *La venganza del asesino par.*

On a philosophical and professional level, Lola takes her responsibility as a judge seriously and obviously supports the redefining and redistribution of power from solely the masculine sphere to include women also. In fact, Jaime even says to her, "te empeñas en controlarlo todo. Haces planes, diseñas estrategias, negocias" (*Venganza* 11), something she later admits: "no me gusta delegar completamente el control sobre mis cosas" (*Venganza* 70). She becomes quite upset at Iturri when, in *Los crímenes del número primo*, he, unsolicited, takes control of the investigation and begins to order the priests around as well (338). In fact, she is not as sure as Iturri that the former novice at the monastery should no longer be considered a suspect (343) and demands that he remain on the list of suspects. She also becomes quite upset when Iturri cuts her off during the questioning of the monks at the monastery (346), resulting in his ultimately apologizing and promising to let her be the one in charge (350).

Godsland's comments concerning detective fiction writer Maria-Antònia Oliver also apply to Lola even though she seldom is belligerent or pugnacious.

> Oliver's crime fiction [. . .] articulates strongly feminist sentiments. [. . .] it is [the female] who decides which cases to accept and how they will be investigated, and she who gives the orders to her male employee, Quim. On the one occasion that she hands over a case to a male fellow investigator, she takes the initiative to contact him to offer information, and she cedes her case notes only in exchange for something beneficial to her. (89–90)

Lola may consult with Juan Iturri, her husband, or other males from time to time concerning various aspects of the cases, but in all of the novels (save the first, in which she is the accused) she is most often the one in control, the one who writes down the various clues and organizes the files, and she plays an important part in ultimately wrapping up the investigations in spite of her own demurring comments to the contrary. She may, in *Número primo*, think about ceding the case and, in *Venganza*, have to be forced into joining the investigation, but in both instances she comes back and proves herself equally as capable as the men. In fact, it is worth noting that her recounting of the events leading up to the assassin's taking of the priests' lives ends when "Jaime y Tagliatelli me miraban con la boca abierta" (*Número primo* 544). In *Venganza*, when she, Iturri, Jaime, and Joe meet with Dr. Hernández to hear his version of why Rodrigo has returned, Lola is the one who first vociferously remonstrates the psychiatrist (203). Additionally, Lola's feminist leanings lead her, on two occasions, to go against the wishes of her own husband, Jaime, that she withdraw from the case:[5] After Iturri is poisoned by the pedophile at the gay bar, she argues that "[t]engo que resolverlo" (*Número primo* 486), and, after Lola is kidnapped, Jaime adamantly vociferates to Lola's superior, "¡Busca otro juez, Gabriel! Lola está de baja" (*Número primo* 500). In spite of all his protests, however, Lola decides to remain on the case. It is the same novel, as well as in *Canaima*, in which Lola chooses Iturri to be her investigative partner instead of another detective. In fact, in *Número primo* Lola has a public stare-down with Álvarez—the policeman who wants to lead the investigation—before he finally must accede to her authority and withdraw (294–96). And, in *Dr. Wilson*, Lola confronts and overcomes both Jaime's and Iturri's initial beliefs that the manuscript she has received is more than merely the fantasy of a morbidly creative mind.

"Feminist" can also be understood as the viewpoint of a committed movement, "un intento de desbaratar el sistema patriarcal y [. . .] de erigirse como signos de discontinuidad con la tradición" (Fernández Rodríguez 124). As Korsmeyer explains, "feminist artists share a political sense of the historic social subordination of women and an awareness of how art practices have perpetuated that subordination" (Korsmeyer). That is, the destruction of the "silencing of women and making them and their experiences invisible is a common theme in feminist theory" (Rakow 288). Lola obviously plays this role as well; in fact Jaime states that Lola "Lleva la reivindicación feminista en los genes" (*Venganza* 258). Perhaps for that reason, and even though she recognizes that she has been named to the Supreme Court because she is a woman (*Venganza* 16, 25) and suspects such to be the case when she was named presidenta of the Sala Penal de la Audiencia Nacional (*Canaima* 98), Lola is very much in favor of a quota system (*Venganza*

16). This desire to establish herself outside of the realms of patriarchal protection also becomes apparent in *Venganza* when she tells Iturri "¿Protegerme? ¿Quién te ha nombrado mi protector? ¡Ya me cuido yo solita, gracias, no necesito a ningún inspector de la Interpol!" (280), reflecting what she had already affirmed in *Dr. Wilson*: "Me saca de quicio que la gente tome decisions por mí, aunque sea mi marido y lo haga por mi supuesto bien" (228). But it is not just in the professional arena where Lola is committed to destroying the historical subordination of women; she also carries out the same in her personal life. When Lola perceives that Jaime is seeking more and more fame and power, and his quality time with the family has diminished to practically nothing, Lola "[l]e había obligado a escoger. Y [él] había optado por el poder" (*Venganza* 59), with Lola then forcing "a Jaime a abandoner nuestra casa e instalarse en un hotel" (15).

Lola's commitment to feminism, while perhaps more subdued than the more militant, or radical, second-wave feminism, is not just aimed toward increasing the number of women in the workplace, giving women a voice, or the destruction of those patriarchal values such as the objectification of women; rather, she goes to the point of even subverting the patriarchal "male gaze" (Mulvey) into an instrument of her own, becoming herself, then, a "female gazer." In fact, one of the very first descriptions that the reader has of her in the series is her being awakened by her husband, still in her "estrecho pijama de batista que marcaba las pronunciadas formas de sus caderas" (*Hemingway* 79). A few paragraphs later, Jaime comes out of the shower and Lola, who "conocía al milímetro su anatomía" (80), indulges herself: "a Lola le encantaba contemplar el cuerpo desnudo de su marido" (81). When Jaime asks her what she is looking at, she replies "'Mis posesiones' replicó ella. 'Tengo que proteger mi inversión'" (83). Evidently, from all textual indications, this female gaze has been present from the beginning of their relationship some twenty-nine years ago (*Venganza* 230) and continues even in the last novel of the series when Lola goes to be with him in Boston (*Venganza* 153). Further evidence of the fact that she converts the "male gaze" into a "female gaze" for her own pleasure are her multiple adventures with Iturri which, by her own admission, "representaba el feliz pasada" (*Canaima* 277). In *Dr. Wilson*, she admits that from the first time she met Iturri "su porte exudaba una pizca de extraña elegancia, un no sé qué que me atrapó. Sus facciones eran bonitos, como perfiladas y retocadas por un artista clásico" (179). When he comes to her house to discuss the Canaima case, it is quite evident that she has spent time in the past gazing on him as more than just an investigator under her authority, and with her own husband sitting at the same table, Lola

> se entretuvo contemplándole [a Iturri]. No había cambiado apenas. Mantenía todavía la barba corta, perfectamente cuidada. Llevaba el cabello oscuro y liso cepillado hacia atrás y engominado, como antaño. Sin embargo, se le notaba la madurez. Las canas de las patillas, la barba y la nuca hacían su porte más elegante. Aunque no estaba gordo, su estómago obligaba al último botón de su chaleco a aferrarse con desesperación a la hebra que lo unía a la pieza. (*Canaima* 279)

Lola's relationship with other males involves more than just a gaze. While she is not one to resort to violence or abusing criminals'/suspects' rights, she does fairly frequently employ trickery and fabrications in order to ensnare them or throw them off her real intentions. Her manipulativeness and deceit are evident from the first novel of the series. When Iturri is investigating the murder charges against her and meets with her to get her version of the events, "[t]raté de componer una mentira creíble empleando retazos de verdad. Todo lo que dije se acercaba notablemente a la realidad, todo salvo que omití lo fundamental. Le narré los hechos accesorios e hice permanecer, toscamente oculto, el fundamental" (*Hemingway* 201). Later on in the same novel, she is less than forthright with her own husband Jaime saying she does not know the relationship between the secret society with which her professor-mentor is involved and herself when, in fact, she is fully aware that it was her mentor's involvement with the group that led to his demise (314). In *Número primo*, she leaves the rural church where the two mutilated corpses of the clerics have been found and walks over to where Father Lucas is resting, telling him that "ninguna de las preguntas que le formulo está destinada a inculparle. Sólo quiero aclarar las cosas, únicamente. [. . .] yo no creo que usted tenga nada que ver con estos hechos—mentí" (213). In *Canaima*, she successfully, and secretly, retrieves the materials from Herrera-Smith's hotel safebox by sending her male student guide off on a mission to retrieve a conference poster and distracting the others by giving them a box of candy in the cafeteria (219). She then hands the safe box code to the front-desk staff only five minutes before shift change and ensures her ruse by sending her male FBI escort to ask the students in the cafeteria if her poster has arrived yet (219). In the same novel, and immediately prior to María's internment, she tells her secretary that she has not decided if she will go to the funeral celebration or not, even though both of them know clearly that she will attend (*Canaima* 129). In *Dr. Wilson*, she is the one who comes up with the idea of her, Jaime, and Iturri pretending to be journalists in order to interview the psychiatrists at the conference in an attempt to determine which one is really Doctor Wilson (260). And in *Venganza* she repeatedly tells people that Jaime is not at her investiture on the Supreme Court due to a flight delay when, in fact, he is on his way to Boston for a three-month period (52). In spite of this, however, she is not a pathological liar; quite the contrary. Her deceits are merely a means to an end, an intentional manipulation of facts and events in order to operate most successfully in the masculine world, and they reveal that Lola is quite capable of subsuming masculine characteristics or traits when such is necessary.

While Lola never resorts to the physical violence so common to the *novela negra*, she can be quite combative and aggressive—a "masculine" trait according to López-Sáez, Morales, and Lisbona (613), and, thus, another indication of Lola's feminist agenda—when she perceives personal slights, even if they are of a non-physically threatening nature; that is, she suffers no remorse, awkwardness, or weakness in showing dominance over males. When she discovers that the police have entered her Singapore hotel room unauthorized, she remonstrates the policeman, denying that Ng is her lawyer (*Canaima* 208) and insists that she be called "señoría" and not "señora" (*Canaima* 211). She also threatens to file a formal complaint against the Singapore police (*Canaima* 209) and tells the ambassador that she wants in writing an apology from the attorney posing as her lawyer (*Canaima* 216). When she learns that the black car she has seen on multiple occasions parked outside her house belongs to the FBI, she gets on the phone with the FBI agent Kalif, whom she had met on the Singapore trip, exclaiming that "voy a poner fin a todo esto inmediatamente" (*Canaima* 325). She fulminates against him, blaming the FBI for all the murders even remotely related to the case and for coming after her too. Intuiting that her phone and house are bugged, she orders him to remove them all (*Canaima* 332). When she learns that the envelope she placed in the trash can was not the original "Canaima file" the extortioners have demanded, and that Iturri and Kalif have switched the envelopes, she realizes the potential physical danger to her family and reacts violently: "Lola lloraba mientras con los puños golpeaba a Iturri en el pecho" (*Canaima* 382); she lambasts Kalif as a "canalla" (*Canaima* 382) who does not care at all about her or her family, and castigates him by asserting that: "Sólo quiere vengarse de los que atentaron contra un compatriota. ¡El FBI, son todos unos matones!" (*Canaima* 382). And in *Venganza*, when Iturri refuses to help Jaime resolve the attempted extortion case against him unless Lola agrees to go to the prison to visit Rodrigo, she explodes: "¡Cabrón, hijo de puta! [. . .] ¿Sabes lo que te digo? ¡Que no eres más que un cabrón! [. . .] El cabrón eres tú, Iturri. Mucho más que eso" (159–60).

As a feminist, Lola is especially combative and fierce with matters that deal with gender-related cases.[6] She is very much in tune with the bonding of women, and it is in these matters where she most clearly approximates the feminist cause of solidarity among women and fighting for women's rights, causes, and issues: "Algún tipo de delito, sobre todo los de naturaleza sexual, o los relacionados con el género, despertaba a la MacHor combativa, fiera y, al mismo tiempo, casi miedosa" (*Canaima* 133). She is especially bothered by criminals who escape punishment, such as Ariel, the drug lord who preys on young girls and, ultimately, is responsible for the death of Telmo's granddaughter María: "'¡Mierda, mierda, mierda! ¡Esto no tenía que haber pasado!' se reprochó dolorida" (*Canaima* 115). But this passion also extends to the personal as revealed, to cite only one example, when Lola wishes her secretary Susana luck in her quest to get her boyfriend to propose marriage (*Canaima* 67). When Lola sees Ángela in the court hallway with evidence on her face of having been beaten, "Enseguida apreté los dientes; de no haberlo hecho, la erupción volcánica en mi interior había salido con toda virulencia" (*Número primo* 357), and "[e]mpleé todas mis armas" (362) in an unsuccessful attempt to get her to file charges against, and divorce, her husband.

IV Postfeminist Values

"Postfeminist" is another type of critical framework that rejects as too restrictive both the stereotypical, traditional values of patriarchy and the women-united-against-oppressive-males focus of feminism for one in which the woman plays an important role both in society and in the home but with marked ramifications. As Tasher and Negra point out: "postfeminism [. . .] incorporates a negotiation with hegemonic forces in simultaneously assuming the achievement and desirability of gender equality on the one hand while repeatedly associating such equality with loss on the other" (108), and "the continuing contradiction between women's personal and professional lives is more likely to be foregrounded in postfeminist discourse than the failure to eliminate either the pay gap or the burden of care between men and women" (108). What then, constitutes "postfeminist discourse"? In clarifying such a definition, and demonstrating how such does and does not correspond to Lola MacHor, for purposes of this chapter I will examine Lola MacHor in relationship to various characteristics/motifs generally agreed upon by the critics as corresponding to a postfeminist ideology.

Godsland comments that "nesting" is "one of the notions that underpin postfeminism: the idea of woman's (re-)moval to a well-tended domestic space" (86) with "intentions to become a latter-day domestic goddess" (87). This differs from the patriarchal role of women as keepers of the home since the earlier ideology was imposed upon women, and they had/have no other choice. Postfeminism "nesting" represents a voluntary escape from public life into a place where the woman wishes to be. Obviously, in the first novels of the series Lola is no latter-day domestic goddess: She becomes so engrossed in attempting to solve one case that she fails to hear her invalid son "llamando a grito pelado: tenía que hacer pis" and forgets that the family has plans to celebrate the Noche de San Juan (*Número primo* 529–30). In fact, she even admits that "Soy mujer de asfalto; ni siquiera cultivo geranios en el balcón" (*Número primo* 371). As the novels progress, however, Lola assumes more and more that role. In fact, in *Canaima*, the subsequent novel in the series, she is planting "dos docenas" of red and white flowers in her flower garden when she receives the phone call threatening her son Javier (348–49). In *Venganza*, "contemplé de nuevo mi pequeño jardín [. . .]. No era gran cosa. El césped tenía varias calvas y zonas en las que crecían las malas hierbas y unas pequeñas flores amarillas. Las hortensias se habían abrasado el año anterior y los minúsculos brotes presentaban mal aspecto; el cerezo no crecía. Pero era mío" (122). And in the same novel she is the one who initiates the reconciliation with her husband—thereby attempting to reconstruct her concept of domestic space—by flying to Boston to be with him.

Godsland posits "the postfeminist as a commercially motivated and commercially constructed individual" (89); i.e., the woman is a materialistic being. Faludi addresses this idea, as well, saying that "postfeminist-minded [. . .] women who are shown with 'careers' and economic power but use these gains primarily to shop, obsess about their weight, and whine about loser guys" (Faludi 1647–48) and that

> postfeminism is very much the offspring of modern American advertising. [. . .] Given postfeminism's origins in advertising [. . .] A *commercial* response to the women's movement, postfeminism offers women an adman's Faustian pact: the promise of "powerful" sex appeal and "choices" you buy with your very own credit card, in exchange for genuine power and self-determined choices for all women. (Faludi 1647)

Almost all of these, Lola consistently rejects. She may occasionally be preoccupied with her weight—frequently ordering a "café con leche y sacarina, para compensar," at the various bars—but never does it rise to the level of an obsession.

Godsland also argues that postfeminism exalts the "individual over the collective" (90), adding that "given the differences that exist between women, feminism cannot and never could successfully articulate the demands of women as a collective" (Godsland 95), and Piepmeir notes that "Postfeminism relies on competitive individualism and eschews collective action." Lola's competitiveness is almost exclusively individualistic in nature; while she does, as noted previously, suffer a special twinge of compassion for crimes relating to abuse of young girls, there are no young, female professionals whom she mentors. With the exception of Jaime's commenting that Lola is in favor of the quota system, the reader fails to see her supporting women's causes in general, nor are the gains she has made in breaking the glass ceiling ever globalized as favorable toward women as a whole, other than the one comment that "Somos ya muchas las mujeres que ejercemos en este juzgado" (*Número primo* 501).

Violence, in the postfeminist work, often arises from the female. Godsland postulates that the postfeminist woman "denies the gendered nature of their victimization" (91) and that "women are as capable of violence as men" (92). While Lola herself does not fit this characterization, two women in the novels do, and of both Lola is horrified. Lola goes to visit Jimena Wittman at this one's apartment in order to see if she can obtain the name of the assassins; Jimena, during the course of the conversation, attempts to get Lola to name the sum of money that it will take for Lola to drop the case, to which "Lola se echo a reír. '¡Increíble, té con el diablo!'" (*Canaima* 370). Sarah Shibata, in *Venganza*, is manipulated by Rodrigo into having her personal valet carry out the various murders, including that of her own son. Lola has a hard time believing that Sarah is guilty of such, and Lola, when she finally is able to accept such, "chilló [. . .] fuera de sí" (409). In *Canaima*, Lola hits her son with a candelabra, requiring him to receive five stitches, but such is entirely an accident that occurs when Lola thinks that she is swinging at an intruder who has entered the house. That is, while Lola herself may not subscribe to this particular aspect of postfeminism, at least two of the novels in the series do demonstrate this tendency.

Pérez and Pérez state that "in the post-feminist economy [. . .] the dichotomy between private and public space is no longer so clearly marked" and "[women's] conversations tend to revolve around the workplace as never before" (17). Lola frequently carries work home in order to get it finished; in fact, such is true in all four novels of the series where she is a judge (in *Hemingway* she is the accused, not the investigating judge). In *Número primo* Lola first converses in her home with Jaime about the case; then after the clerics have departed her house following their stay there while the police are sweeping the Archbishop palace for a bomb, Iturri, Jaime, the Nuncio and Lola all discuss the case. Later, at her home she questions Chocarro concerning aspects of the case and further discusses the investigation with the Nuncio when he returns to her house to answer a theological question she has asked him to clarify. In addition, she actively works on the case at home and becomes so engrossed writing up the various points and attempting to understand exactly the various nuances that she forgets completely about taking care of her injured son Pablo (529). In *Canaima*, Lola is described as working on the investigation from home on at least six occasions, even though she does not take on the case until chapter 8 of "Libro Segundo" (page 232 of a 422-page novel): discussing the case with Jaime (259) and with Iturri, (278, 317), talking on the phone with the tax auditor Roque Castaño (309), and comparing notes with Jaime, Iturri, and FBI agent Kalif Uber (322, 355). Obviously, however, Lola works on many other cases at home as well since Susana, Lola's secretary, "la observaba cuando abandonaba el despacho, cada día más tarde, arrastrando los pies, con el traje arrugado y la cartera repleta de documentos por si, por la noche, podía adelantar trabajo atrasado" (*Canaima* 132). On eight occurrences, in *Dr. Wilson*, the reader observes Lola involved with the investigation at home, frequently in consultation with others: alone (288), with Chocarro (282), with Jaime (292, 298), with Iturri (304, 326), with Jaime and Iturri (319), and with the architect Cristóbal Ezponda (309). And, in *Venganza*, even though the events of the novel transpire primarily in the U.S. (74% of the novel's pages, quantitatively speaking) and Lola refuses to become involved with the investigation except under duress, Lola does read at home Rodrigo's latest missives (94).

Pérez and Pérez note that in postfeminist works "[t]he majority of women characters are now working women, [. . .] most of them struggling to balance family and career" (16). Lola certainly reflects such a tendency. She is employed outside of the home and struggles mightily to balance the conflicts. In *Número primo*, she and Jaime get into an argument about such, and she casts in his face, "Eres la única persona que no comprende que como juez tengo obligaciones inaplazables. Te recuerdo que hay alguien ahí fuera matando gente, y no a cualquiera, ¡a tus queridos curas!" (409). And, in *Dr. Wilson*, Lola comments that "El trabajo—el de la Audiencia y el de casa—tiraba por igual de mí" (18). In addition, she frequently suffers not only from the conflict between work and family obligations but also because she views her work as less than satisfactory. In fact, such is her frustration that in *Canaima* the narrator notes: "Definitivamente, se había equivocado de camino. Había corrido, había escalado, había ascendido, no obstante, todo aquello la había conducido a una tierra de nadie. ¡Cuánto había perdido! Antes era una mujer agradable, alegre, que se permitía ser despistada o instintiva; ingenua, incluso. Eso había quedado atrás" (54).

V Conclusion

While it may be true that there are certain residual elements of a patriarchal, feminist and postfeminist mindset within the novels, the preceding analysis of the narrative elucidates both how Calderón denies each as her sole aesthetic and goes beyond those ideologies in creating/reflecting a new paradigmatic—or non-sexist ideological—structure. That is, Calderón seems to reject ultimately the masculine-oppressive patriarchy and the masculine-as-oppressor feminist, as well as the liberated-professional-suffering-woman postfeminist aesthetic. Relations between the sexes demonstrate more clearly Calderón's presentation of an almost gender-neutral—although certainly not libido-absent—narrative. Having said such, there is a fair amount of traditionalism still in her works. Clearly then, the novels closely reflect the changing role of women in Spain at the beginning of the third millennium.[7]

Notes

1 The first female P.I. in Spain, Bárbara Arenas, was created by Lourdes Ortiz in her *Picadura mortal* (1979). Among the other, more-widely recognized female detectives prior to the appearance of Reyes Calderón's Lola MacHor are those created by—in no particular order—Maria-Antonia Oliver (Apol.lònia Guiu), Isabel Franc (Emma García), Carme Riera (Teresa Mascaró), Adelaida García Morales (Silva), and Alicia Giménez-Bartlett (Petra Delicado). Lola MacHor, however, is the first *juez de instrucción* among the group.

2 As of December 2012, women in Spain constituted only 7.62% of the incarcerated population, 7.35% of those convicted of crimes, and 9.24% of the prisoners on remand (Secretaría General de Instituciones Penitenciarias). While the disparity between the number of female and male criminals may be great, the gender difference between those in overseeing the investigations, defense, and prosecutions of those criminals is quickly shrinking. The Council of Bars and Law Societies of Europe (CCBE) reports, for example, that as of October 2011—the most recent data available—40.2% of members of the bar in Spain are female. And while the International Association of Women Judges (IAWJ) boasts membership from 103 countries, none of which is Spain, Ekberg Fredell and Dahlerup do report that 36% of the Spanish judiciary is comprised

of women judges in 2000 (12). In that regard, Lola is a quite veridical representation of the changing face of the Spanish judiciary throughout the years in which the various novels of the series were published.

3 Even today, only two of the current twelve members of the Tribunal Constitucional de España are women; these are Adela Asua Batarrita (from Bilbao, Professor of Penal Law, appointed December 2010), and Encarnación Roca Trías (appointed July 2012; Vicepresidenta del Tribunal since June 2013). Only three of the forty-eight Magistrados Emeritos listed on the Court's website are women: Gloria Begué Cantón, serving 1980–1989 (Vicepresidenta del Tribunal, 1986–1989); María Emilia Casas Baamonde, serving 1998–2011 (Presidenta, 2004–2011); and Elisa Pérez Vera, serving 2001–2012.

4 "En España, las mujeres tuvieron prohibido el acceso a la carrera judicial hasta 1966. Y tuvieron que pasar 11 años para que ingresara la primera mujer" (Lafuente).

5 That Lola, a woman whose formative years were under the Franco dictatorship, would vigorously oppose her husband is especially revealing of her feminist beliefs in a country such as Spain which had long had laws on the books concerning "patria potestad (legal authority of the father or husband over the female)" (Pérez and Pérez 8) and where "uxorcidio por causa de honor [. . .] se mantuvo en vigor en el ordenamiento jurídico español hasta la aprobación de la ley 79/1961" (Martínez) at the end of 1961.

6 See Cook and Fonow for a more in-depth discussion of the techniques used in standard sociological, feminist research, which helps to explain how and why events in Lola's past profoundly affect her gender relations and desire for consciousness-raising for the empowerment of women.

7 For further reading concerning the changing society in Spain, see John Crow's *Spain: The Root and the Flower*, in particular, pages 418–22.

CHAPTER THREE

Narrative Ethos: From the 19th to the 21st Centuries

I Dehumanization and Animal Imagery

Naturalism, a late nineteenth-century literary movement, evolved out of the earlier literary movement of Realism as a result of the studies by Darwin, the philosophy of Comte, and the sociological impacts of the Industrial Revolution. These writers' works purportedly "objectively" examined life without the interference of authorial directives guiding the plot to its ultimate denouement in a literary experiment influenced by the scientific method. In reality, however, most of these authors ultimately produced literature of social protest employing what has now become known as Naturalist techniques or characteristics, the most important of which include: a desire to replicate a believable everyday reality, a devaluation of religion and exaltation of science, a positivist objectivity in which there is an attempt to explain everything through science, an emphasis on the sordid subject matter which exposes the harshness of life, an inherent social criticism, and dehumanization.

That Reyes Calderón employs fairly frequent usage of 19th-century narrative forms and techniques is the focus of this chapter, but even a superficial reading of the novels reveals that the two main male characters do not necessarily belong wholeheartedly to the contemporary world. Iturri, in fact, uses "la antigua fórmula—'permiso'—" (*Hemingway* 258) prior to sitting in a chair to talk with Dolores and Gonzalo at the café and believes that men need ideals to "compensar, al menos en parte, el peso de su animalidad denigrante" (*Venganza* 310). The case of Jaime is stated even more explicitly: "Al conocer más a fondo a Jaime Garache en su entrevista en la cárcel, al inspector Iturri le había parecido retrotraerse a más o menos el siglo XIX" (*Hemingway* 254). Such, then, provides ample justification for a character examination based on one of the primary tenets of Naturalism, dehumanization, and its tangential offshoot, animalization. While Chamberlin is speaking of another novelist from a different time period, his comments are just as true in regards to the MacHor series: Dehumanization, and in particular animalization, or the portrayal of humans via animal imagery, helps to "ilustrar, poner en relieve y reforzar el tema y la tesis de la novela" (24). Jeremy Medina explains that animalization in the Spanish naturalist author Blasco Ibáñez's works has as a common purpose "to emphasize man's similarity to the brute force and primitive irrationality of animals, to demonstrate that the pressures of environment and heredity have reduced man to a sub-human level" (204). In a similar fashion, animal imagery plays an important role in the five novels of the Lola MacHor series, and the association of animal characteristics/attributes to humans has as a major function that of social commentary, social critique, and a call for social justice.

Los crímenes del número primo is the Lola MacHor series novel for which the author is perhaps most widely recognized. It is also the novel which contains the most varied use of animal imagery with every major character (except for Nuncio Tagliatelli) and many minor characters being described in this manner. In fact, some sixteen different characters (including two collective nouns) are depicted via thirty-two animal images, two plants, and nineteen other elements in a total of seventy distinct, dehumanizing portrayals. Even the title of the novel itself dehumanizes the criminal, but it is the assassin who applies that clue to who he is as a reflection of his prime nature; i.e., his homosexuality.

The assassin, who the reader learns at the end of the book to be an antiquities art dealer, decides to exact revenge upon the Leyre Monastery official who expelled him ten years prior due to his sexual orientation. He perceives himself to be the one carrying out justice against Satan, a being described in the narrative as dressed in cleric robes, whose smoke has invaded the entire temple, and whose infiltration of the monastery is evidenced through the clerical officials' involvement in the merchandising of church antiquities (497). One of the initial descriptions of the assassin occurs in the first chapter; when he kidnaps the monastery abbot and draws back the habit's hood in which he has concealed himself: "Sus ojos felinos resplandecían con el metálico brillo de las luciérnagas" (15). This triple imagery—cat eyes, metallic gleam, and fireflies—all lead to dehumanize even further someone who has just kidnapped a cleric with the obvious intentions of murdering him. Somewhat later in the narrative, the assassin, in fact, places two Persian cats in the lap of the abbot and watches while the cleric's allergic reactions lead to his death.

The first clues that Lola MacHor obtains concerning the suspect come from Fermín Chocarro, the sacristan of the Leyre Monastery, who has dreams concerning the investigation, the assassin, and events which either have happened or soon will happen to Lola and/or Juan Iturri. In his dreams, he envisions the assassin as a dehumanized man with two faces, one benevolent, the other extremely malevolent. But what the faces have in common are "los ojos; son verdes y en ellos se puede leer la palabra *muerte*" (373). These "ojos verdes" become an epitaph for the character in the remainder of the novel, with the character being referred to in this manner some sixteen times—only two of which occur after Lola arrives on the suspect's ranch in the closing pages of the narrative.

But a close textual analysis reveals that even the "nice" appearance of the assassin that appears in Chocarro's dreams is additionally dehumanized through the use of the word "faz" (372, 398), a word more commonly associated with buildings, topography, or coins than with humans, with which it generally carries a negative connotation.[1] Regardless, the particular use of "faz" in this context is revealing in that the assassin believes himself to be the exactor of justice and commanded to eliminate Satan from the monastery. The assassin's intentions are good—dare we say "holy"?—corresponding to his "faz agraciada, suave, dulce" (372), but his murderous methods are represented by his "rostro, esta vez duro y amenazante: dos pequeños cuernos asoman en su frente, y de su boca salen largos colmillos afilados" (372).

Lola first "meets" the assassin in the Archbishop's Palace toward the conclusion of the funeral service for the abbot and the Archbishop. She has left the church and gone to the palace because the archbishopric has received another package containing a severed finger. Since Monsignor Tagliatelli, the Nuncio who is officiating the service, is to lodge in the palace—and Lola suspects him to be the next target for assassination—a bomb squad is called in for security measures. While Lola and Iturri are discussing the case, the assassin, dressed in a bomb squad suit, passes by them and purports to be making one last sweep to collect in his bag any remaining tools (380). However, when Lola goes to the "tercera planta" of the palace, she once again sees the bomb squad member, who now is wearing only head protective gear and has no bag in which to place the "missing tools." She quickly intuits who the man is, but she is unable to arrest his escape or to observe the suspect's eyes through the face mask (382). Picking herself up from the floor, after having fallen in the chase, she is left simply to call for another bomb squad sweep, which does discover an artifice in the Nuncio's wardrobe set to explode at eye level.

The assassin, at this point in the novel, is a virtual non-entity; his name is not known. To the staff of Faustino Gorla, the assassin's lover who lives in Málaga, the suspect "es como un fantasma" (430). They have never seen him at all, and there are no pictures of him anywhere in Gorla's house; Gorla always sent the staff away or told them not to come to work when his lover was to be in town. It is only at the end of the novel that Lola is finally able to meet the suspect in person when she goes to meet the President of the Spanish Art Dealers Association on his ranch outside Toledo. Once on site, she quickly realizes that the art dealer himself is the assassin and in an attempt to save her own life argues that his mother would not be proud of his exacting of revenge.[2] Such evidently is effective as he quickly takes a gun, aims it at his own head, and "[l]os bellísimos iris verdes, el elegante óvalo de su rostro, los rizos azabaches, la dulce piel morena, la angustia encerrada, todo saltó por los aires. Se convirtió en una masa sanguinolenta que se desparramó por la habitación" (565). That is, with the exception of very brief periods—such as Lola's recapping of his biography as a novitiate at the Leyre Monastery and as an adult interested in antiquities—the assassin is always presented in dehumanized fashion: he assumes other names and professions as an adult, his feline, green eyes predominate any discussion or description of him; his being concealed in a monk's habit and/or bomb squad suit/mask at every crime scene, and even his shadowy, phantom-like presence in Málaga, all work together to present a character of the basest sort far from the realm of normal humankind.

Given the nature of the assassin's objectives (revenge for his mother's suicide brought about by his being expelled from the monastery due to his homosexuality and the expelling official's later use of a Church reliquary as collateral for a gambling debt), the principal targets of his actions are clerics associated with the Catholic Church, and the Leyre Monastery most particularly. Pello Urrutia, the Leyre Monastery abbot, is an old man suffering from dementia (57). In fact, it is just that which causes the monastery's Rector and Maestro de Novicios to hesitate/refrain from calling the authorities when the abbot, the abbey's vehicle, and the church's paten and host, all inexplicably disappear at the same time. Little is revealed in the novel about Urrutia—other than he was the abbot when the future-assassin was expelled and who, along with the Archbishop, presided over the funeral service for the lad's mother (511)—but dementia is not the only dehumanizing characteristic attributed to him; he is also tangentially dehumanized when he dies upon inhaling cat hair (47). Furthermore, even in his younger days, when he was well respected, the physical characteristic of his that most stood out was "su nariz aguileña" (31).

And in his last moments in the monastery immediately before being kidnapped, "sus piernas tiritaron como hojas de otoño [. . .]. Hasta su nariz, de por sí aguileña, se incline peligrosamente hacia su boca, abierta por el estupor y la sorpresa. [. . .] su mente se apagó como claudica la pasión: de improviso. Ciego, trastornado sin remedio, hizo lo que nunca habría aconsejado a otros: abandonó raudo el templo en dirección al infierno" (13). Certainly legs trembling as autumn leaves, an eagle-beak nose inclining dangerously toward one's mouth, and one's screaming for mercy because one is ingesting cat hair are not positive portrayals of a normal person in his/her right mind. In effect, Urrutia is dehumanized through both plant and animal imagery which further elucidate his growing mental incapacity before his death.

Blas de Cañarte, the Navarra Archbishop, is the second cleric killed and mutilated in the novel; the assassin cuts a finger off of each priest with a cigar cutter and includes it in the subsequent "ransom" note (48). No negative animalization, however, is directly related to the Archbishop, the assassin's distant cousin. But, rather, all animal associations are a positive description of him as a cleric who "cuidaba de su grey" (117) in the best way possible, as a true representative of Christ, the most holy Shepherd. The narrator's descriptions of him reflect that positive view, portraying him as a cleric concerned with even those "dentro de su rebaño" (118) who are part of a dissident sect, but for whom Cañarte would leave the "noventa y nuevo buenos animales" and go in search of the "oveja negra" (118). In fact, the only negative dehumanizing characterization of Cañarte is in the discussion with his advisors about how to deal with the ransom note, and he, believing the threat to be somehow caused by, and directed toward, him, "el rostro del prelado simulaba un sudario blanco y muerto" (127). This single, direct, negative dehumanization occurs only a few pages before his demise and, as the case with the Abbot Pello Urrutia, corresponds to an unstable cleric about to make a decision and act in a manner which will lead to his own death. Archbishop Cañarte does not tremble as an autumn leaf; neither does he have a genetically-imposed eagle-nose nor die by ingesting cat hair, but possessing a face that appears to be a white shroud and already dead both dehumanizes the cleric and foreshadows his proximate future.

On three occurrences Lucas Andueza, Blas de Cañarte's secretary, is portrayed through animal imagery; on all three occasions he appears in a negative light. When he agrees with the Archbishop's advisors and recommends trying to buy off the kidnappers, Lucas "[d]irigió sus pequeños ojos de crustáceo hacia el arzobispo" (127). Lucas is, in fact, "trapped inside his shell," unable to express himself while serving as a mere secretary to the Archbishop and one who normally would not even be included as an active participant in the Council of Advisors meetings. Later, he drives the Archbishop to within walking distance of the appointed place, hears the assassin's shotgun blasts and, devastated, remains at the crime scene. When Lola arrives and introduces herself, he notices the blood on his hands and "la altivez de su rostro aquilino se esfumó" (205). While the proud eagle may disappear, during the course of the interview, animalization recurs when "sus pequeños ojos de insecto se clavaron en mí" (214) before Lola is finally able to get him to disclose what he knows about the crime. There are two other dehumanizing descriptions of the secretary: "sus ganchudos dedos" (159) when he reaches for what he perceives to be a ransom note delivered to the Archbishopric, and his being "carcomido por algún profundo sufrimiento" (203) when Lola first meets him at the crime scene. Through these dehumanized descriptions of the secretary, the narrator presents in a negative light a priest collaborating and supporting a bad decision to attempt to negotiate with kidnappers and unwilling to voluntarily assist in the criminal investigation.

Two other important priests at the Leyre Monastery are initially also unwilling to participate in the investigation: the Rector, padre Ignacio, and the Maestro de Novicios, padre Francisco. When they are being unhelpful to Lola, even disingenuous in their responses (not yet aware that the abbot has been murdered), it is abundantly clear through her verbal expressions and the dehumanizing imagery that Lola does not like either of them. In fact, she markedly points out what she believes to be hypocrisy, obstruction of justice and outright lies, adding that "¡Se supone que son cándidos como palomas!" (277), but she believes them to be "aquellas cucarachas marrones" (277). That is, their teachings and actions are quite disparate, in her view. And while Ignacio's eyes are blue, as opposed to green, the narrator's employment of identical animalistic imagery in describing the Maestro de Novicio Ignacio's and the assassin's eyes ("ojos felinos") demonstrate both the past and present relationship between the two while further dehumanizing the cleric through "esos ojos azules que parecen taladrarte el alma cuando te miran" (326) and "sus bellísimos ojos felinos" (259), respectively.

Contrasting with these two priests is the Leyre sacristan who discovers the missing paten, host and abbot, Fermín Chocarro. His first discovery is the missing paten and host, at which point "el temor volvió a embestirle con la fuerza de un toro bravo" (22). Instead of acquiescing to this fear, as well as to his perception that someone/something is still in the church, he "bramó" (25), telling the "intruso, hombre o demonio" (28) to show himself, that "tengo la fuerza de un oso" (24). Later, when it is discovered that Urrutia as well is missing, Ignacio temporarily incarcerates Chocarro in his chambers and forbids his communication with anyone for having opposed his decision not to notify the authorities, accusing the sacristan instead of "embestir contra las puertas como si se fuera un buey" (59) and having "su cabeza llena de pájaros y ensoñaciones" (60). Interestingly, this "bull in a china shop" description and actions reflect a survival of the fittest character trait which ultimately leads to his salvation—and, in the novel's epilogue, election by the monks as their new abbot to replace Urrutia—and contrasts so sharply with the presentation, actions, and deaths of Urrutia and Cañarte, the two "weak" priests who wind up assassinated.

Lola's perception of Chocarro, while also occasionally described in dehumanized terms, is not that of a raging bull; hers is one that corresponds to "un monje de profundo amor, con la delicadeza y el primor de los números decimales" (34). When she demands to speak with him, under threat of handcuffing and immediately carrying to jail both the Rector and Maestro de Novicios, she notes his "fornido cuerpo de oso" (267) but cannot believe that he is the "oso asesino" (273). In fact, he takes on more of a "teddy bear" imagery with his "cándidos ojos color miel" (270) and amiable demeanor, leading MacHor to confirm Chocarro's dream that Urrutia has died. In fact, such is Lola's belief in his assistance to the investigation and his gift of prophetic dreams that Lola states that "por Chocarro pondría la mano en el fuego. Y no me quemaría" (*Dr. Wilson* 287).

One other cleric also voluntarily participates in the investigation and assists in the resolution of the mystery, the Nuncio Tagliatelli, who is never described via either dehumanizing or animalistic portrayals, either positive or negative. Such lack of animalization may owe itself, in part, to Lola's positive impression of him and his assistance in resolving the investigation; in fact, Lola meets with him twice in her home and discusses the case even though she knows she should not be doing so, and he is the one who suggests to Lola that she contact the artist guild president, leading her directly to the assassin himself. Additionally, by refusing to present the Nuncio—Rome's representative in Spain—in a negative light, the author is further demonstrating that it is only certain Church officials, and not the Church as an institution, with whom the assassin is angered: "él no iba contra, digamos, la base de la Iglesia; iba contra la jerarquía porque no había entendido" (personal interview with the author).

While *Número primo* does have the most varied animalization and dehumanization, both quantitatively and qualitatively, *Venganza* contains an approximate quantitative equivalent in overall dehumanizing imagery (70 vs. 67). Of the allusions to animals in *Venganza*, however, one-half are similes, whereas the use of that narrative device in the other novels is relatively minor; in them the use of metaphors prevail. In fact, while clearly not every animal–human combination in *Venganza* is a simile, every single character in the novel who is ever portrayed via dehumanizing imagery receives at least one of those associations via a simile: Rodrigo says that Lola pursued him around the world "como un perro de presa" (422). Iturri confesses that he would like to "trepar por [Lola's] ropa, como una araña" (300). Jaime realizes that without Lola he is "Como una botella sin sacacorchos que solo sirve para que la exhiban" (229). Dr. Wilson "se comporta como un corderito, es un paciente modelo" (81) in prison. And Joe says that Rodrigo está loco, como una cabra" (304), to name only a few examples. What these similes all seem to have in common is the fact that they simply reiterate, or reinforce, previous descriptions or portrayals of said characters through animalistic imagery; they do not alter the already-established portrayal of the characters.

Three of the principal characters—Lola, Jaime, and Iturri—are present in all of the novels of the series, and the imagery associated with them remains quite stable. Deviations from such, in fact, generally reveal significant changes in the character, his/her circumstance, or the relationship(s) that said character has with others. All three, with only minor variations, represent the positive side of the equation in the various investigations. Lola, while serving as the investigating judge in the four latter novels, is a victim in the first novel, a role that she additionally fulfills to a lesser extent in the majority of the other narratives as well. Jaime, while generally not directly involved in the investigations, frequently offers advice, in large part because of his medical training. Iturri is the investigator who clears Lola in *Hemingway* and serves as her assistant in the remaining works.

The animal imagery associated with each is therefore representative of their function in the novels. Lola admits her obsessive-compulsive nature in an email to Jaime: "estrategia del avestruz: meter la cabeza en el trabajo y en las rutinas" (*Dr. Wilson* 174). Later in the same novel she calls herself "una idealista, tozuda como una mula. [. . .] Me siguen sacando de quicio las injusticias, los desafueros de los prepotentes y las iniquidades de los poderosos" (235). Her secretary, in *Canaima*, conveys the same idea to Jaime, saying "ya sabe que es terca como una mula" (145). And Iturri throws the accusation in her face: "¡Mira que eres burrica!" (*Venganza* 102). In fact, on several occasions Iturri simply leaves information concerning the Rodrigo case within Lola's reach, and she "sumisa como un cordero, o como un perro apaleado, abriría ese sobre y devoraría ávidamente su contenido" (133). Her sense of justice, empathy toward others, and hatred of violence is such that when Iturri, completely exasperated with their inability to obtain information about Rodrigo from Dr. Wilson in *Venganza*, suggests that: "¿Qué tal un tiro en la rótula? Wilson canta seguro [. . .] Lola saltó como un animal salvaje. '¡Ni hablar!'" (391). But everyone admits that her investigative abilities are second to none; the politician/extortioner Lorenzo Moss and the FBI agent Ramos both call her a "mosquita muerta" (216, 226) for retrieving the Canaima file without their knowledge and discovering the identity of the criminals.

As a victim, in *Hemingway* Lola is totally exhausted: "Ahora era tan dúctil como un flan de arena de playa" (187) and "El calvario había instalado en mis sienes un zumbido persistente y tremendamente molesto" (228). In *Canaima*, while she perceives both herself and her children to be in imminent physical danger at different stages of the narrative, there is no concurrent animal imagery. Such is not the case in *Venganza*; in this work, Lola believes that Rodrigo is determined to kill her and that, once Kimio dies, she is in fact the next one on Rodrigo's list. When Jaime then receives a phone call that Kimio is dead, Joe and Iturri immediately return to pick up Lola and Jaime from the airport. Iturri notes that "[m]e parecieron dos pajarillos, ateridos de frío, perdidos porque se habían caído del nido" (389). And when Sarah grabs Joe's pistol and commits suicide, Lola is so overcome that she freezes, "sin mover un músculo, como un maniquí enfundado en su traje oscuro y su camisa de chorreras" (410).

Many of the remaining animal imageries associated with Lola are personal in nature and do not reflect either positively or negatively on her professional career; they serve, in fact, to make her appear more similar to a normal person and not a stock character. Her snoring is legendary and is described in increasingly powerful imagery; in *Hemingway*, Jaime tells her that at night "te convierte en rana" (83), later saying that she is "como un tren" (124). In *Número primo*, she herself admits, however, that "Ronco con una intensidad digna de un tren y con las formas de un perro en celo" (423). And by the end of the series, Jaime simply says that "Parece que, al dormirse, la poseyera un demonio vengativo de voz cavernosa. O un animal prehistórico, cuyos rugidos taladrasen tus oídos hasta alcanzar el cerebro. Es un sonido insoportable. [. . .] Levantaría a un muerto de la tumba" (*Venganza* 227). Lola, surprised and upset that she is, in her late 40s, pregnant, questions why "la naturaleza me había dotado con genes de coneja" (*Dr. Wilson* 55), especially since she is unhappy with "la zanahoria que tengo por pelo" (*Venganza* 90) and "mis patas de gallo" (*Venganza* 122).

Jaime is not often portrayed via animalistic imagery; in fact, in *Hemingway* and *Canaima* there is a total lack of such. Surprisingly, for the frequency in which he appears and assists in the investigation in *Dr. Wilson* and *Número primo*, there are only three total animal associations attributed to him. In *Dr. Wilson*, Lola needs to talk to someone concerning her belief that the manuscript she has received recounts real murders, so she calls her husband Jaime from her Barcelona hotel room: "Es de los que reviven por las noches, como los vampiros" (171). In *Número primo*, realizing that he has placed his own work ahead of his family, Jaime begs forgiveness from Lola: "Lo siento, Lolilla, de veras; a veces puedo ser tan bruto como un buey" (482) and "Te quiero; soy un mulo, pero te quiero" (486). It is the last novel, *Venganza*, in which dehumanizing associations to Jaime are most frequent. Contemplating his life, he notes that without Lola he is "Como una botella sin sacacorchos que solo sirve para que la exhiban" (229) and that he would never have an extramarital affair in spite of the fact that "soy, como todos, bioquímica con patas" (229). When he goes to Iturri's hotel room, Jaime notes his own poor appearance "[d]elgado como un galgo" (237). Interestingly, the three other dehumanizing references to Jaime in *Venganza* are also narrated by a male, never by Lola. While obviously Iturri has ulterior motives—he would like Jaime simply to disappear so that he could be with Lola himself, his dehumanizing portrayals of Jaime all portray Jaime as powerless from either cold or fear. When the investigation carries them to the dead Russian's estate, Jaime comes back to the car and "[t]emblaba como un flan" (323). Iturri is the one who observes Jaime and Lola waiting at the airport: "Me parecieron dos pajarillos" (389). And Jaime is further described as "[t]enía los ojos del color de los carabineros cocidos: rojos y brillantes" (389).

The imagery associated with Iturri, the third "good" character in all the novels, is somewhat more complex; such follows, however, from his dual roles in the narratives. As a member of the police/Interpol force, he assists the intervention of criminals and represents a positive force for change in the society. Because of his obsession with Lola, and multiple attempts to have carnal relationships with her, he represents a negative or, as the author herself has noted, "Iturri representa la tentación" (personal interview). Professionally, "Juan Iturri se sabía un cameleón" (*Hemingway* 253); his ability to pass undetected allows him to uncover clues to crimes not available to other uniformed policemen. Lola, in fact, says that he has the "mejor olfato que cualquier perro sabueso" (*Número primo* 293) and that his dedication to, and focus on, crime interdiction is such that he is "Como un toro brava recién salido de toriles" (*Número primo* 401). An allusion to Iturri's "bull-ish" nature had appeared once before when Iturri, frustrated at his inability to determine the reason behind Alejandro's murder, "bramó" (*Hemingway* 277) that the professorship position keeps reappearing as a common thread.

Other dehumanizing allusions occur in relation to emotional and physical battles that he suffers: When outside Lola's hotel room in Málaga, suffering from the effects of the poison slipped into his drink, he is "hecho un ovillo" (453), and in the hospital in Barcelona, suffering from a reaction to anesthesia, he references how he feels, all alone in the hospital with no friends, family, or colleagues around to visit, when he tells Lola that she is on the phone with "el lobo solitario" (*Dr. Wilson* 176). When Jaime unexpectedly leaves for three months to the United States, Lola tells Iturri that Jaime is not at the ceremony for her investiture as a Spanish Supreme Court judge because of a flight delay; immediately, however, she notices his "mirada felina" (*Venganza* 48) and admits the truth. Later, after Iturri becomes drunk at a dinner to which he has invited her, in part, in an attempt to get her to engage with the Rodrigo investigation, Lola admits to herself that she really knows nothing about him other than his "nombre, su apellido y la inteligencia contenida en sus felinos ojos verdes" (111). The other reason for his inviting Lola to dinner is that with Jaime's unexplained departure his own chances with Lola might be improved. But such is not to be; she resoundingly rejects him, telling him that once this case is over she wants nothing else to do with him ever. Realizing that Lola will remain faithful to her marriage vows, Iturri bemoans his failure: "¿Quién sino un estúpido teje una tela de araña y queda enredado en ella? La presa era Lola, pero yo era quien estaba atrapado" (*Venganza* 297). And when he and Joe say good-bye to Lola and Jaime at the airport, "Me quedé allí, frío y quieto, como una estatua sin cabeza y sin corazón. [. . .] La maldije para mis adentros" (386).

Corrupt policeman and journalists are always referred to via negative animal, or dehumanizing, imagery. Ruiz, the Madrid policemen who goes to Pamplona to investigate Alejandro's murder and incarcerates Lola and Jaime on unsubstantiated charges, is a friend of the assassin's. Obviously, however, he is not as strong as he would appear: He "bramó" (*Hemingway* 156) that nothing is wrong with Lola (who is suffering a heart attack); one of the policemen immediately comments to another that Ruiz "[e]stá bufando" (157), to which another responds: "Eso intenta, pero con la voz de pito que tiene, lo que realmente hace es cacarear" (157). This emasculation of Ruiz is further emphasized by Lola, who, when writing the story, remembers only his deformed body and "su voz de flauta efeminada girando alrededor de su incipiente calvicie" (163). Inspector Álvarez is the policeman initially involved with the investigation in *Número primo.* Lola, however, has no remorse in demonstrating her dislike for him and considers him a corrupt officer: "Si el inspector Álvarez nació dotado de algo parecido a un alma, desde luego la perdió por el camino" (232). In fact, immediately prior to dismissing him from the case, she tells him that "No sé si usted juega habitualmente en el equipo de los buenos o en el de los malos" (295). At the crime scene where the two violently murdered priests are found, Lola objects to Álvarez's use of the word "curioso" to describe the case, to which he responds that policemen are "pacientes águilas que patrullan el techo del mundo, esperando que los ratones abandonen confiadamente su madriguera y delincan" (232) and that such a case "alegran [sic] el día a cualquier investigador que se precia" (233). Obviously, Lola does not esteem him as highly as he does himself, and when she dismisses him from the case, "[s]us ojos aparecieron tan repulsivos como su boca. Sus rasgos, propios del ave rapaz que era, se afinaron hasta enmarcar la estructura de su calavera" (295). Iturri, meanwhile, is also involved in a pedophile case in which he is convinced that one of his superiors is continuously informing the suspect of the investigation's progress; he tells Lola that "continuaré abriendo manzanas . . . hasta dar con el gusano" (321). In the same novel, Clara refuses to leave the hospital to smoke due to the large "enjambre" (94) of journalists—"cantidad de buitres" (*Hemingway* 97)—outside. And while it may be Lola's archenemy who calls them such, obviously Lola is of the same opinion: "¡Qué bárbaro, estos tipos [los periodistas] son como los buitres!" (*Canaima* 125). In fact, the narrator further explains that "Lola MacHor no apreciaba a los periodistas. Presumían de ser los voceros morales de la sociedad, la conciencia del pueblo, y al final acababan por absorberlo todo bajo sus letras de imprenta" (*Canaima* 34). Lola's escort at the conference in Barcelona opines that Justino Sandoval, another of the invited speakers and an investigative reporter is a "*self-gay* [. . .] solo es feliz junto a un hombre: Justino Sandoval. Sólo se divierte escuchando a Justino Sandoval, leyendo a Justino Sandoval, amando a Justino Sandoval: un *self-gay*" (*Dr. Wilson* 108–9).

Murderers are often presented as animals, or with animal imagery. Rodrigo Robles, in *Hemingway*, has a tattoo of a snake on his groin (116). The as-yet unnamed priest-killer in *Número primo* has "ojos felinos [que] resplandecían con el metálico brillo de las luciérnagas" (15). Ariel, who had raped the 15 year-old María Bravo (she subsequently dies shortly after giving birth) "no deseaba ejercer de cabeza de un ratón escuálido, encerrado en su gueto" (*Canaima* 107) and so becomes a major drug dealer/importer. Lorenzo Moss, the corrupt politician who orders the assassination of witnesses and whose blackmailing leads to Herrera-Smith's suicide, is nicknamed David "en referencia a los antiguos dibujos animados" (*Canaima* 49), David el

Gnomo. Rodrigo, the murderer attempting to conduct a psychology experiment in *Dr. Wilson*, is warned by Dr. Wilson that someone carrying out such an experiment "irá poco a poco trasformándose en un animal ávido de sangre" (67), a "vampiro" (68) and "un monstruo" (68). Later Iturri tells Lola that "[Rodrigo] está como una cabra" (*Dr. Wilson* 390), and Dr. Wilson confirms that Rodrigo es "un animal" (469). Joe, the North American policeman and friend of Iturri who assists in the investigation, says that Sarah Shibata, the intermediary between Rodrigo and the murderer, is "más loca que una cabra" (*Venganza* 414). Rodrigo writes that she "Me recuerda al corderito que se dirige al matadero dando saltos de alegría por caminar junto a su amo" (424), and that she "cayó como una fruta madura" (428) in agreeing to order the various murders. Meanwhile Itoo, the actual exactor of Rodrigo's murderous plans has "ojos [. . .] fríos. Impenetrables e inquisitivos, como hielo negro" (365), and Sarah admits that "¡Él es un monstruo, pero yo le supero!" (409).

In sum, Reyes Calderón's utilization of dehumanization plays an important role in the narratives and characterizations in the Lola MacHor series. The two clerics who are unable to maintain their strength of character, Urrutia and Cañarte, succumb to their animalistic attributes and are soon thereafter murdered. The Archbiship's secretary, padre Lucas, is also described via negative, animalistic portrayals and, although not assassinated, is rendered ineffectual. Ignacio and Francisco, when opposing Lola's investigation, are likewise dehumanized through negative animal imagery, subtly referencing the social reality of today's Spain where civil law has become more important than clerical law. This latter fact is reinforced through positive, animal portrayals of Chocarro—animals are not inherently negative—and the lack of negative dehumanization in the characterization of Nuncio Tagliatelli, who assists the investigation in multiple manners. Lola, Jaime, and Iturri, as representatives of the law, are presented in a positive light while acting in ethically responsible manners. And criminals are almost always associated with negative animalist imagery. That is, the resultant revelations concerning how the author uses this technique in her development and portrayal of the characters parallel her dynamic portrayals of animal and other dehumanizing elements. In short, the association of both positive and negative animal characteristics/attributes to humans has as a major function that of social commentary, social critique, and a call for social justice, while paralleling the portrayal of the various characters in either a favorable or negative light.

II Pathetic Fallacy

Another stylistic technique common to many of the novels is the use of pathetic fallacy. According to Holman and Harmon, pathetic fallacy is a "phrase coined by Ruskin to denote the tendency to credit nature with human emotions. In a larger sense, the *pathetic fallacy* is any false emotionalism resulting in a too impassioned description of nature. It is the carrying over to inanimate objects of the moods and passions of a human being" (347). Calderón's use of the pathetic fallacy, while not extensive, generally becomes more apparent throughout the series. Its relative infrequency of use, however, does point out to the alert reader significant points in the plot and foreshadows important moments in the development of the novels' denouements.

The two occurrences of the pathetic fallacy in the first novel, *Las lágrimas de Hemingway*, bookend the various crimes, deaths and plot twists of the narrative and the resolution of said mysteries. As the novel opens, Pamplona is on the verge of beginning its annual San Fermines festival. The two hours between 6:00 a.m. and the first running of the bulls encompass the first three pages of the book, where the narrator describes nature through the use of multiple animalistic vocabulary and instances of personification: While dawn is breaking, "tímidas luces van seccionando la negrura de la noche" (15). But a storm is brewing, threatening to put a damper on the festivities: "estrapajosos nubarrones, negros como toros de lidia, merodean por el cielo" (15). In fact, the conflict in the weather foreshadows the bad events about to occur at the *encierros*: "en el cielo porfían sol y nubes" (16) until the rain is able to "adueñarse de la plaza" (16). As if this were not enough, the narrator reemphasizes the negative through the mind of the bull farmer, who "tiene la experiencia de un anciano sabio" (17) and who opines that "esa lluvia no es buen presagio" (17).

The storm returns at the close of the novel. Don Niccola, prior to his death, has willed Lola a bound collection of Sherlock Holmes stories, and Lola has discovered in the book binding the letter from Niccola which implicates his law school colleague Rodrigo Robles and the secret society. After Lola and Jaime are subsequently released from jail, the narrative immediately turns to Robles, reading in his home office, unaware that all his plans have been discovered and his own father-in-law is about to appear and tell him to be honorable and commit suicide. Nature, however, is very much in alignment with the impending conflict: "Fuera, un viento avieso y amenazador descomponía [. . .] la tórrida tarde. Con creciente enfado, el viento planeaba sobre la capital a toda velocidad. Parecía que, molesto con el mundo, estuviera buscando un blanco certero [. . .]. En su tercera pasada, las ráfagas consiguieron secuestrar la luz del atardecer" (303).

Número primo opens with the narrator, Lola, seemingly affirming a disbelief in the pathetic fallacy: "Nada ocurre por casualidad. Ni la impávida luz que se filtra tímidamente por las rendijas de tu ventana" (7). Later, she unequivocally reconfirms her earlier belief and her current disbelief in such: "por aquel entonces, creía que cuando el sol penetraba ardorosamente al día, procreaban una jornada sin delitos graves. He cambiado de opinión; la hipótesis de que una meteorología favorable contribuye a vaciar cualquier servicio de urgencias [. . .] no es más que una estúpida hipótesis" (169). In spite of this, the author employs the aforementioned narrative technique on at least six occasions throughout the work, establishing a direct relationship between the events of the novel and contemporaneous weather conditions. The first of these is Lola's initial visit to the Leyre Monastery. After not receiving an invitation to enter the monastery and, instead, conducting an increasingly frustrating preliminary questioning of the three ranking officials "a la puerta de la clasura" (246), Lola notes that "El día, nacido caluroso, iba poco a poco derivando en un gris amenazante" (253), and she worries that a sudden downpour will mess up her coiffure. After further obfuscating by the clerics, finally resulting in their admission that their superiors have not been informed of the abbot's disappearance, "la tarde se volvía plomiza" (256). Lola stays at the monastery several more hours, interviewing the monks individually, but no additional meteorological conditions are noted until she is, close to nightfall, well on her way back to Pamplona and "la oscuridad arañaba al día" (280).

The next day Lola and Iturri visit the monastery and inform the superiors of the particulars concerning the abbot's death. Shortly thereafter, "el temporal dejó caer su furia sobre la tierra" (330). While rain is frequently associated with sadness, Calderón's usage of such serves an additional purpose as well: "el frescor de aquella cortina de agua tuvo efectos balsámicos sobre todos nosotros. Pareció como si mientras mojaba la tierra, enjugara también las lágrimas del alma [. . . y el rector] estaba mucho más tranquilo" (331). This rain, then, serves a cleansing, and calming, effect, and the investigation soon centers on an earlier client of the monastery lodgings whose distinctive perfume aroma had made an impression. In fact, Lola and Iturri leave the monastery believing that they finally are making headway; at the same time, "el cielo parecía recién pintado; su azul lo llenaba todo con su brillo esperanzador [. . .] y el calor campaba nuevamente a sus anchas" (487).

Following this is a series of sunny and hot days until Lola's job requires her to drive outside the city to a site where a body has been discovered on a roadside embankment. Suddenly, the reader discovers that there is an "amenaza de lluvia [. . . which] descargó cuando estaba en un paso de cebra" (490), a change in environment which is emphasized by "tuve una premonición. Se me metió en la cabeza que lo que iba a encontrarme en aquel barranco estaba relacionado con el fatídico caso que llevaba" (491). What happens is that the "body" turns out to be a plastic, life-size doll—the "bait" that the assassin uses to ensure his means of accessing, and kidnapping, the judge. That there is a strong narrative correlation between the plot and meteorological events cannot be denied; when Lola awakens from the beating suffered at the kidnapper's hands, she immediately notices that "era casi de noche y había dejado de llover" (497).

Conversely, the night of June 20–21, when Lola meets with the Nuncio and explains the case, its history, and its protagonists, "era preciosa. El cielo se insinuaba con un azul añil casi transparente ante miles de diminutas estrellas encendidas por el espectáculo. Un leve viento refrescaba la tórrida velada hasta hacerla agradable" (531). And one final association between the plot and the weather combines with other imagery of nature to foreshadow a violent ending to the novel: "mientras nos acercábamos a Toledo, nubes parduscas [. . .] comenzaron a echar fieros [. . .] la brisa [. . .] empezó a encresparse levantando al pasar remolinos de polvo que impedían la vista. En realidad, el tiempo no hacía sino vestir de duelo los acontecimientos: no lo sabíamos, pero era día de entierro" (556). When Lola and Jaime finally make it to the assassin's house—a long driveway bordered with cypresses and rosemary[3]—"había empezado a llover" (557), and "[f]uera llovía suavemente" (560), foreshadowing through a soft rain that Lola's intended death will not be so violent after all.

In the third novel, *Canaima*, the author continues the use of overt personifications of the weather (i.e., rain storms) corresponding to death. "Comenzaba a llover" (91) the very instant when Lola arrives at the building where she works. Psychologically buffeted by her inability to change society and impose true justice, Lola observes María Bravo's—who reminds Lola of her own experience at the hands of a pedophile—folder on her desk; this is Lola's secretary's way of telling the judge that María has died, and the funeral will be that evening. Immediately, "La tímida lluvia había ido ganando intensidad hasta adueñarse del cielo. Más que llover, diluviaba" (100). Shortly later, Lola "[s]e alegró de saber que tanto María como su abuelo eran católicos" (115), since this will provide a known funeral ritual and afterlife, and Lola takes a short walk for coffee. "La última nube se retiró y el sol le abofeteó el rostro. [. . .] Ni siquiera una pequeña nube" (115). That same afternoon, shortly after 2:00 p.m., "[c]aía un fuerte aguacero cuando Lola llegó a la parroquia" (129) for the funeral. That such is directly related to the funeral and the pathetic fallacy becomes even more apparent at the end of the service when "[h]abía dejado de llover y volvía a lucir el sol. El cielo, vestido de añil, ya no lloraba por María" (132).

Interestingly, another instance of rain in the novel parallels an impending death. Herrera-Smith, not wanting to accede to the extortioner's demands, is on the hotel terrace contemplating his next move; outside, "[l]lovió torrencialmente durante una media hora. Goterones enormes" (111). He decides that the only resolution will occur if he can discover the reason behind the attempted extortion, at which point "[e]n un instante, sin casi avisar, la lluvia cesó y apareció un sol de justicia" (111).

Another weather event, a snowstorm, occurs the day when Lola places what she thinks to be the file demanded by the extortioner in the designated hiding place. This serves the narrative structure as a reason for Lola's covering the file with other trash in the trash bin and as an excuse for not appearing for her deposition in court. Interestingly, however, there is no other mention that day—the same day as the FBI calling Cerda, his calling of Moss, and Moss's threatening call to Lola—of snow.

Dr. Wilson, as is the case with four of the five novels of the Lola MacHor series, also opens with the narrator's use of the pathetic fallacy. Instead of rain or a snowstorm, however, this novel employs color associations with nature. "Había algo extraño en aquel atardecer, algo fuera de lo común, completamente extraordinario. Lo notaba en el color de la brisa y en los gritos de la luna. Y en la brusca forma en que el sol penetraba el horizonte y se derramaba naranja sobre el mar" (5). Simultaneously, the narrator decides to kill someone else, Act II of *Madame Butterfly* finishes, and "la patina naranja del mar elevó su intensidad; luego, como por ensalmo, murió. Permaneció extasiado contemplando aquella brusca despedida, la tristeza de Puccini hecha vida" (6).

The pathetic fallacy, however, fails to reappear in *Dr. Wilson* until late in the narrative when Lola, Jaime, and Iturri finally explain to the Shibatas that they believe their house to be somehow connected to the Rodrigo murders case: "La enorme cristalera no lograba amortiguar la cólera de las olas al chocar contra las rocas. [. . .] Había empezado a llover. Sin prolegómenos, con furia. Las rachas de viento barrían el agua y la lanzaban contra el ventanal" (412). Mrs. Shibata finally agrees to call Rodrigo's—and her—psychologist, Dr. Ross i Roví, in an attempt to identify Rodrigo, but Dr. Ross is uncooperative. The next morning Lola rises early, emotionally drained due to her inability to solve the case; what greets her is "lejos de aminorar, la tormenta engordaba por momentos. Fuerte marejada. Mar gruesa, quizás. Las olas parecían gigantes levantándose enfadadas del suelo" (425). It is in this environment that the Shibatas' maid provides conclusive proof that Dr. Ross does know Rodrigo and that Rodrigo, in fact, had visited the ocean-side home while the psychologist had the run of the building.

The fifth novel of the series, *Venganza*, contains multiple, overt utilizations of the pathetic fallacy. The novel begins, unlike *Número primo*, with a statement of affirmation of Lola's belief in the pathetic fallacy: "Cuando abrí los ojos aquella mañana, tenía el convencimiento de que iba a ser un día inolvidable. Hasta los elementos se sumaron: amaneció radiante. Ni una nube" (11). That day is the investiture of her judgeship on the Spanish Supreme Court. Her peace, however, is soon broken as this is the day when she receives notification that Rodrigo—of whom she is immensely terrified—has begun another series of assassinations, this time from behind prison bars in New York, and Rodrigo's letters to Lola implore her to take up the case.

Approximately one-third of the way through the novel, the reader sees Lola on a plane in route to Boston, accompanied by Iturri. Shortly before landing, the plane runs into a storm: "Turbulencias . . . Aquello no fueron turbulencias, parecía el Juicio Final. La tormenta zarandeó el aparato como si fuera de papel" (139), and both Lola and Iturri end up vomiting. This storm, which continues much of the time that they are in the U.S., foreshadows the attempted extortion of Jaime, Lola's rupture with Iturri due to this one's blackmailing her into joining the Rodrigo investigation, and Rodrigo's machinations. In fact, the storm only abates once Lola has visited Rodrigo in prison (217).

Twice, light is employed as a positive reflection of events in the narrative. Jaime, happily reunited with Lola, watches her sleep: "Su cara quedaba parcialmente iluminada por un rayo de la luna que lograba filtrarse por la contraventana. ¡Cómo la había echado de menos!" (227). After Rodrigo names Elena Polvoskha as the latest victim, Lola, Jaime and Iturri drive to the Russian's mansion to visit the crime scene *in situ*. "Pese al frío, el sol brillaba en lo alto. Sus rayos caían a plomo sobre la nieve y provocaban un brillo insólito. El mismo que descubrí en los ojos de Lola" (288).

In sum, Reyes Calderón's use of the pathetic fallacy serves as a means of highlighting the emotional nature of events occurring in the novels, or to nature as it reflects the emotions resulting from those events. The pathetic fallacy also emphasizes key moments and turning points in the novels and foreshadows events yet to occur. That is, Calderón's employing the pathetic fallacy both aids in creating a more mimetic environment and characters, and strengthens the reader's emotional response to such.

III Sexism and Stereotyping

While not necessarily a narrative technique *per se*, the presence of overt sexism and stereotyping in a novel does reveal a mindset tied to a traditional ethos which distances the offending character from the progressive values of a more modern civilization. In these novels, Lola, as well as the other women, almost exclusively performs the stereotypical roles traditionally relegated to the woman, such as preparing the meals and watching the children. But it is the thoughts and subtle, if not unconscious, actions and word choice of the various characters which reveal the depth of those engrained stereotypes.

In *Las lágrimas de Hemingway*, Clara appears to contradict stereotypes. She is the philanderer, going from bed to bed and telling Lola that "perteneces al tipo de mujer que permanece anclada en el pasado y atada a estúpidas supersticiones" (99). However, closer examination reveals Clara herself to be the stereotypical *femme fatale*, but one who is acting out of a desire for vengeance for the suffering she endured as a physically malformed child. Men stereotypically fall for her charms and wind up paying the price in separations or divorces. And even the one man who resists her on repeated occasions, Jaime, "veía aquellos lances a su manera, como un hombre. Le había dicho que no y todo acabado" (*Hemingway* 123). Lola, however, "[i]mpotente para impedir que los celos la embargaran, primero se derritó llorando" (81) and is never totally capable of viewing Clara in any other way than as competition. Lola also demonstrates a certain sexism when she notes "las dotes de observación de su género" (91).

The sexism and stereotyping in *Canaima* are more complex, generally double-edged in nature. When Lola goes to Jaime's lab to pick him up for the benefit dinner, Lola tells him to hurry, to which her responds: "No tardo nada. Soy un hombre" (337). While the comment is positive concerning men, it is a back-handed negative stereotyping of women with the implication being that women are slow dressers. And when Lola leaves for work, and to hand over a copy of the Canaima file to the sitting judge, knowing that such will cause an explosion of stress and bad publicity, she asks Jaime if he is happy. Taken aback, his response is to remark that "¡Pero mira que sois raras las mujeres!" (333). Kalif, meanwhile, has commented to Lola that the FBI "nunca abandonamos a uno de los nuestros [conciudadanos]. Ése es uno de nuestros signos de identidad más características, por encima de las hamburguesas o el béisbol" (328). The narrative includes the stereotype of minorities as primarily criminals when Lola picks up the file of Ariel, who is accused of having raped 15 year-old María Bravo, observes the picture of his "presuntuoso rostro chocolate" (107), and notes that he had "[u]na adolescencia difícil, como tantos otros de su raza [. . .]. Norberto Rosales anhelaba vivir como los blancos, gastar su dinero con ellos" (107). And when Lola finally tires of the FBI car "tailing" her around town, she calls Kalif and chews him out "en plen ebullición irlandesa" (326).

In *Número primo* Lola unsuccessfully attempts to use traditional sexist stereotyping to her advantage when she does not want to be the investigative judge of the priests' murders. Her protestations that "Además, soy mujer, ya conoces que los estamentos eclesiásticos no nos ven . . . " (238) are interrupted by the chief judge—a male—who asks: "¿Y eso qué importa? La justicia carece de género" (238).

Lola, in *Dr. Wilson*, is the one who typecasts most frequently, noting that the manuscript concerning the psychological experiment that she has received contains a hand-written plea for help which "[e]mpleada letra capital, temblona y fea, como de zurdo" (85). When considering the story related, and how one would be able to create said accounts, she says that she "[i]nvitaría a un café con bollo (lo del bollo es esencial [. . .]) a un policía [. . .] y le dejaría hablar" (164). And when Josep María is overcome by emotion and starts crying when telling Lola about his son's brush with the law, "Los turistas que pasaban se le quedaban mirando, extrañados. Hasta unos orientales le dedicaron sendas fotos" (140). One sexist observation is attributed to Jaime, who, according to Lola, "piensa con la cabeza. Para él, el corazón es un órgano femenino, disoluto, voluble, débil, maleable" (439).

La venganza del asesino par, however, has the highest number of sexist and/or stereotyping comments—sixteen—with at least one appearing, on average, every 28 pages, or every five chapters of the novel.[4] While one might be inclined to think that such owes itself to the novel containing four different first-person narrators, three of whom are male, 65 percent of these, or eleven, appear in the "Primera parte," which is narrated by Lola. Additionally, 41 percent of the stereotypes, seven, are comments that Lola herself makes; Rodrigo stereotypes four times, Jaime thrice, and Iturri twice. Quantitatively, then, Lola reveals herself to be more bound to traditional ideas—or at least more free to express such overtly—than the men.

The most frequent stereotype in *Venganza* is negative caricatures of women; all four of the main characters participate in such. Rodrigo, when relating why he dislikes Dr. Wilson's behavior in prison, comments that "llora como una mujer, se queja como una mujer . . . Creo que, dentro de poco, se le declarará la menopausia y empezará a tener sofocos. [. . .] lo que no soporto es que haya permitido que su razonamiento decayese hasta volverse poco menos que femenino" (62). He further adds that "Sí, ciertamente es fácil vencer a una mujer. Cualquier fruslería sirve" (62). After Lola visits Dr. Wilson in prison, Rodrigo writes her a note and, commenting on how afraid she had been, adds "No se preocupe. Es normal. Las mujeres son asustadizas" (223). Obviously, Rodrigo's opinión of the female gender is not very high; he even admits to Lola that when he was first trying to understand her interest in finding him, "[p]ensé en una histeria, tan típica del sexo femenino" (422). Iturri's opinion of women is equally negative:

> Las mujeres me atraen físicamente, pero no las soporto. [. . .] Lo que me ocurre es que su comportamiento me repele. Son orgullosas, pesadas, entrometidas y empalagosas. Intentan saberlo todo de ti, te absorben y, cuando lo han logrado, te reabsorben. Quieren conocer hasta tus pensamientos. Se sienten con derecho a invadir tu espacio, tu aire, tu paz." (298)

Jaime comments that "en ocasiones, resulta difícil confiar en una mujer. No siempre saben asumir responsabilidades. No siempre son de fiar. Te dejan en la estacada en demasiadas ocasiones. Lo quieren todo, pero no están dispuestas a pagar el coste." (258–59). And while Jaime tempers his remarks somewhat by immediately adding that some men act in the same manner, he finishes the thought by reaffirming his chauvinism: "creo que el porcentaje es menor. Yo, para ser sincere, me siento cómodo trabajando con mujeres. Pero no creo que soportara que una fuera mi jefa" (259).

Lola's view of women ranges from negative to positive, with sexism, stereotyping, and traditional gender roles being a frequent expression of belief. Besides being the one who prepares the meals for her family, in order to keep from vomiting during an autopsy, "[l]o único que se me ocurrió fue hacer mentalmente la lista de la compra: leche, cereales, café, magdalenas, chocolate" (*Venganza* 72). And she goes shopping on Saturday simply to pass time, knowing that at El Corte Inglés "pude devolver todo aquello sin dar explicaciones" (103). She supports the traditional, sexist roles when they are to her advantage: after dinner with Iturri, she is upset because he is too drunk to drive and "Se suponía que Juan iba a llevarme a casa" (110). But her sexist views are displaced from the female gender itself onto the parking garage and its "dichosas rampas, que parecían diseñadas para fastidiar a mujeres" (111). At the same time, the aforementioned traditional stereotypes are also tempered, and women are stereotyped in a positive manner. When Lola sees the condition in which Jaime has fallen, suffering from a blackmailer's threats, she notes that she wishes she could exchange positions with him: "Las mujeres encajamos mejor el dolor. Y la vergüenza" (151). And when she visits the prison where Dr. Wilson is encarcerated and sees the building named with letters of the alphabet, her sexist thoughts both praise women and denigrate men: "de quién fue la feliz idea de emplear letras para identificar sitios. [. . .] Seguro que no fue una mujer quien escogió ese sistema" (172).

There are, in *Venganza*, at least two other observations that correspond to racial/ethnic stereotypes. When Lola is recounting how she had become upset with Jaime and ordered him out of the house, she notes that "yo me había limitado a comportarme como una anglosajona civilizada" (18). Jaime utilizes a racial expression, and then immediately wonders why: After Rodrigo angrily says that Elena Polvoskha has just died, Jaime does not believe him, stating that he is a compulsive liar, and telling Joe, "La vez pasada nos engañó como a chinos [. . .]. Me quedé pensando en el porqué de esa expresión. Conozco a algunos chinos y son, sin excepción, magníficos negociadores" (273).

Traditional sexism and stereotyping, in fact, actually work in Lola's favor on one occasion and play a major role in her becoming, in *Venganza*, a judge on the Spanish Supreme Court. She is originally chosen as a candidate simply to fill out the ballot (23), but a journalist writes a short article saying, "Una vergüenza. La justicia debería sonrojarse por que exista una ala cuya historia nunca haya escrito una mujer" (24). The comment soon becomes fodder for vociferous protests by the feminists, and under the clamor of double stereotyping—the journalist also says that Lola "viene de provincias"—the feminists and Basques raise such an outcry that Lola winds up "siendo nombrada por ser mujer y vasca (o vasca y mujer, si se prefiere)" (25), a fact of which she is very much aware and which causes her some consternation. In fact, Lola tells Fernando, the judge who originally had asked her about being a place-holding candidate, "Creo que no voy a encajar en este ambiente vuestro, tan selecto. Formas. Protocolo. Exquisita educación. [. . .] Quizá no sea capaz de civilizarme y ser como tú" (31). At the moment, such is not a facetious comment.

IV Narrative Structure

As opposed to the narrative tropes in the Lola MacHor series which demonstrate a profound attachment to traditional dehumanization, pathetic fallacy, and sexism/stereotypes, the narrative structure of the novels themselves in general demonstrate a remarkably modern, or progressive, angle. Only with *Las lágrimas de Hemingway* does the author construct a work that approximates the classical norms of plot, time, and place. But even here, while the events of the novel occur in Pamplona, the work transpires during the entire week of the *Sanfermines* festival, and there are additional subplots concerning Lola's various conquests and a surprising denouement which reveals a dark side to some of the "good" men. In addition, the novel contains two narrators: the first half is third-person omniscient while the second half is Lola, employing the first-person singular. Also worthy of note, in an examination of the traditionalism/progressiveness of the series, is that the novels all contain multiple characteristics of the rather modern literary subgenre of the thriller, and even more specifically within a subgenre of the subgenre: academic (*Lágrimas*), political (*Canaima*), religious (*Número primo*) and psychological (*Dr. Wilson* and *Venganza*).

With *Los crímenes del número primo*, Calderón makes several changes to the narrative structure which reveal an even more progressive mindset. The author retains a division of the work into three main sections, plus an "Epílogo," but calls each division a "Libro" and adds a "Prólogo" which serves as an introduction to the novel. While the novel basically retains a linear chronology, nine of the twelve chapters of "Libro Primero" begin with an introductory place and time indicator. In addition, the author dramatically increases the use of the first-person narrator with Lola acting in such capacity in the "Prólogo," the "Libro segundo," the "Libro tercero," and the "Epilógo." Lola, now an investigative judge, travels in the course of her investigation fairly extensively outside of Pamplona: to the outskirts of the Navarra capital, to the Leyre Monastery, to Málaga, and to Toledo, where the novel's denouement occurs. An even closer approximation of globalization enters the novel with the Vatican's nuncio coming to Pamplona for the cleric's funeral, the assassin's relating to Lola of his time in Budapest, and the assassin's lover moving to the U.S. Additionally, the subplot of the pedophile case that Iturri (who now works for Interpol) is heading, which is ultimately solved in Malaga and directly linked to Lola's case, corresponds to a much more modern and progressive narrative structure.

Canaima develops even further a progressive narrative model throughout the entire work even though, except for the three-page "Epílogo," it is recounted by a third-person narrator. The setting, however, corresponds to a more global environment with the "Prólogo" becoming, in essence, the first chapter of the novel and detailing Jorge Parada's murder in Caracas, chapter one relating the

World Bank offices' break-in in Madrid, the FBI's collaboration in the ultimate resolution of the crime, and the remainder of the work taking place in Pamplona, Singapore, or Madrid, to where Lola moves at the end of "Libro Segundo" when she takes a job on the Tribunal Supremo. Interestingly, even the topic of Lola's presentation at the World Back conference in Singapore, and the main plot itself—public corruption—distances from traditional themes and anticipates through a fairly extensive account of an attempted extortion of Herrera-Smith what later occurs with Lola herself. Additional foreshadowing, and simultaneous reflection back on Herrera-Smith, is Lola's positive thoughts regarding her own death (143), suicide being something she will later attempt to carry out in *Dr. Wilson*. There are, as well, multiple subplots, with the child-rapist Ariel's threats against Lola and Telmo, and Iturri's infatuation with Lola comprising a significant amount of space. Calderón reveals even more clearly a more progressive narrative structure through her use of a parallel narrative, with alternating chapters recounting simultaneous events in Singapore and Pamplona in "Libro primero" until chapter twenty-three when the plots merge with Herrera-Smith calling and Jaime arranging for Lola to catch a flight to the Singapore conference that same day.

This parallel narrative structure becomes, in *El ultimo paciente del Dr. Wilson*, a braided narrative which corresponds to both Hutcheon's definition—"the doubled or 'braided' narrative of the past in the present" (304)—and Fischer's original idea of this narrative structure as a combination, or alternating between, history and analysis in a single text. While at a conference in Barcelona, Lola receives a manuscript detailing a psychological experiment which involves the murdering of people in different places around the globe. The odd-numbered chapters of the "Primera parte" of the novel are a first-person narrative detailing the quest by Lola—eventually joined by Iturri and Jaime—to capture the murderer while the first ten even-numbered chapters are first-person narratives, written by the assassin Rodrigo, detailing the experiment. "Segunda parte" and "Tercera parte" continue the plot in almost a continually chronologically linear fashion—chapter four of "Tercera parte" flashes back to relate the Vietnamese prostitute's death—and the novel ends with both an "Epílogo" and an "Epitafio." Obviously, the issue of globalization plays an extensive role with the theme of the panel Lola chairs at the conference in Barcelona being crime and globalization (16); Lola going to the nearby Starbucks to drink coffee in Pamplona instead of a local café (378); her receiving Google alerts and PowerPoint (378); five of the seven deaths occurring in non-Iberian countries; the psychologist being a Catalan whose practice is in New York; a key clue appearing when Lola, Iturri and Jaime visit the Aegean island of Santorini; the appearance of the FBI and Interpol to assist in unraveling the crimes; and the actual arrest, trial, and incarceration of the suspect occurring in the U.S.

Dr. Wilson contains several subplots which parallel or closely relate to, and foreshadow, the principal plot of the novel: Rodrigo's killing of a gorilla anticipates, and is reflected in, the death of multiple of his victims. Lola asks the journalist and the sociology professor at the conference dinner the exact same question that the psychology experiment in the manuscript is attempting to answer: can a sane person voluntarily kill people and remain sane? Josep María's son drives the car for his friends who torch a junkie and are seen laughing about it on tape. Additionally, Lola's own psychological instability and attempt at suicide turn out to be a micro "psychological thriller" which anticipates the novel's end and serves as a rationale for Lola's eventual understanding of the assassin (352). And, finally, there are several instances of events that anticipate the novel's end, leading the reader to believe something other than what will eventually be revealed as the truth: When Lola, Iturri, and Jaime visit the Shibata family, Sarah interprets their suspicions that Dr. Wilson knows who the murderer is as an accusation against the psychologist himself; the tension in the room is broken by Jaime suggesting that they call Dr. Wilson and ask him concerning the murders (415). During the phone call, Iturri multiple times directly accuses Dr. Wilson of being Rodrigo, to which the psychologist responds "¡Es usted idiota, lo mismo que sus amigos, una colección de idiotas! ¡Entérense de una vez: yo no soy Rodrigo!" (421). And while all the people at the Shibata house apparently believe, at the end of the conversation, that Dr. Wilson is not the killer but that he knows who the assassin is, the novel's denouement proves that they supposed correctly with their initial thoughts.

La venganza del asesino par also departs from the traditional novel structure in a myriad of manners. While the novel is for all practical purposes linear in nature, it also pertains to the subgenre of the psychological thriller with the assassin attempting to prove that the perfect crime does not exist (43). It contains multiple twists and turns in two parallel plots—one consisting of Jaime's unexplained flight to the U.S., and the other being Rodrigo's detailed recounting of murders of important people around the world from the confines of his jail cell. While the two plots never merge into one, the investigation of both continue in a parallel and simultaneous fashion as Iturri is the only one who can resolve the attempted blackmailing of Jaime, and he refuses to assist unless Lola agrees to join in the Rodrigo investigation. Unlike the majority of parallel narratives, both of the plots in *Venganza* continue until the end of the novel; dual, unrelated plots running simultaneously with the same characters definitely do not match the characteristics of a traditional novel.

The work has four principal sections, each narrated in the first-person singular; the narrators, respectively, are Lola, Jaime, Iturri, and Joe Lombardo, the Interpol agent in Washington, D.C. who had assisted in Rodrigo's capture in *Dr. Wilson.* Contained within the observations of the principal narrators are other narrations by other characters which also demonstrate the progressive nature of the novel; the various genres it contains, besides the normal dialogue, include three letters that Rodrigo mails to Lola (38, 61, 96), a congratulatory note from Sarah and Kimio Shibata when Lola starts her duties as a Supreme Court justice (56), a newspaper article which corroborates Rodrigo's version of Vadertucci's death (84), blogs which detail the deaths of other victims (117, 134, 437, 439), Rodrigo's hand-written note to Lola (222), and a SMS that Iturri sends to Jaime's blackmailer (444).

Additionally, for all intents and purposes the novel takes place in the U.S. At the beginning of "Primera parte," chapter 19, Lola and Iturri board a plane for Boston, and the reader fails to see again any of the characters or action in Spain until the penultimate page of the novel, when Iturri calls Jaime from France to ask him if Jaime sent the lab test results to the blackmailer or not.

The narrative structures of Calderón Reyes's Lola MacHor series, then, parallel the characterization contained therein. Lola grows professionally throughout the novels, moving from law professor in Pamplona to Supreme Court justice in Madrid, setting her own path and developing as an individual. In her journey, she becomes more affected by a globalized society but manages to retain what she considers positive, traditional traits. In a similar fashion, the novels of the series become increasing more complex, more global in theme and setting, and with an ever more progressive structure—culminating in two parallel plots. Yet, at the same time, the novels retain certain traditional aspects, techniques and structures that help them to retain their high artistic value.

Notes

1 The most overt example of "faz" not carrying a negative connotation in the Spanish language when referring to a person's face is "faz santa," the face of Christ. But even this usage normally is in reference to Jesus's image on Saint Veronica's veil, i.e., no longer a living human being.

2 Lola is also included as a target of his assassinations since her name is on the file as the judge who ruled—with no official investigation—the death

of the mother of the assassin to be a suicide due to "una enfermedad mental repentina" (544).

3 In addition, the combination of rosemary—a symbol of memory (The Herb Society)—and cypresses—a symbol of death (Reynolds)—combines the assassin's attempt to avenge his mother's death and the planned death of Lola herself.

4 For computational purposes, I am counting as one multiple stereotypes found in contiguous sentences. Rodrigo's extended paragraph, for example, concerning the various "womanly" ways in which Dr. Wilson is acting are counted as one (*Venganza* 62).

CHAPTER FOUR

Criminality: Causes, Motives and Public Perceptions

Given that the principal crime to be solved in all five novels of the MacHor series is murder, and that two of the five works contain characteristics of the psychological thriller, it is no surprise that the question of criminal motivation and culpability would arise in the narratives. Psychologists and criminologists have long debated whether malevolent personality aspects, traits, and actions owe themselves primarily to heredity or environment and which is more important in the formation of both the criminal mindset and the criminals themselves. Saul McLeod offers a brief summary of various psychological approaches to the debate, and each one's stance on such, ranging from "Biological Approach" (Nature) to "Behaviorism" (Nurture). And while "[i]t is a commonplace of the history of psychology that the use of the terms nature and nurture to frame this debate can be traced to [the 19th-century writer] Francis Galton" (Groff and McRae) in the 1800s, these same two critics note and examine the usage of the two terms as far back as the French author Heldriss of Cornwall in the 1300s. As were many progressive thinkers in the 19th-century Western World, the aforementioned Galton was influenced heavily by (his cousin) Darwin's *On the Origin of Species* . . . (1859) and, in 1883, "coined the term eugenics" (Carlson). By then, however, Zola had already published "Le Roman expérimental" (1880), and Taine's positivist theory about art being motivated, or conditioned, by *race-milieu-moment* had taken the world by storm, resulting in a pseudo-scientific, literary period known as Naturalism which "took as its subject the matter of atavism (ancestral influence as a product of genetic recombination) and a universe of force (cosmic or political) that was almost always subterranean and disruptive" (Lehan xx–xi). Today, however, the rejection by Naturalism of the element of free will is viewed by most psychologists, thinkers, and authors as too restrictive and bound in a 19th-century ethos that does not adequately take into consideration more progressive theories and scientific advancements which favor a continuum ranging from stability to plasticity somewhere along the nature-nurture divide (Berk 9).

In agreement with more modern theorists, Reyes Calderón's Lola MacHor and other major characters do not generally perceive the issue of criminal culpability to be simply a matter of nature, nurture, or free will—or even that these three are mutually exclusive. In fact, many of the characters believe that the elements of fate and destiny may also play a role, at times, in one's thoughts and actions. In *Canaima*, Telmo enters Lola's office and throws the decomposing fetus of his great-grandchild on her desk. Upset because of his granddaughter's rape and the judicial system's lack of finding the perpetrator guilty, Telmo is relieved, at least, that the child will not fulfill its destiny:

> "De haberlo dejado crecer, no hubiera sido más que un cabrón, un cerdo violador" aclaró el hombre, más calmado. "Éste ya no podrá hacer el daño que hizo su padre. No puede decir, señoría, que no se lo advertí. Debía haberla obligado a abortar; eran malos genes, genes de diablo. Usted y ese mierda a quien protege han tenido la culpa: María tiene sólo quince años." (*Canaima* 38–39)

While the assassin Rodrigo proclaims to Dr. Wilson in their first meeting that "No creo en el destino" (*Dr. Wilson* 44), this statement of disbelief in the inescapable effects of fate and genetics is tempered in *Venganza* when Rodrigo attempts to reassure Lola concerning the prisoner Steven, who, as the initiator of a prison-house brawl, had come close to ending Lola's life: "Está muy enfermo. Sus genes están muy dañados" (223). The jailer, on the other hand, seems to agree that the prisoners are merely beings controlled by deterministic influences and that Lola therefore cannot enter the cell block itself: "Estos tipos son como animales, se mueven por instinto" (*Venganza* 173).

Josep María, the Chief Justice of the Catalan Supreme Court who invites Lola to be the moderator of a panel at a Barcelona conference on crime, later attempts to explain the reasons for his son's criminality, telling Lola that the youth's malevolence is a congenital characteristic that has no correspondence to a low IQ:

> Ese chico es así desde que nació. Cuando no levantaba dos palmos del suelo, ya le gustaba torturar a las pobres lagartijas. En el colegio, pegaba a los chavales más pequeños, como un matón de pacotilla . . . Un día entré en su ordenador; lo tenía lleno de pornografía. Y de vídeos extremadamente violentos. Es listo, su coeficiente intelectual es notable. Saca buenas notas, no tengo nada que decir en ese sentido. (*Dr. Wilson* 139)

Fate, as well, plays a fortunate role in the youth's life as it is such that results in his driving the car and dropping his friends off at the ATM. When there is no available, near-by parking space for him, fate thereby results in a sufficient delay for Josep María's son to avoid being with his friends when they pour gasoline on a fifty-year old junkie, light the match, and burn the victim to death. Justino, a fellow panelist at the aforementioned conference, would blame—and excuse—such actions as an indomitable essence of the human being: "ínsito en nuestra naturaleza, hay un germen incoercible que nos inclina hacia la violencia y la destrucción. Nos esforzamos, incluso con denuedo, por lograr la paz, la tranquilidad y el orden, pero somos seres transgresores, incapaces de domeñar nuestra esencia" (128). But Josep María would totally reject that theory, squarely placing the blame on the youths themselves, and their exercising of their own free will to do evil:

> ¿Te lo imaginas? ¿Puedes hacerte una idea de lo que te cuento? ¡Estamos hablando de un asesinato a sangre fría! ¡Se quedaron mirando cómo ardía! Es más, lo grabaron con el móvil. ¡Airearon la llama con ginebra! . . . Y se reían. ¿Tú lo entiendes? ¡Se reían! . . . ¡Por todos los santos, es mi hijo pequeño! [. . .] Según ella [the FBI], la inmensa mayoría de los asesinos en serie presentan al menos dos de estos tres elementos: enuresis, piromanía y crueldad con los animales en la infancia. (*Dr. Wilson* 141)

On the other hand, free will is deemed to be nonexistent, almost irrelevant, or unconsciously overridden at various points in the novels. Even someone as educated and cultured as the gene researcher Jaime Garache himself evidently is incapable of always controlling the totality of his own thoughts and actions: Jaime admits that when Iturri had mentioned the perforated plug in the Garaches' bathroom shower, "Algún resorte se rompió en mi interior sin que yo pudiera hacer nada para evitarlo. [. . .] Cuando quise darme cuenta [a Iturri] le sangraba la nariz. [. . .]. De pronto, me sentí ridículo. [. . .] Ridículo y avergonzado. Porque no soy del tipo de personas que van batiéndose por el mundo. No creo en las espadas ni en los golpes" (*Venganza* 247). Later, Lola as well demonstrates a deficiency of free will when she succumbs to the forces of heredity; in fact, Jaime smiles when he remembers how Lola's face had contorted when the jailer said that women were not welcome in the jail: "Lolilla, mi revolucionaria . . . No puede evitarlo. Lleva la reivindicación feminista en los genes" (*Venganza* 358). In *Número primo*, Jaime discovers that Lola had visited a homosexual bar in Málaga, and he questions her concerning such. She responds that the visit has impacted her and that her appreciation of destiny is such that she now considers herself to have been lucky "al caer en este ambiente, contigo y con los niños . . . ¿Qué hubiera sido de mí si el destino hubiera sido otro?" (486). And when Lola awakens on April 6, in *Venganza*, the day of her investiture as a judge on the Spanish Supreme Court, in her mind it is going to be a great day, "uno especial, plagado de horas alegres" (11). However, "olvidé facturar al destino y a su maldito cabo suelto" (12), and fate turns the day into one quite different from what she had been anticipating.

Such occasional limitations or restrictions on, or simply lack of, free will, on the other hand, are not the sole factor in determining a person's conduct and/or converting said person into a criminal. When commenting on Clara's personality in *Hemingway*, Lola proclaims that "Los caprichos del destino son difíciles de entender. Pero más lo son nuestras respuestas a sus inesperadas embestidas" (223), obviously demonstrating, in the first novel of the series, a belief in personal responsability. Dr. Wilson tells Rodrigo about one of his patients who casually wrote in a web blog "¿Es que la maldad existe?" (51). As a reply, he receives an anonymous note telling him to connect to a certain web site if he really wants an answer. Exercising his free will, he completes the Faustian pact that he finds on that web site and soon discovers that he does indeed reap the benefits of having voluntarily and consciously sold his soul, but that, as a consequence, he also loses his free will and "empezó a hacer cosas que no deseaba" (52). Indeed, just as in society at large, not everyone in the novels believes in the existence of a malevolent divinity or the ability of a person to give herself/himself freely over to such. Rodrigo even interrupts Dr. Wilson's recounting of the experience with the client stating that "Ese ser no existe: es una invención de curas y frailes" (51), but the psychiatrist refuses to debate that issue in particular.

As a novel with a plethora of "curas y frailes," *Número primo* does represent the Church's view of criminality with the abbot, Pello Urrutia, invoking God in his quest against a demonic presence he perceives to have invaded the monastery: "El humo de Satanás, Señor, se ha vuelto a colar en tu casa . . . ¡Protégeme!" (13). When the sacristan Chocarro first enters the monastery chapel and senses something amiss, "Le embargó el miedo [. . .]. Sí, pareciera como si el enemigo, el ángel negro, se hubiera colado en la casa del Padre y acechara ladinamente desde las sombras" (21). But he soon becomes bolder after discovering that something has entered the sanctuary and absconded with the consecrated host, screaming at the unknown and unseen robber to return his Lord. As no one appears, however, his vociferous raging continues, ranging from remonstrations against a human thief to challenges against the divine: "'¡Sal, alimaña corrupta, asqueroso demonio de los infiernos!' [. . .] Hasta el momento, había buscado al ladrón blasfemo: un hombre, quizás algún demonio" (25). Quickly, however, he becomes convinced that Satan has profaned the monastery: "Chocarro tenía la certeza de que algún espíritu cargado de malvadas intenciones se había colado en su monasterio con algún inconfesable propósito" (51).

To a lay person, the genesis and plot of *Número primo* revolves around a church administrator using a reliquary as collateral for a gambling debt and the Archbishop attempting to pay off that debt and retrieve the church property. To the artisan-assassin, however, the Archbishop's involvement is something quite different and is the catalyst that both brings back repressed memories and converts the former clerical student into God's avenger on earth. That is, the assassin returns to his religious upbringing and references the evil divinity when explaining the deaths to Lola, refusing to accept his own culpability: "¡Yo no soy el asesino, sólo soy el verdugo! ¡Busque a Satanás; está dentro, su humo mezquino se coló por las rendijas del templo invadiéndolo todo! ¿Es que no alcanza a descifrar que el diablo viste de clérigo? [. . .] Le hablo de Satanás. Tiene cara dulce y voz melosa, pero no es sino el diablo" (497). While the assassin believes himself on a mission from God to destroy Satan's influence in the Church, the reader merely sees someone who has gone mad either from religious zealousness or some other cause.

This juxtapositioning of the idea of zealousness, a malevolent divinity, and lunacy is especially noticeable in the last novel of the MacHor series. When Lola, Jaime, Iturri, and Joe go to visit Rodrigo in prison, Lola nearly loses her life at the hands of the prisoner Steven and his fellow inmates. Shortly after the civilians enter the cell block, Steven meets the group and, foreshadowing future events, addresses their escort Susan stating that "tú sabes que hay gente como [Lola] encerrada en el infierno" (178). As they continue through the building, the escort explains that Steven is not as affable or normal as he may appear, that his residency in the prison owes itself to a "religious lunacy": "Siete palizas, dos de ellas con resultado de muerte. Todas mujeres de mediana edad . . . Cree que es un ángel enviado a la Tierra para meter a las mujeres pecadoras en cintura. A golpes . . . " (*Venganza* 179). Later, as they depart Dr. Raspy's office, a group of prisoners pass by on their way to dinner. El Profeta sees Lola and initiates a group action against Lola and her companions by yelling: "¡Antes de que cante el gallo, le habrás negado tres veces!" (193) and "¡Arrepiéntete, pecadora! [. . .] Todos vosotros, arrepentíos ya. El gallo acaba de cantar" (194). In spite of the guards' best efforts, the other prisoners listen to El Profeta and Steven, who announces that "¡El Profeta tiene razón ¡[Lola] Es una bruja, mirad su pelo!" (193) and "¡A por ella, nos traerá una maldición" (195). Susan attempts to convince "a Steven de que [Lola] no era la encarnación de ningún demonio, pero sus buenas palabras recibieron por respuesta un bofetón" (195). And it is only after a considerable effort on the part of the prison officials—along with a fortuitous proclamation by Rodrigo—that Lola and her colleagues are able to escape.

Clearly more than merely involuntary psychological imbalances cause the mêlée; the environment also plays a role in the prisoners' lives as they easily follow El Profeta's and Steven's lead in their religious lunacy. Environment, as well, is also important in the lives and actions of "normal" people under stress. Iturri comments to Jaime that psychiatrist and policemen both suffer such influence: "Por lo general, los psiquiatras me parecen tan locos como sus pacientes. También les pasa a los policías que pasan mucho tiempo con criminales peligrosos: ellos mismos se vuelven violentos e inestables, y terminan siendo tan pendencieros como la gente a la que custodia" (*Venganza* 240). Jaime ponders the depths to which humans can fall when their surroundings "demand" such:

> Las guerras, especialmente la segunda guerra mundial, han puesto de manifiesto lo bajo que puede caer el alma humana. ¡Más que bajo, bajísimo! Buenos, respetados y modélicos ciudadanos que habían acudido con nocturnidad y alevosía a locales policiales o paramilitares para denunciar a quienes habían compartido con ellos escalera, piso o incluso mantel. Y no por miedo (lo cual, aunque no es una excusa, permite justificar o, al menos, entender muchas cosas) sino por un pequeño beneficio, monetario o en términos de reputación. Primero, franceses que habían denunciado a judíos. Después, judíos o franceses que habían denunciado a colaboracionistas. (*Venganza* 253)

And even Ross i Roví's dissociative identity disorder ultimately stems from a terrible experience he witnessed as an adolescent; i.e., the environment in which he lived:

> El conflicto interno que aquel niño de once años experimentó fue tan insoportable, el dolor resultó tan desgarrador, que su mente se negó a aceptarlo. Pero los hechos estaban ahí. Si cerraba los ojos, podía evocarlos una y otra vez. De modo que, inconscientemente, separó la información y los sentimientos. [. . .] Esas personalidades tienen la particularidad de que interactúan en un complejo mundo interior. No ven lo que hacen las otras, y viceversa; de esta manera se forma algo así como una colección de vidas paralelas. (*Venganza* 206)

Dr. Wilson seems to concur with Rodrigo's initial assessment of environment as an important determinant of criminality and intent—or lack therof—but that once a person consciously crosses the boundary between "good" and "evil," escaping future malevolent tendencies becomes ever more difficult. When Rodrigo questions the psychologist concerning whether a sane person can take someone else's life and remain sane, Dr. Wilson responds that "ese hombre irá poco a poco transformándose en un animal ávido de sangre" (*Dr. Wilson* 67), which Lola also notes as being in agreement with "la ciencia criminalística [que] acierta [que . . .] pasada la línea divisoria entre el bien y el mal social, lo normal es reincidir" (*Número primo* 351). In Dr. Wilson's mind, committing evil is addictive and initiates an appetite which demands more and more in order to be satiated: "el mal produce un efecto similar al de este magnífico ron que nos han servido, aunque mucho más rápido. Si lo toma a menudo, se volverá un alcohólico. Del mismo modo, si alguien derrama la sangre de otro, y saborea su hazaña, se convertirá en un enfermo, en un psicópata . . . " (*Dr. Wilson* 53). When Rodrigo then summarizes Dr. Wilson's views, asking "¿el mal es como una droga dura, que te engancha hasta hacerte perder la cabeza?" (64), the psychiatrist responds, "Yo no lo habría expresado mejor." In fact, according to Dr. Wilson, repetitive intentional ignoring of one's conscience has extremely grave effects: "mi experiencia me indica que quien siega voluntariamente varias vidas o bien se hunde en la culpabilidad o bien reniega completamente de su humanidad y se transforma en un monstruo" (*Dr. Wilson* 68). Later, he goes even further and tells Jaime that voluntary serial murderers—including Rodrigo—are little other than merely animals: "Sin embargo, no lo estaba [Rodrigo] cuando todo esto empezó. Él quería probar una teoría, y lo ha hecho: cuando arrancas la vida a tus semejantes, pierdes tu humanidad y te conviertes en un animal" (469).

Rodrigo, in *Dr. Wilson*, is not so easily convinced and urges Dr. Wilson to collaborate in a scientific experiment to prove the veracity of the theory. Obviously, Rodrigo has to subjugate his own free will and force himself to violate the principles of his own conscience:

> ¿Y qué mayor tragedia que la suya? Tenía que volver a matar. No deseaba hacerlo. Su espíritu se resistía. Sus manos se revelaban. Sentía náuseas. Pero sabía que había llegado el momento. Era su deber, un deber inexcusable. Debía arrebatarle al mundo una nueva vida, crear un nuevo mártir. [. . .] Fue entonces cuando sintió la reconvención de su conciencia: "No es tiempo de escrúpulos: necesitas tomar prestada una nueva vida." (*Dr. Wilson* 5)

And even though he is able to carry out the murders for the sake of science, "[d]esde el primer instante, y llevaba ya cinco muertes a la espalda, había soportado una terrible angustia" (*Dr. Wilson* 8). In fact, it soon becomes quite apparent that Rodrigo has transformed into, simply, just another serial killer, albeit one with a delusional, grandiose concept of his own self importance. As such, he plans to the extreme what type of person is to be killed, the murder weapon, and even—as it becomes obvious at the end of the novel—the city in which the attack occurs. His attention to detail borders on the maniacal:

> los asesinos en serie se pueden equiparar con los depredadores. Matan, pero no de cualquier manera ni en cualquier sitio. Tienen sus zonas, territorios donde creen que pueden atacar con impunidad; lugares que conocen, en los que las posibilidades de la huida planeada se incrementan. En todo caso, la escapatoria en una situación de riesgo no es la única, ni la más importante razón. Matar es una acción que incluye un tinte obsceno y que requiere, por ello, de cierta intimidad. (*Dr. Wilson* 100)

In *Venganza*, Rodrigo seems to corroborate Dr. Wilson's beliefs concerning the addictive nature of criminality when he explains to Lola how committing multiple murders has affected him. He uses his own experience as proof of his belief that the assassin in this novel will not stop with the death of only one or two of the world's wealthiest individuals, but that the assassin will carry out his promise of killing five people, plus the shadow:

> En todo caso, mi perfil decía que el autor de este crimen pronto se embriagaría con la sangre. Lo sé porque yo mismo he pasado por ello. He sentido esa fiebre, esa calentura que te sube por el cuello hasta llegar a las orejas y alcanzar luego la frente . . . Un volcán esperando para entrar en erupción. He notado esa sed, inmensa, como de vampiro, más dura cuando sabes que al alcance de tu mano hay una fuente que mana agua fresca. Toda para ti si pagas el precio . . . (97)

Rodrigo, however, terrifies Lola, and in *Venganza* she does not want to go see someone she believes to be an inveterate murderer with unclear, present motives. When Lola refuses to answer Rodrigo's petition and go visit him, he insists that her communicating with him is the only way to thwart additional deaths: "Este hombre, si es que es un hombre, está verdaderamente decidido, tanto que sus manos están ya manchadas de sangre. Y una vez que ha comenzado, no se detendrá.

[. . .] Póngase en contacto conmigo, señoría. Mejor, venga a verme. Necesito que alguien dé fe" (67–68).

Iturri, as a professional policeman, has his own beliefs concerning motives that lead people to turn to crime. In the first novel of the series, he explains to Lola's mother that he believes Lola to be innocent of Alejandro's death because she neither fits the profile of a murderer nor can he establish a clear link between her and any of the three motives for criminal activity, which he condenses as follows:

> Verá, sin contemplar la hipótesis de un comportamiento criminal patológico, hay tres motivos fundamentales por los que una persona mataría a otra: el primero poseer algo que el muerto tiene: dinero, sobre todo, pero también es posible que sea un cargo, una posesión intangible o el mantenimiento de un poder. [. . .]
>
> El segundo motivo más frecuente de asesinato es el pasional, pero tampoco parece que sea lo que buscamos. El tercero es el miedo: alguien podría desear silenciar a Alejandro Mocciaro. Eso explicaría que se exigiese al delincuente que le robara el móvil. (*Hemingway* 272–73).

Interestingly, all three of these reasons are exemplified within the series. Iturri's first motive, "poseer algo que el muerto tiene," corresponds perhaps more readily to what we would call either covetousness or ambition. This is a frequent inspiration in seven of the narratives. Miguelón Ruiz, the Madrid policeman who maliciously impugns Lola on the law professor Rodrigo's behest, "era algo torpe, pero se había comportado fielmente: la esperanza de poder tiene la facultad de crear sólidas lealtades" (*Hemingway* 306–7), marry Clara, and live in high society drive him to criminal behavior. Inspector Álvarez, in *Número primo*, is so ambitious that his egotism leads him to be universally despised and even threaten Lola in her capacity as *juez de instrucción* (232, 295–97). Covetousness leads Lorenzo Moss, in *Canaima*, to skim money for personal gain off the amount illegally obtained in the Canaima project (396, 399). In the same novel, Norberto Rosales, a.k.a. Ariel, "no deseaba ejercer de cabeza de un ratón escuálido, encerrado en su gueto. [. . .] Él tenía aspiraciones de más calado. Dinero, posición y clase . . . Una cierta modalidad de respeto. Norberto Rosales anhelaba vivir como los blancos, gastar dinero con ellos" (107). Ambition is also what drives Lionell Cobbin, the pharmaceutical company executive, to attempt to extort Jaime so that the ineffective drug SCMR-E3 can be approved and his company reap huge dividends (*Venganza* 328).

Closely related to, and often intertwined with, covetousness is vengeance. In fact, the narrator in *Número primo* explains that the assassin's motive is revenge: "No lo hacía por sí mismo, sino por ella. Se lo debía; y ella estaba por encima de todo, incluso del mismo Dios" (33). But it is abundantly clear that the assassin is even more motivated to his actions because the Archbishop enjoys respect in the community and is able to live a monastic lifestyle in spite of collusion with the pawning of holy relics, a sin much more serious—in the assassin's eyes—than that for which he had been denied a monastic lifestyle (549–58). The law professor Rodrigo, himself, also portrays this character flaw:

> Rodrigo, por el contrario, no había nacido rico. Quinto entre siete hermanos, se había visto obligado a correr tras las oportunidades sin preocuparse de quién o qué quedaba en la cuneta. Sus métodos habían resultado notables; eso había reforzado su idea inicial: lo importante es saber dónde quieres llegar, no cómo vas a alcanzar ese puesto. Había dado amplia cuenta de su talento hasta la fecha y no estaba dispuesto a que los estúpidos Mocciaro le amargaran otra vez la vida. (*Hemingway* 304)

Hill and Hill define "crime of passion," Iturri's second stated motive of pathological criminal behavior, as:

> a defendant's excuse for committing a crime due to sudden anger or heartbreak, in order to eliminate the element of "premeditation." This usually arises in murder or attempted murder cases, when a spouse or sweetheart finds his/her "beloved" having sexual intercourse with another and shoots or stabs one or both of the coupled pair. To make this claim the defendant must have acted immediately upon the rise of passion, without the time for contemplation or allowing for "a cooling of the blood."

Jaime's punching of Iturri certainly fits within the definition of this type of crime as even Jaime does not realize what has happened until he seems blood streaming down Iturri's face. In *Venganza*, as previously mentioned in the discussion of crimes involving a lack of free will, Iturri comments on the perforated plug in the Garache's bathroom shower, and "Algún resorte se rompió en mi interior [Jaime speaking] sin que yo pudiera hacer nada para evitarlo. [. . .] Cuando quise darme cuenta le sangraba la nariz. [. . .]. De pronto, me sentí ridículo. [. . .] Ridículo y avergonzado. Porque no soy del tipo de personas que van batiéndose por el mundo. No creo en las espadas ni en los golpes" (247). In fact, Jaime compares his "crime of passion" to the dissociative identity disorder from which Marc Ross i Roví suffers: "Yo también parecía haberme disociado. Aquel Jaime no era yo" (265). While the filicide of which Sara Shibata is guilty has no sexual element, it is an action "due to sudden anger or heartbreak" resulting from a verbal exchange with Dr. Wilson, an action of which she almost immediately repents after ordering it carried out, but it is already too late. Tigris, another fellow prisoner of Rodrigo, is guilty of crimes of passion before his incarceration, but it is his sudden and unprovoked attack on the music therapist in the cell block itself when she plays a recording of African drums that draws the most attention: "No fue más que un mecanismo reflejo: cree que es un tigre de Bengala y trata de cazar como ellos cuando algún sonido le recuerda a la India. Tiene tres muertes a su cargo, todas fruto de la misma patología" (*Venganza* 188).

Fear, Iturri's third motive, is portrayed as a cause of criminal actions less frequently in the MacHor series. Lucio Lescaino is killed by hired-assassins when he discovers corruption involving road construction in Venezuela and anonymously reports such to the World Bank; the same fate awaits the World Bank investigator Jorge Parada when he goes to South America to check out the allegations (*Canaima* 7–12). Ariel beats Telmo to within an inch of his life because he fears the old man has seen the drug cache that he is dividing up to sell (*Canaima* 191). And it is a fear of non-acceptance by her peers which leads an unnamed, young girl—whom Lola scolds and then sets free—to shoplift in *Número primo* (489).

Lola's early concept of criminality involving the taking of human lives corresponds remarkably to Iturri's list of motives. Having not yet solved the assassinations of the priests, in *Número primo* Lola writes down a series of unanswered questions concerning the cases and, frustrated, finally concludes that "En definitiva, la vida parecía obsequiarnos con un nuevo capítulo de una serie vieja: ambiciones, dinero, venganza" (*Número primo* 524). As Lola is involved in cases of increasingly more global corruption, her views of criminal motivation become more slanted in the direction of being tied to materialistic gain with few risks: "La corrupción debe entenderse como la coincidencia de tres circunstancias muy diversas: oportunidad, beneficio y bajo riesgo" (*Canaima* 94–95). These motives are exhibited on various occasions. World Bank President Woolite gives favors to a female friend against institutional rules and is forced to resign (*Canaima* 305). The hired assassins of Lucio Lescaino, Jorge Parada and Lorenzo Moss evidently earn a considerable salary for their services and are never found (*Canaima* 408). And Leon offers an exciting, and confidential, human hunting expedition to Dr. Wilson during an illicit gorilla hunt (*Dr. Wilson* 23–25).

Twice in the series the theme of criminal culpability is discussed in-depth. In *Número primo*, the Nuncio delays his departure from Lola's home in an effort to learn more about the priest assassinations and questions he has concerning the ability of psychology to construct a profile of an assassin. Jaime responds that such is not really possible, especially when the criminal is a repeat offender, to which the Nuncio wonders: "¿qué es lo que opina: los asesinos nacen o se hacen?" (389). After briefly expositing how past beliefs in eugenics were replaced in the 19th century by the more complex naturalist determinism which, in turn, has also proved to be less than satisfactory in assigning responsibility to either nature or nurture, Jaime simply summarizes the debate with, "Como ocurre en todo lo que circunda la conducta humana, los distintos factores se presentan mezclados, es difícil diagnosticar el mal" (390). And even the cleric admits that he does not believe that criminality owes itself totally to free-will actions: "Creo que matar es siempre un acto que exige la entrada expresa de la voluntad; no se mata por instinto. No obstante [. . .] en la mayoría de los casos [. . .] se esconde un grave trastorno de personalidad provocado por muchos factores, algunos de los cuales no son responsabilidad del individuo" (390).

Lola participates in a similar discussion over dinner with the other conference panelists in Barcelona in the fourth novel of the series. The journalist Justino Sandoval initially allows for no bivariate or multivariate analyses, asserting that the scientific theory of "una cierta animalidad patológica del hombre [. . .] es una tontería" (*Dr. Wilson* 131) while arguing that "el ser humano posee libre albedrío: decide, actúa, no se comporta siguiendo un patrón preestablecido" (131). Meanwhile, the sociology professor Pablo Tasso counters that "Nada es blanco o negro. Digamos que la maldad tiene una base moderadamente hereditaria, moderadamente social y moderadamente voluntaria" (132). Lola's strong opinions expressed in *Hemingway* concerning personal responsibility have evolved to the point that now she seems to accept uncontrollable causalities for criminal conduct, under certain conditions: "en el caso de los asesinos en serie, el ambiente no parece ser el elemento esencial. En los pocos asuntos de esta clase en los que me he visto obligada a intervenir, los informes forenses señalaban influencias hereditarias y factores somáticos como coadyuvantes en la conversión del individuo en un psicópata" (134). After further questioning by Lola, her dinner partners concede that "existe un nexo causal entre criminalidad y patología orgánica [. . .] que sólo se verifica en un porcentaje del total de los casos. En el resto, los genes están al margen" (134–35). Tasso, furthermore, remains adamant that environmental influences play an important role in criminality:

> La criminalidad es el resultado de la interacción de muchos factores físicos y sociales o culturales. Algunos hombres habrían sido normales de haber vivido en otros ambientes, pero alguien los maltrató en tal grado que los hizo unos criminales vengativos. En otros casos, los factores genéticos interaccionan con el ambiente, o con otros elementos, como el consumo de drogas, haciendo que salte la chispa y se declare el incendio. (135)

Interestingly, these arguments and debates provide information which foreshadows the eventual resolution of the narrative plot of *Dr. Wilson,* in which the assassin turns out to be a person who suffers from an extreme case of dissociative identity disorder, and *Venganza.* In fact, while Lola plans actions that may not be described as "criminal," even she herself is unable to explain rationally, after the fact, why she would attempt to take her own life (*Dr. Wilson* 351), other than to suggest that her actions owed themselves to a chemical imbalance following an unexpected miscarriage.

The preceding arguments, of course, are opinions expressed by professionals such as the clergy, doctors, policemen, and a judge concerning the reasons, causes and/or precedents of the crimes and criminal mentality. Public perception often varies greatly from such and, as reported by Duffy, Wake, Burrows, and Bremner, in 2006, 81% of Spanish people surveyed agreed with the statement that "Nowadays there is too much tolerance. Criminals should be punished more severely" (40).

Additionally, a study on Spain's criminal law reforms carried out between 1996 and 2011 by José Luis Díez Repollés concludes that "una de las cualidades que mejor caracteriza el desenfrenado proceder legislativo penal de los últimos 16 años es la cada vez más acentuada tendencia hacia la expansión y endurecimiento del sistema penal español" (4). Such sociological concerns become apparent, as demonstrated in *Hemingway* and *Venganza,* and most often correspond to a reversal of presumed innocence into "guilty until proven innocent" and "not in my backyard" mindsets. Lola, upon contemplating her arrest for having supposedly killed Alejandro, has faith in ultimately being exonerated, but she knows that public opinion may forever be against her: "Es verdad que la ley se alía necesariamente con la justicia, pero no siempre lo hacen la sociedad y los ciudadanos. La presunción de inocencia es sólo un concepto jurídico. En la vida ordinaria, impera un principio mucho más simple: cuando el río suena . . . " (*Hemingway* 185). And it is only shortly after coming to this realization that the other patients in the hospital ward begin their verbal assault of her. One even loudly proclaims, "¡Que se la lleven!

¡Corremos grave peligro con ella aquí! Hace unos años hubo muertos en el hospital por un caso similar. ¿No lo recuerdan?" (*Hemingway* 188–89).

The convicted face even worse treatment and are ostracized, cast away and forgotten; penal institutions as capable reformatories is a concept long out of favor.[1] Susan, the prison guard who escorts Lola *et al.* to Dr. Raspy's office behind the walls, states: "Esto debería ser un hospital, pero lo han convertido en un almacén. Aquí guardamos lo que la sociedad no quiere. Lo importante no es curar; de hecho, muchos empeoran. Lo que la sociedad espera de este tipo de centros es que los internos den la menor lata posible a los que están fuera" (*Venganza* 180). Interestingly, it is this description and commentary that seem to overshadow Lola's visit to the prison and the trauma she suffers while there.

In sum, as in society in general the debate concerning the causes and motivation of criminal action remains unresolved. There is no conclusive evidence or decision about the true reasons, catalysts, and/or causes of malevolent behaviors/personalities nor can Lola, Jaime, or Iturri agree on such either. In fact, Lola's opinions evolve from the first novel of the series, where she appears to emphasize most strongly personal responsibility, to the fifth novel, in which she appears to lean toward accepting more environmental or physiological causalities as the culprit. At the very least, throughout the series criminal motives range from ambition to vengeance, from demonic mandates to thrill seeking, and from voluntary manslaughter to lunacy-induced malfeasance. All of these, in fact, are portrayed at different points and in different manners in the MacHor series. But what distinguishes this narrator—if not author—from her peers, and from society in general, is that her narratives are not universally negative against all criminals, or supposed criminals; those crimes resulting from psychological or physiological abnormalities merit our sympathy. In this manner, the author thereby finds herself in the position of advocating for better mental therapies and treatments.

Note

1 Monica Aranda Ocaña, in *Prison Conditions in Spain*, offers a fairly comprehensive description of detention data, description and conditions in Spain. Among her findings, she notes that

> The Spanish prison system has two different penitentiary administrations: Catalan administration (which depends on Department of Justice) and Spanish administration, from the rest of the country, which depends on Ministry of Home Affairs since 1992. [. . .] There are 68 Spanish prisons and 11 Catalan prisons, actu-

> ally in Catalonia there are two prisons built that cannot be opened for lack of funds.

Aranda Ocaña goes on to add that some of the seventy-nine aforementioned prisons are so old and run-down that they are barely inhabitable. (16)

CHAPTER FIVE

Social Criticism in the Lola MacHor Series

I Leitmotif

In a September 2010 interview, Reyes Calderón seems to separate herself from many of the "classical" detective fiction writers—such as Vásquez Montalbán, Juan Madrid, or Andreu Martín—stating that "a mí no me interesa la violencia por la violencia" (Stegmeier). Later in the same year, she went even further, rejecting the categorization of her novels as "novela negra" while emphasizing the importance of characterization over plot development: "Siempre he dicho que mis libros no son novela negra. No importa tanto quién mata o quien [sic] muere, como la vida de estos personajes" (Rubio 60). While this may, in fact, distinguish her from the traditional *novela negra*—which "suele desenvolverse en ambientes marginales con dosis de crimen, sexo y violencia" (Cercas)—this does correspond to what Kalen Oswald notes about other detective writers from Barcelona: "in many contemporary Spanish detective novels the mystery and investigation can turn out to be of less overall importance than the social commentary expressed by the words and actions of the characters and the critical description of the urban space that serves as context" (11). Reyes Calderón's social criticism, however, often appears more subtly in the narrative and frequently comes across as a tacit, nearly hidden, almost didactic moral compass which might assist the reader in making the world a better place. The author, in fact, noted in an October 2011 interview that books are not just to be "consumed" or lightly viewed as mere entertainment:

> Los libros te obligan a detenerte: [. . .] Los libros te ayudan a ponerte en la posición de otros: [. . .] Los libros se leen y releen, se aconsejan y se prestan: toda una lección en un mundo de consumo y caducidad instantáneas. [. . .] Los libros enseñan con profunda humildad, algo muy necesario en una cultura de éxito arrogante como la nuestra. Los libros, si son buenos, te hacen mejores, aunque no se note. (LESEG)

In a personal interview with the autor in May 2012, she avoided directly answering the question of "¿Cree, entonces, que sus novelas tienen un elemento didáctico, una moraleja?" (see Chapter Eight), responding, instead, that "Si las novelas son buenas, te hacen mejores," and "Yo me conformaría que la gente sería más contenta." It is my contention, however, that these novels are more than mere entertainment, and that there are, in fact, various motifs—if not lessons to learn—in each of the Lola MacHor novels. At the very least, one overarching theme is present in all of the narratives: humankind's need to have compassion and understanding for fellow citizens.

The clearest example of that moral stance in *Las lágrimas de Hemingway*—the first of the series—comes at the climax of the novel, while Lola is still in the hospital and not yet officially cleared of the charges of homicide unjustly filed against her by Miguelón Ruiz. Miguelón, an ambitious Madrid police officer whom Clara manipulates into taking on the investigation of her brother Alejandro's death, is intent on solving the case quickly in order to please Clara; at the same time, however, as is revealed in the final pages of the novel, Miguelón is also working at the behest of the one who hired the murderer. Meanwhile, Clara and Alejandro's father, Niccola Mocciaro, has charged his lawyer and executor of his will Gonzalo Eregui with, after his death, personally handing to Lola a collection of first editions of Conan Doyle's stories which he has bound and dedicated to her. Because of the perplexing wording of the dedication—"No te olvides de que Vermissa tenía 61 miembros" (270)—both the local police detective Juan Iturri, who is conducting a parallel, extra-official investigation unbeknownst to Miguelón Ruiz, and Lola suspect that Niccola is attempting to convey a message about Lola's not winning the coveted professorship and/or his own, mysterious death. After an exhausting page-by-page examination of the volume, Lola finally perceives that there is an unusual bulge in the binding, and upon slitting open the membrane, "lo que ocultaba [the hidden letter] amputó la mitad de mi alma" (293). Up to this point, Lola's bitterness has been directed more toward higher education in general, but upon reading the letter she realizes that her former academic and professional mentor, Niccola Mocciaro, had unsuccessfully become re-entangled in the convoluted web of a secret society at the university in an attempt to win Lola the coveted professorship, something which creates "en mí un vacío inmenso, mezclado con un sentimiento de extrema repugnancia" (293). Despite such emptiness and repugnance, Lola immediately states that "Sé que todos creemos tener derecho a juzgar a los demás, especialmente cuando se equivocan. Pero en realidad no somos quién para juzgar a nadie" (293). Of course, this forgiveness and compassion toward all other humans are not necessarily Lola's first thoughts upon reading Niccola's letter. In fact, Lola notes that the evolutionary process of her thoughts has taken some time to develop when she acknowledges that "[p]oco a poco, la amargura que todos los 13 de julio sembraban en mi ánimo ha ido cediendo" (163) and "[p]asado un lustro, puedo narrar [ahora] aquellos hechos sin que mi corazón dé vuelcos. Aquella situación fue terrible; en muchos sentidos, la experiencia más angustiosa que jamás haya vivido. Desde entonces, no soy la misma, pero creo que a pesar de todo fue positiva porque ahora soy mejor: más segura (o menos insegura), más fría y más feliz" (163).

Lola's expression of her commonality with, and compassion for, humankind in *Los crímenes del número primo* also occurs toward the end of the narrative, shortly before the climax. The now-Interpol agent Juan Iturri has convinced Lola to go with him to Málaga to investigate, and possibly reopen, the case of the designer Faustino Gorla, who had been found floating in the Mediterranean Sea. Although the death has been officially ruled a boating accident, Iturri believes it to be a homicide connected to the murder of various clerics associated with the Leyre Monastery. Once in Málaga, Iturri and Lola go to Brothers, a *local de alterne*, where the unidentified pedophile whom Iturri is seeking recognizes him and slips a poison into his drink. Lola is forced to leave Iturri in the hospital in grave condition and return to Madrid to work on the case alone. A few days after Lola arrives home, Iturri suffers liver failure, and unable to contact Lola, the authorities call Jaime to communicate the news. Jaime goes home, attempts to convince Lola to abandon the case, remonstrates her for the visit to the gay bar and wants to know exactly what happened there. Lola tells him and then admits that the experience has impacted her, that she feels fortunate for her life situation which has let her escape the "fiesta de carnaval, donde todos los presentes podían disfrazar sus frustraciones, desfigurándolas para que la realidad pasara desapercibida, pero con un elemento de artificiosidad que de alguna manera los delataba" (442). At the same time, she recognizes that, at the core, the people in the bar are human, as well and she is no better than they:

> Me afectó . . . No consigo despegarme de esas imagines, de esos recuerdos . . . Yo no soy mejor que ellos, ¿sabes? No soy como tú te crees . . . No soy como tú . . . A veces, cuando recuerdo aquellas imágenes, pienso que he tenido suerte al caer en este ambiente, contigo y los niños . . . ¿Qué hubiera sido de mí si el destino hubiera sido otro? Muchas veces me siento sola. Me imagino cómo se sentirán ellos. (*Número primo* 486)

Compassion for humankind is the main thrust of the entire narrative of *El Expediente Canaima*; it encompasses both the minor plot involving María Bravo and the more central plot involving the World Bank official David Herrera-Smith. María Bravo is a 15 year-old girl under the care of her grandfather Telmo Bravo, and who has been sexually assaulted by a local drug dealer, Norberto Rosales, aka Ariel. María, innocent to the point of explaining to the judge the impossibility of the newborn being hers—"Ya le he dicho que era negro, señor juez, ¿cómo iba a ser mi hijo? Yo soy blanca, ¿es que no lo ve?" (66)—suffers a postpartum hemorrhage and dies, something that causes Lola to remember a "lista negra" (106) of various criminal cases, each of which has ended badly and with which she was involved. Her remorse causes her regrets because the legal system, followed strictly, lacks the element of human compassion which could have changed the various outcomes:

> Andrés Hidalgo Gil, diez años, colgado por el cuello hasta morir. El padre se había negado a ingresarlo tras el primer intento de suicidio. [. . .] Aurelio Aldaba, cuarenta y dos años, padre de tres hijos, víctima del ladrón a quien la policía había capturado en dos ocasiones y ella había soltado otras tantas, debido a errores de procedimiento del Fiscal. Ángela Armisén, veinticinco años, cinco recibiendo palizas, y otros tantos perdonando a su maltratador; muerta en la bañera de su casa, desangrada. Estaba embarazada de doce semanas.
> (*Canaima* 106)

But it is not just the strict limitations of the law which upset Lola; she also is angered at María's funeral by the seeming callousness of the cleric eulogizing the youth, his lack of sympathy at the taking of her life, and his focusing on death itself instead of on María as an individual:

> El sacerdote, un hombre rechoncho de avanzada calvicie, expuso las más conspicuas reflexiones que sobre la muerte había compuesto, quién sabe para qué muerto. A Lola le invadió la rabia ante la prédica. El cura no se refería a María; no decía lo joven que era y lo injusta que resulta esta vida nuestra. Sólo juzgaba la muerte y la vida, y hablaba del juicio final y de la misericordia de Dios. En el fondo María era inexistente, por eso dejó de escuchar el sermón y se concentró en la muchacha. (*Canaima* 130)

In the last chapter of the novel, the narrator unites María, and what happens to her, to the case of David Herrera-Smith, the World Bank official who chooses suicide over allowing himself to be extorted by those who want the investigation into the money laundering in Venezuela to be abandoned. After much investigation, and with the help of Juan Iturri and the FBI, Lola discovers that the person behind the crimes is Lorenzo Moss, a former law-school colleague and current Secretary of the Ministry of Economy for Spain. After the discovery, and the FBI informs the businessman Ramón Cerda that Lorenzo is having an affair with Jimena, Ramón's wife, Lorenzo is fatally shot by the gunmen formerly under his charge. Recognizing that many people would judge Lorenzo's death as merely a settling of scores between criminals, Lola's explanation at the end of the novel excoriates both society in general and individuals in particular:

> Se lo ganaron a pulso, dicen los ciudadanos decorosos. Lujuria y ambición. Yo sólo veo cien quilos frente a cincuenta; veo vergüenza frente a negocio; veo dinero cambiado por vida. Y esta vez no tengo dudas: el culpable lleva nombre de detergente y de político y de VIP. Y de este mundo desleal y miope que encumba a Jimenas y abandona a Marías.
>
> Pero las mofetas huelen aunque cambies de acera. Y el lenguaje de los hechos impera: ¿cuántas Marías, cuántos Parada, cuántos Herrera-Smith han de caer por cada Jimena? (*Canaima* 420)

But Lola does not stop with a simple question; she continues with an admonition that humans are, in fact, responsible to be their brother's keeper and that each should strive to improve the world for others:

> Antes de conocer a María Bravo y a David Herrera-Smith, [yo] pensaba que había cosas que no tenían solución. Condición humana, que diría el filósofo; ley de vida. No tenía entonces plena conciencia de que ése era precisamente el problema. Ahora, ante la funda de un hombre que creyó en la justicia, la tengo. Ahora sé que hay cosas que permanecen porque nosotros lo permitimos y miramos hacia otro lado. (*Canaima* 419)

In her world view, human beings must get involved in society and helping others; suffering, crime, and "bad luck" can be remedied.

In the fourth novel, *El último paciente del Doctor Wilson*, Lola suffers a stillbirth after falling off a chair while attempting to reach a book on the top shelf of the bookcase. Despite her doctor's assurance that she is in no way guilty of the miscarriage, that the fetus had been dead for some time in her womb, and that the fall and abortion occurring in such proximity is a pure coincidence, Lola is unable to overcome the psychological trauma she suffers and goes into a state of clinical depression. The depression ends only when Iturri abruptly appears at Lola's house the day she is intending to overdose on sleeping pills, and he takes action. He realizes what is happening and recounts to her his experience of being cloistered in the monastery to recover after the poisoning he suffered in *Los crímenes del número primo*. Ultimately, he is able to convince her to agree to follow his advice and get some rest, only after finally adding that if his plan is unsuccessful in relieving Lola's depression, he will loan her his pistol so that she can shoot herself. Several weeks later, looking back on those life-changing events, Lola admits that "[f]ueron momentos de delirio; esperpénticos [. . .]. Ahora, [. . .] todo aquello me parece una locura. Y lo fue. Lo malo es que se trató de un dislate que creí cordura. Soy incapaz de explicar cómo llegué a esa situación" (*Dr. Wilson* 351). Then Lola philosophizes that "Fue una mala época . . . Y, no obstante, agradezco haber dormido en esa cueva. De no haberlo hecho, nunca habría comprendido al doctor Wilson, ni al cuerdo asesino llamado Rodrigo. En realidad, ahora tampoco puedo entenderlos, pero ya no me siento capaz de juzgarlos. Que sea el tiempo el que lo haga" (*Wilson* 352).

At the end of the work, she returns to that motif in a four-paragraph "Epitafio" in which she speaks directly to the reader—using the second-person singular forty times in the 286-word passage—saying, "Hablo de ti, que crees dominar tu juicio, que te tienes por un tipo racional y razonable" (481). She tells the reader that "Desconoces que hay muchos yos dentro de ti" (481) and that "Es tu vida: la vives, la sientes, la disfrutas, la sufres. Es tuya, pero estás lejos de controlarla. No la dominas del todo. A veces, ni siquiera puedes entenderla" (481). Some might argue that as an epitaph, the narrator is speaking to Dr. Wilson, whose alter ego, Rodrigo, has been described on the prior page as on his death bed. While, in fact, such could theoretically be the case, given the author's proclivity to speak directly to the reader, urging her/him to act in certain ways, it is just as credible that the epitaph is a moral direction directed to the reader on how to live. And given that both Dr. Wilson and Rodrigo reappear in the next novel of the series, very much alive, this "didactic" explanation gains even more plausibility.

II Other motifs and social criticism

In addition to the previously studied leitmotif of the "Golden Rule" found throughout the Lola MacHor series, the various novels offer additional examples of social commentary or social criticism which, while loosely related to the immediately surrounding narrative, is largely independent of such and could be easily excised from the text without any significant change in the novel itself. As an academic thriller, the world of education comes under intense scrutiny in *Hemingway* and, while deeply criticized, is also considered of utmost importance. The nun who visits Lola in the hospital, Sor Rosario, comments, in fact, that the lack of education is devastating to humans: “ignorancia y pobreza, dos de los mayores males de la humanidad” (176). Lola, however, has lost faith in higher education, telling Iturri that “la liturgia de cada día es más bien ésta: largas mentiras soportadas con ánimo estoico y forzada sonrisa; áspiras y groseras discusiones [. . .]. ¡Si usted supiera qué hercúlea es la tarea de convertir a un sabio en catedrático! . . . Aunque, ahora que lo pienso, quizás sea más titánica la empresa de hacer de un catedrático un sabio” (210). Iturri, taken aback by her comments, notes that “[m]e sorprende su ácido lenguaje” (210). But she is unrelenting, adding that “ya no buscamos la sabiduría, sino los honores, las glorias, los reconocimientos; las subidas, en definitiva, de categoría y sueldo. [. . .] Somos, en definitiva, una especie de vampiros” (211). And her additional allusion to Roman gladiator fights establishes a connection between bullfighting, the winning of a professorship, and the inhumanity of the higher education system:

> aquí de lo que hablamos es de otro tipo de competencia. Esto es la arena romana. El emperador siempre tiene el pulgar inclinado hacia abajo. Es una lucha a muerte, vencer de una vez para siempre. [. . .] Ese dulce y tierno discípulo que trae pastas el día de tu onomástica y te abre las puertas con sumisión y modestia te apuñalará por la espalda en el preciso momento en que, colmadas sus aspiraciones, ya no le seas útil. Así de cruel, así de real. (212)

Hemingway is a novel situated in Pamplona during the week of the Sanfermines festival; thus, it is no surprise that both the running of the bulls and bullfighting itself would earn additional scrutiny. Sanfermines.net details the medieval creation of the festival as an October commemoration of the martyrdom of the first bishop of Pamplona and its eventual conversion into more of a secular, July celebration coinciding with the cattle markets. Tellingly, by setting the novel in the Sanfermines festival, and having the murder occur during the *encierros* themselves, the author juxtapositions celebration and death, the traditionally sacred and evil, and the commonly known with the mysterious. This duality is accentuated by the narrator’s dubitative stance toward the merits of the *encierro*, a stance that both questions the playing with death while recognizing its economic and cultural importance to both the city and its citizens:

> Todos los allí presentes son capaces de captar la soberbia esencia de ese juego con la muerte que acontece siete días al año cuando se rompe el alba. Pero ante un nuevo cadáver, vuelven a preguntarse si aquel macabro e irracional juego merece la pena. Son sólo tres minutos frente al resto de tu vida. Jugarte la piel y miles de kilómetros de sentimientos a cambio de soltarte la coleta y ducharte con adrenalina a granel durante 848 metros. Sin embargo, ¿qué sería de Pamplona sin esos ratos? ¿En qué quedarían julio, agosto y hasta enero sin la esperanza de que el espíritu de San Fermín volviera a emigrar a su lecho de Santo Domingo? (*Hemingway* 38)

Bullfighting itself comes under a harsher criticism; in fact, the wording and symbolism associated with the sport relegate it to a level inferior to that of a civilized society. On one hand, bullfighting is associated with the most violent aspects of Roman culture: "A la hora en punto, comenzó el paseíllo: monosabios, areneros y mulilleros se unieron a los trajes de luces y a los aplausos en aquel desfile triunfal. Fue como si Roma renaciera de sus cenizas y Julio César clamara al cielo de su Hispania ofreciéndole otro festejo de gladiadores: pan y circo; bocadillo y toros" (*Hemingway* 131–32). On the other hand, the narrator simply compares bullfighting to another social gathering where much of the audience is unconcerned, and unlearned, about what is happening on stage; it has become, in essence, another idolatrous sacrifice:

> Olía a puros habanos y a perfumes caros; espesos, dulzones. Las mujeres, muchas de ellas de pie en el estrecho pasillo de sus asientos, sonreían aireando sus cabellos, esperando que comenzara el festejo. Quizás buscando al hombre de sus sueños, miraban y saludaban a diestro y siniestro, cuchicheando con sus vecinas. Los caballeros, tratando de aparentar indiferencia, observaban furtivamente al sexo opuesto, al tiempo que repasaban el cartel pues, aunque allí había gente a la que los toros ni fu ni fa, había muchos a los que ver dominar una muleta les encendía. Todos, ellos y ellas, de una u otra manera hablaban de lo mismo: el nuevo sacrificio al *dios*. (*Hemingway* 131)

Society's attitude toward death itself is also examined in *Hemingway*. In spite of society's playing with death, enjoyment in having "cheated death," and even tempting such by running through cobblestone streets in front of horned animals multiple times larger than oneself, few individuals consider death's true ramifications, and that everyone, some day, will die. Perhaps for that reason, society tends to separate itself from the physical proof of its mortality as the forensics doctor

Ramiro Gómez states: "Verás, no sabemos si viviremos mañana, pero hacemos minuciosos planes para ese día. Sin embargo, lo único que sabemos con certeza—que nos vamos a morir—tratamos de olvidarlo. Por ejemplo, acostumbramos a situar los cementerios lejos de los núcleos de población" (*Hemingway* 59). At the same time, and as noted by Iturri, the somewhat-conservative nature of the text and main characters lead humankind to long for the certainty that death is not final, that something follows death, and that there is a higher power than the earthly:

> Pero puedo decirte que en la medida en que se decreta la muerte de Dios, toman su posición las hermandades, sociedades secretas, asociaciones diabólicas . . . Resulta comprensible: los hombres necesitamos creer que hay algo más y formular hipótesis acerca de nuestro destino. Despreciando lo auténtico, los substitutos emergen como las setas, tratando de ofrecer el mismo servicio, las mismas respuestas a esos deseos de inmortalidad que nos corroen. (*Hemingway* 291)

The second novel of the series, *Número primo*, continues in this vein of the spiritual, the belief that humans search for something more than simply the physical on this earth. Lola, even while in the gay bar in Malaga, views the people awaiting the "magical hour" as actually on a quest to escape reality and become, for a moment, something else: "me habría gustado poder hacerles preguntas cara a cara. ¿Cuál era la verdad de aquella gente? [. . .] ¿Se encontrarían a gusto consigo mismos? ¿Tendrían miedo a la muerte? [. . .] ¿Desearían el amor verdadero" (442). Obviously such parallels the Church's position on the subject as well.

Additional social commentary in *Número primo* relates to both the Church and society's support and opposition to that institution. Church secrecy and desire to protect itself, as demonstrated through its unwillingness to risk a public airing of either questionable activities or occurrences that might result in uncomfortable questions and/or explanations by the Church, play a role in the early part of the novel. Both Lola and Iturri lament the Archbishop's attempt to negotiate with the kidnapper instead of turning the matter over to the police. Father Chocarro is upset that "lo que importaba a ambos padres [his superiors] era no poner en un brete al monasterio y correr el riesgo de que aquellos acontecimientos llegaran a la opinión pública" (59) instead of calling in professional assistance in an attempt to get to the bottom of the profanation. And Lola is even more enraged when she learns that the robbery at the monastery has been concealed by Chocarro's superiors because "[c]reen que este asunto debe permanecer velado, porque de divulgarse la noticia, es posible que el monasterio salga malparado" (274). Such commentary and Lola's "acusando formalmente de encubrimiento, delito tipificado en el artículo 451 del Código penal, amén de otro delito de coacción a un testigo" (276), however, are not merely indictments of the Church for its unwillingness to cooperate with secular authorities, they are really a critical commentary about society at large and its propensity to rush to believe anything negative concerning the Church, if not other institutions and individuals as well. Such is abundantly evident after Lola finally explains to the clerics that blood has been found in the front seat of the abbey's car and that a witness has seen someone dressed in a Benedictine habit fleeing the scene: "Supe enseguida que terrible remordimientos arañaban su conciencia" (278).

The Church's reluctance to "air dirty laundry" in the novel is simply a reflection of real life and the Spanish society's distancing of itself from the institution.[1] As noted in a 2009 study by Braulio Gómez Fortes and Irene Palacios Brihuega less than one year after the publication of *Número primo*, confidence in the Church in Spain is rated at 2.9 (on a scale of 0 to 10 points), approximately the same number as say that religion is very important in their lives (Pew Research Center). Antipathy toward the Church is not documented in that report, but an October–December 2008 survey by the Spanish Centro de Investigaciones Sociológicas indicates that 22.7% of Spaniards claim that "La Iglesia y organizaciones religiosas" inspire "Ninguna confianza" (4); 51.3% state that "la Iglesia y las organizaciones religiosas de este país tienen" either "Un poder desmesurado" or "Demasiado poder" (6), and 19.8% agree that "Hay muy poco de verdad en cualquier religión" (18). This secularization of society is noted by the narrator when Lucas Andueza, the Archbishop's secretary, is on his way to the archbishopric and becomes frightened upon passing a group of "extraños personajes ataviados con vestimenta de guerrilla y paraphernalia metálica clavada en el cuerpo" (61–62). While they do nothing against him, he is very nervous, trembles, takes off his glasses in case of attack, and ponders that "[a]ntaño, esa alcurnia le hubiera granjeado reverencias al pasar, pero los tiempos habían cambiado y el péndulo de la historia se hallaba en el extremo opuesto: ahora los curas eran objeto de mofas, dianas improvisadas cuando se presentaba la ocasión" (62). Later, he tells Lola that "casi todos los días, llama alguien haciendo una broma, pero son mensajes inofensivos. [. . .] Insultos a los curas, a la Iglesia, al celibato" (216).

The obvious social commentary in *Canaima*, the second novel of the series, both echoes the series's leitmotif and criticizes the weaknesses of the political and judicial systems. Lola's concern for humanity in general is blatantly obvious, and her desire to help the less fortunate frequently is front and center. In fact, she has often dreamed of making a difference in society,[2] and when she sees such efforts thwarted by the technicalities of the legal system, she is quite upset, even to the point of ranting against the intricacies of the law and how such intricacies do not correspond to reality:

> la ley puede ser realmente injusta. Injusta y ciega, y sorda. Decir que una violación es un acceso carnal opuesto a la voluntad de la víctima es no entender nada. Decir que es un delito contra la libertad sexual implica carecer de perspectiva. [. . .] Violar puede implicar cópula, sí, pero sobre todo es un ejercicio de dominación. Ejercer poder. [. . .] Pero la ley no entiende esa lógica. (106)

And one of the reasons for her decision to solicit the position on the Audiencia Nacional in Madrid and leave Pamplona is her sense of futility in resolving such cases and being able to deliver true justice: "Un sentimiento de inutilidad la hostigó. Llevaba meses abrumada por las dudas, cuestionándose la eficiencia de la institución que presidía" (92).

But it is not just the judicial system that Lola thinks is not living up to its potential; she considers the political system in much the same way. In fact, Lola's lack of political activism closely parallels the growing apathy of the Spanish people at large during the early years of the third millennium. Omar Encarnación notes that "studies of contemporary Spanish political culture show a clear disinterest in politics bordering on apathy and cynicism" and that "since the early 1980s the percentage of Spaniards professing an interest in politics has rarely exceeded 25 percent [and during the early 1990s this] actually fell to the mid-teens" (47). Tellingly, on the night that José Luis Rodríguez Zapatero was elected Presidente del Gobierno, March 14, 2004, even his supporters greeted him in a mass demonstration of victory chanting "No nos falles." And Lola feels much the same way about politicians, that they cannot be fully trusted and are really only going to do whatever is necessary in order to retain power:

> MacHor estaba convencida de que los políticos, sin distinción de credo, hacían leyes con el único fin de atraer hacia sus filas a ese número de indecisos votantes que puede inclinar definitivamente la balanza de una elección. El voto joven, el voto gay, el voto de la tercera edad, el voto emigrante, el voto femenino eran calibrados, pesados y diseñados a ritmo de subvención. ¿Qué desean? ¿Qué debo hacer para que me voten a mí y no a ellos? (93)

The fourth novel, *Dr. Wilson*, contains very little extended social commentary extraneous to the series's leitmotif other than Lola's anti-abortion stance.[3] In large part, this is most probably due to the fact that the novel revolves around an obviously deranged serial killer and the narrative spends a considerable amount of time detailing the psychological aspects of the psychiatrist and his patient-murderer through page-turning plot scenarios. This, in effect, only occasionally allows the narrator to pause—generally just for a sentence, often for even less—to offer very brief social comments such as "La vida es mayoritariamente una cesta de fruta dura: las piezas en sazón escasean" (353). Perhaps, however, more so in this novel than in any other, the reader notices intrinsic social commentary that the world is increasingly globalized.[4] Lola no longer goes to the local café, but instead goes to Starbucks (378); she moderates a conference panel in Barcelona on crime and globalization (16), and her email is full of spam, Google alerts, and "seis reenvíos de Power Point" (378).

The fifth novel, *Venganza*, is a sequel to *Dr. Wilson*; thus, all the main characters are already known to those who have read the fourth novel. This allows the narrators more freely to offer social commentary since there is less need to focus almost exclusively on psychological character development. In additional, the novel has four narrators—Lola, Jaime, Iturri, and Joe Lombardo—and each has her/his own perspective on social conditions. Lola quotes Susan, the social worker at the prison where Dr. Wilson is incarcerated, as explaining that "Esto debería ser un hospital, pero lo han convertido en un almacén. Aquí guardamos lo que la sociedad no quiere. Lo importante no es curar [. . .]. Lo que la sociedad espera de este tipo de centros es que los internos den la menor lata posible a los que están fuera" (180). And, apparently, Dr. Raspy, the prison psychiatrist, has finally succumbed to the realities of the privatization of the penal system and the lack of true interest on the part of the public and politicians in rehabilitating the prisoners; Susan reports that he "[d]ice que bastante hacemos con sobrevivir y evitar que [the prisoners] se maten entre sí o que nos maten a nosotros" (182). And while such comments are made by Americans, they do parallel society's perception in Spain as well. Nick Lyne summarizes, for example, the various criminal code changes occurring in Spain since 1995 which increasingly mandate hasher penalities such that, in 2010, "Spain now has the highest rate of imprisonment in the European Union [. . . at] 166 prisoners per 100,000 [inhabitants]." People, in essence, just want criminals out of sight, out of mind.[5]

Lola recognizes that she is appointed to the Spanish Supreme Court "por ser mujer y vasca (o vasca y mujer, si se prefiere)" (25), and she is in support of a quota system intended to increase the number of women in certain jobs. However, she also recognizes that such is due to a strong push by minority groups for such and that "sin comerlo ni beberlo, me había convertido en piedra de toque de una batalla que no era la mía" (25). In effect, she recognizes that a fellow judge's attempt at humor has a certain amount of truth and social commentary: "Si fueras negra o musulmana, mañana te ofrecerían la presidencia" (25).

The Free Will Baptist International Missions website details the growth of the evangelical movement in Spain, but even that site notes that Spaniards are "reactionary" against Evangelicals and "most Spaniards do not appear to be willing to listen to any message presented by Evangelicals" ("Current Religious Climate"). Not surprisingly, then, is Lola's implied criticism of non-Catholic clerics through the relating of a humorous airplane incident on her trip to Boston: "Turbulencias . . . Aquello no fueron turbulencias, parecía el Juicio Final. [. . .] Un señor sentado en la fila anterior a la nuestra, que hablaba inglés y dijo ser pastor de no sé qué confesión religiosa, se desabrochó el cinturón y se puso en pie para entonar una oración. El pobre salió despedido. Se dio un buen golpe contra el techo y decidió rezar en silencio" (*Venganza* 139).

Jaime's social commentary appears more didactic in nature and involves a warning against excessive dedication to one's career; in fact, such is what ultimately leads to his becoming the target of extortion. His career becomes all-absorbing, taking him away from family, recreation, and any social activities in a continual quest to reach a higher level: "con el trabajo pasa como con el dinero: nunca es suficiente. Siempre hay un coche con más caballos, un barco con más metros, un nuevo reto y un puesto más apetecible donde puedes brillar como mereces" (231).

Iturri is a chain smoker; in fact, in the entire series his taking out his packet of tobacco, filling his pipe, and starting to smoke runs parallel to his thinking process and a breakthrough in the investigation. Lola's anti-smoking stance, however, is quite strong, and she frequently forbids his smoking in her presence. Iturri is even more upset at her because she used to smoke and "[d]ebería entenderme, ya que ha sido una fumadora empedernicida. Pero ya se sabe que los ex son los peores" (302).

The last chapter of *Venganza* prior to the "Epílogo" ends with Lola's final letter to Rodrigo. In it, she expands even further upon the series's leitmotif, here stating that the assassin's actions have all been in vain. "Y te digo que te equivocas: el cordero es más fuerte que el lobo. [. . .] No puedes matar la bondad. El amor termina atrayendo con su imán a todo hierro humano" (441). With such, Calderón closes both the novel and the series[6] and adds an exclamation point to the leitmotif of the series promoting something more than just the Golden Rule; she is promoting action.

In conclusion, each of the novels of Reyes Calderón's Lola MacHor series extols the virtues and humankind's responsibility to take seriously the Golden Rule. Caring for one's neighbor is not just an abstract concept in the author's narratives; she treats the idea through several means, situations, and geographical locales. Each novel more strongly personalizes the motif, with the author ultimately replacing the desire for the reader to simply infer her ethical stance to a direct call for action through multiple usage of the second-person singular, social commentary and an overt mandate for more compassion for others because the reader really does not even truly know her/himself entirely.

Notes

1 Note, for instance, that even the United Nations' Committee on the Rights of the Child reported, regarding the Vatican's 2014 report on disciplinary measures taken against pedophile priests, that "the Committee regrets that the report was submitted with considerable delay, which prevented the Committee from reviewing the implementation of the Convention by the Holy See for 14 years" (1). It is interesting, at least to this critic, that a secondary plot structure of this novel involves Iturri's search for the leader of an international pedophile ring (non-Church related).

2 In *Venganza*, Lola tells her mentor Fernando on the day of her investiture on the Spanish Supreme Court that "[d]e pequeña soñaba con cambiar el mundo" (30).

3 See the discussion of Lola's conservative values in Chapter Two.

4 The series seems to be ever-increasing in both its examination and utilization of globalization. *Hemingway* is a fairly local novel but with obvious references to the American author and a Madrid police officer leading, for a while, the investigation. *Número primo* is set, to a large extent, a few kilometers from Pamplona, but the murderer has traveled to other countries and describes his trip to Hungary. *Canaima* involves a case of malfeasance by Spanish officials in Venezuela and Lola's speech concerning corruption at a Word Bank conference in Singapore. *Dr. Wilson* involves a Spanish psychiatrist involved in murders in France, Russia, Vietnam, South Africa, San Francisco, and Barcelona, with Lola going to Washington, D.C. to arrest the suspect after having spent a weekend investigating Dr. Wilson on an island in the Aegean Sea. And *Venganza* involves murders in Argentina, Japan (two), California, and Boston with the bulk of the narrative occurring after Lola and Iturri have flown to the U.S. In addition, an important, secondary plot line involves the attempt by an international drug company to extort Jaime.

5 See Ruth Pike's study of the multiple garrisons and prisons in Northern Africa to where criminals were sent at least as early as the sixteenth century, two of which were Ceuta and Melilla.

6 While it may ultimately prove to be that the MacHor series is only temporary suspended, and that there will be (an)other novel(s), even the author herself in my May 2012 interview with her was less than sure that she would take it up again: "De momento los vamos a dejar descansar un poquito porque son cinco entregas ya."

CHAPTER SIX

Food as Cultural Symbol

The role of food in society and its representation in literature throughout the ages has been well documented. As Emily Gowers notes in her study of Roman literature, "another of the contradictions associated with food: it can be mentioned both for its own sake and as a symbol of something else" (4) and "[t]he significance of food in its literary representations lies both in its simple existence *and* in a bundle of metaphorical associations, a capacity to evoke a whole world of wider experience" (5). In fact, she goes on to say, "the field of social anthropology [. . .] has taught us that the classification of food, the rituals of cooking, and the arrangement of meals hold clues to notions of hierarchy, social grouping, purity and pollution, myths of creation and cosmogony, and the position of man in relation to the world" (5). Thomas Schoenberg and Lawrence Trudeau further note: "Themes related to food are common among all types of writing, and they are often used as a literary device for both visual and verbal impact. [. . .] Dining rituals often provide a framework that both reflects and expresses human desires and behaviors. Many authors [. . .] have used the ritual of dining to present the powerful conflicts that simmer underneath the surface of order." Carmen Ortiz García carries this idea even further, stipulating that food is both identity and a demonstration of power: "La cocina y la comida, sirven, por tanto, para manifestar situaciones de poder, competencia, prestigio y dependencia. [. . .] Al comer se incorporan no solo las características físicas de los alimentos, sino también sus valores simbólicos e imaginarios que, de la misma forma que las cualidades nutritivas, pasan a formar parte del propio ser" (304). Thus, food metaphors are often used to characterize people and their status in society.

David Knutson posits that "Attention to gastronomy is a common feature of detective fiction" (54). At the same time, as Michael Ugarte proposes,

> the motif of food consumption and preparation is [rarely central to] most detective novels, although its strong presence is a feature that

> many readers look for and expect, depending on the sleuth or the author. Food is both peripheral and essential. [. . .] it is through this connection that the reader enters into a dialogue with the author on Spanish and world politics, national and urban history, the working class, the "disenchantment" years, and a possible future. Meetings, rendezvous, settings for character development often revolve around eating places. (100)

That is, on a macrocosmic scale, food, as a critical point in post-Franco Spanish detective fiction, is well established. Consequently, as is the case in other Spanish detective novels, food also plays a prominent role in the Lola MacHor narratives, with many investigative deductions and plot twists occurring either at a local bar/café, at Lola's family dinner table, or at other venues involving gastronomical consumption. My own examination of food and drink in Reyes Calderón's novels provides a vision of alimentary intake as depicted within these novels, the preparation and intake of which are representative of the continuing cultural, and even sometimes sexist, attitudes and habits of the Spanish people in a general sense.

As the series develops throughout the first four novels, food and drink references quantitatively become more frequent. In *Las lágrimas de Hemingway*, for example, there are fifty-six references to specific foods and drinks—twenty-six mentions of nineteen different foods and thirty of thirteen different drinks.[1] In addition, there are three references to non-specific foods (*alimentación*, *alimento*, *viandas*), two occurrences of the verb "beber" without an indication of what is being swallowed, nineteen references to breakfast, lunch or dinner without further clarification of what is being consumed, and one food metaphor: "[Clara] era una manzana envenenada" (305). The gastronomical references in this novel total, then, eighty-one, or approximately one in every 1,283 words.

The total quantitative references to specific foods and drinks increase almost fifty percent in *Los crímenes del número primo* to one hundred—forty-one and fifty-nine, respectively—while the frequency of those references in comparison to the overall word count in the text decreases slightly. The variety also increases, with this novel containing some twenty-nine different foods and sixteen different drinks.[2] In addition, there is one non-clarified use of the word "beber," three generic references to food (*tentempié* [twice], *pinchos*), eighteen generic meal references with no follow-up specificities (*desayuno*, *almuerzo*, *cena*, and *comer*), and one understood food-related analogy, although no food is overtly mentioned: "Me abalancé sobre el ordenador, como un bebé hambriento sobre el hinchado pecho de su madre" (303). The sum total of all food references in this second novel, then, is 123, or one in approximately every 1,575 words.

In *El Expediente Canaima*, food and drink references are substantially elevated, both in total quantity, at 228, and in overall word-count percentage, at approximately one in every 648 words. Such, in essence, represents a twice-as-frequent occurrence and a three hundred percent overall increase in comparison to Calderón's first novel. The specific references to food and drink number 114 and sixty, respectively, with sixty different foods and twenty different drinks being mentioned.[3] This is a 150% *increase* over the variety of food and drink represented in *Las lágrimas de Hemingway* and a 128% *increase* over the total gastronomical representations in *Los crímenes del número primo*. In addition, there are three references to drinks in a general sense (*bebida*, *bebidas frías*, and *bebidas calientes*), nine references to food in a general sense, thirty-eight generic meal references with no follow-up to specifics,[4] and four food/drink metaphors: "la dulcísima miel del reconocimiento público" (97), "le pasa la patata caliente" (253), "el pan nuestro de cada día" (303), and "el beso es privado, un vino de reserva" (416).

Much, if not almost all, of the narration of *El último paciente del Doctor Wilson* occurs over meals: i.e., Rodrigo's meetings with Dr. Wilson at the Washington D.C. restaurant Clyde, Lola's and Wilson's presence at various academic conference dinners, Lola discussing the case with Iturri and others over coffee or lunch/dinner at her house, Lola, Juan and Jaime's visit to the Shibata manor, etc. Food, then, is placed front and center in this novel. In addition, it is important to point out that the murders that Rodrigo carries out occur in several nations around the globe, and Rodrigo describes, often in detail, meals that he consumes while at these various locations. Consequently, it is no surprise that food and drink references increase dramatically in this novel in every category represented, with a total of 425 references, for a ratio of approximately one in every 448 words referring to either food or drink.[5] There are 174 references to seventy-six different and specific foods; two of these, which I am including as food out of deference to a lady at the psychological ward reporting of their possible gastronomical consumption, are not normally considered so: in reference to the cat, "Si te lo has comido, vomítalo. Son indigestos" (478) and "Eso decía mi padre. Se comió a mi madre" (478–79). One additional liquid which Rodrigo tastes one time in an effort to "fortalecer mi voluntad" (189) I do not include in the list of drinks: "La sangre acudió de inmediato a la herida. La toqué. Estaba tibia, pegajosa. Me la acerqué a los labios. Dudé de nuevo. No quería probarla, pero debía hacerlo. Apreté los ojos y lamí la herida. Tenía un sabor especial, metálico" (189). Otherwise, the dishes and drinks mentioned are typical Spanish and/or of another national culture in nature. There are 200 references to thirty-four different and specific drink items, ranging from the multiple ways in which one can prepare coffee to the more international Montecristo, Coca-Cola, *aguardiente*, White Russian, B 52, Faustino del 96, *vino* Gentilini, or *ouzo*, to name only a few. As well, there are three references to non-specific drinks, eight to non-specific foods, thirty-four generic meal references with no follow-up to specifics, and six food or drink analogies or metaphors: "Me ha ofrecido una Coca-Cola pero se ha reservado el abrebotellas" (49); "En ocasiones—que en mis labios saben dulces como la miel—, logro resarcir a los pobres, restituir a los que sufren ultrajes, y encarcelar a los que se creen inmunes porque tienen a medio país a sueldo" (235); "mi vida se me antojaba como el chocolate amargo: dulce en la boca, pero con regusto a guindilla" (329); "[Wilson's voice was] Profunda, amenazadora pero cálida. Una buena taza de café muy cargado, aromático y azucarado" (342); "La vida es mayoritariamente una cesta de fruta dura; las piezas en sazón escasean" (353), and "Nunca digas de esa agua no beberé" (441).

In *La venganza del asesino par*, the overall quantity of references to gastronomical consumption decreases slightly. This is understandable given that in the previous novel the meetings between Dr. Wilson and Rodrigo (i.e., the principal criminal plot line in the narrative) *always* occurr over dinner at the restaurant Clyde. Having said this, however, there still are more references to food and drink in this fifth narrative than in the the first three novels of the series. The specific references to food and drink total 236, of which 127 are drink related and 109 are food related. Of these, there are forty-three and twenty-nine different and specific foods and drinks, respectively, for an approximate total of one in every 655 words of text.[6] Additionally, there are sixteen different non-specific references to food and drink and fourteen different analogies and metaphors to alimentary intake.[7]

In the entire series, then, there are 1,045 distinctive references to food and drink, with a total of 178 different foods and 63 different drinks being named. The drinks are comprised of thirty-four non-alcoholic types and twenty-nine alcoholic types, with the latter group being comprised of only nine beers or wine; thus, the occurrence of hard liquor is rather frequent. The single, most frequent type of drink is coffee, with fourteen different types and serving styles being named.

Interestingly, the only time in the novels when a character repetitively consumes alcoholic drinks in one sitting is when that person is at a crisis point in her/his life; in fact, the association between such and devastating loss is unmistakable, and it occurs in each of the novels under study. In *Hemingway*, Rodrigo, the secretary of the secret society and the one behind the murders, has already drunk three whiskeys only moments before being betrayed and given a gun with which to kill himself (304). Three whiskeys are also the drink of consolation, or solace, for Lorenzo, in *Canaima*, immediately before attempting to obtain logistical support for the murder of Lola (402). In the same novel, Lola turns to Iturri for help in solving the mystery when she finds her first choice of professional assistance, the judge Galo Morán, "todo alcohol" (263) on the floor of the courtroom storage closet (263), seeking consolation from the professional stress he is undergoing as well as his loss of self-pride after a frustrated sexual encounter due to his impotence. Iturri's third cognac, in *Número primo*, is tainted by the pedophile whom he is seeking to arrest while he and Lola are in a night club looking for clues to the priests' assassination (443); this results in Iturri's hospitalization, near death, withdrawal from the case and eventual need to spend several weeks in solitude and recovery at the remote monastery where the crimes began. In *Dr. Wilson*, Lola herself suffers a mental breakdown after a traumatic miscarriage and plans her own suicide over three beers and a "bolsa grande de patatas fritas" (366). And in *Venganza*, after Lola has told Iturri that Fernando has given her hope that Jaime will return home—and implying that there are no possibilities that Iturri will become her lover—the two of them go out to dinner where "Iturri se bebió él solito la botella de reserva de Cune y que, a los postres, pidió L'Esprit de Courvoisier" (107). He finishes off the drink; "pidió una segunda ronda" (107), and "apuró la copa [Lola's]" (109). In fact, for the rest of the novel, during which time Lola and he remain on distant terms, Iturri is often seen as heavily drinking. When Jaime goes to Iturri's hotel room in order to retrieve Rodrigo's letters, on one of the nightstands "descansaba una botella, más vacía que llena" of "whisky norteamericano" (237). While there, Jaime drinks a "medio vaso" (237) of whisky, serves himself another glass (241), and retrieves three "botellines de distintas bebidas" (241) from the hotel lobby to take back to Iturri's room so they can discuss how to resolve the attempted extortion against Jaime. "Media hora después [Jaime] tenía tanto licor dentro que ya no podía razonar con coherencia" (245), the two of them having finished off all the drinks within sight, and in the room. And it is at this point that Jaime cannot control himself and violently punches Iturri when the detective mentions that the bathroom shower in Jaime's house has a leak. Realizing that he has lost control of his own reactions and injured the person who can best help resolve his own dilemma, Jaime goes back to the hotel lobby and gets "dos botellines de whisky" (248) as an atonement gift, which he takes to Iturri: "Era mi forma de pedir disculpas. Se los bebió seguidos, directamente de la botella" (248).

Junk food is described as normal for North Americans. Such is the belief in the stereotype that, in *Canaima*, when Lola's family is sheltered by the FBI in a safe location, her son Javier's response upon leaving reveals a stereotypical view of North American and police food: "Ha estado bien, aunque te has equivocado: no tienen comida basura. ¡Ni siquiera donuts! Y la Coca-cola es light" (381). Such sociological type casting is accentuated in *Dr. Wilson* when Lola, Jaime, and Iturri go to Washington D.C. to capture Wilson and "tomábamos una taza de café americano" (454), and the undercover agents seated at the bar "bebían Coca-Cola" (457). Hamburgers are consumed quite frequently by the investigative team when, in *Venganza*, they are in the United States: Iturri complains that "[l]a hamburguesa se está enfriando" (159) when Lola calls him from the International Faculty Club seeking his assistance in helping Jaime. Following the second trip to the prison, "ante unas hamburguesas grasientas" (280) Joe, Jaime, and Iturri tell Lola about the visit and Rodrigo's announcement that Elena Polvoskha has died. After they receive a phone call saying that Kimio Jr. has been assassinated, the group decides to go visit Rodrigo again in prison, but they stop "en un McDonald's y compramos unas hamburguesas que nos tomamos en el coche" (392). During the journey through the night, however, they decide that it is probably better to visit Sarah in the hospital first, and Iturri comments, "[a]ntes de llegar al hospital paramos a desayunar y a asearnos un poco. Es inconfesable, lo sé, pero la pura verdad es que me sentaron fenomenal las hamburguesas" (397).

Extensive examples of other nationalistic food and drink are portrayed in Rodrigo's travels around the globe: in France, he samples *calissons*, in Russia *blinis* and vodka, and in the Middle East *souvlaki*, *dolma*, *baklava*, and *ouzo* (*Dr. Wilson*). Lola calls a Chinese restaurant and orders "rollitos de primavera [. . . ,] fideos con bamboo [. . .] y una ternera con setas" in *Venganza* (95–96). The Russian Elena Polvoskha drinks vodka with her visitor and killer before her murder (*Venganza* 290). The refrigerator on the yacht of the leader of the international pedophile ring whom Iturri is investigating has "dos botellas de champán [que] llevaban la etiqueta Möet-Chandon" (*Número primo* 114). In *Canaima*, Lola and Jaime attend a fund-raising dinner for African women hosted by Jimena, of which she says that the meal is "los manjares que ellos sirven en los días de fiesta y bonanza" (341): "Les habían servido viandas típicas de Kenya. [. . .] habían comido [. . .] una extraña mixtura de fécula y alubias y una correosa carne de cabra que flotaba sobre una salsa clara. De bebida, cerveza amarga" (339). Obviously Lola recognizes the inherent sociological associations with food as she decides the best souvenirs to bring home to family and friends from Singapore. In *Canaima*, such gifts are boxes of candy, "unos bombones rellenos de frutas con la forma del dragón asiático" (223), and she later offers Kalif a box of Spanish chocolates when he leaves Madrid headed back to the U.S. (413). Other, "typically Spanish" foods and drinks in the series allude to Iturri's weakness for churros (*Hemingway* 256–57, *Número primo* 96)—and Lola's revulsion at such (*Canaima* 124)—*rosquillas* (*Número primo* 96), *tortilla* (*Número primo* 96), *jamón serrano* (*Número primo* 414, *Dr. Wilson* 60), and Jaime's telling Lola to drink "un Cola Cao" (*Número primo* 301). Even more regional in nature are the *pinchos* typical of the Basque region (*Número primo* 382, *Canaima* 249), the Catalan *pa amb tomàquet* (*Dr. Wilson* 257), the *pisto manchego* (*Canaima* 96), and Faustino, a Rioja drink from a winery with the same name (*Dr. Wilson* 345).

But Lola is not the only one who recognizes either the sociological implications of food or the fact that certain foods can impact in a meaningful way. In fact, fortunately for Lola, it is probably the food on the car floor which causes her kidnapper to view her more as a mother than as a *juez de instrucción*, and such thereby saves her life in *Número primo* (551). Rodrigo's offering of a chocolate to Dr. Wilson is the only way that he can get the psychiatrist to speak about the trail of murders in *Venganza* (5, 62), and Jaime employs the same technique himself for the same purpose (267). And Lola, at the end of *Dr. Wilson*, goes back to Clyde, in Washington D.C., and eats the same meal that Dr. Wilson and Rodrigo tended to share in an attempt to break the nightmarish spell of terror that the memory of them continues to hold over her (475–76).

The author's depiction of varying levels and types of food and drink offerings in relation to the different levels of society increases the effect of verisimilitude in the series. In *Venganza*, even the smell of the greens in the prison is so strong that "En cuanto la puerta metálica se movió, me llegó el olor a comida" (177). And while the prison psychiatrist recognizes the repugnance of his "plato de macarrones con salsa boloñesa y queso gratinado" (183), he says that "la que sirven aquí es mucho peor" (185). When Lola, in *Número primo*, finally understands that the hunter poaching rabbits out of season will not talk about what he has seen without receiving certain accommodations, she tells him that he will not be prosecuted for his illegal activities and his bounty will be ignored: "Quien le cuide sabrá hacer de él un buen guiso" (196). In the same novel, the head of an international ring of pedophiles whom Iturri is seeking has in his yacht refrigerator "dos botellas de champán [que] llevaban la etiqueta Möet-Chandon" (114) and, escaping the dragnet yet once again, "estará desayunando en algún hotel de lujo" (116). Later in the narrative, Iturri protests when Lola tells him to take the priests somewhere safe, insisting that "¡Por Dios, Lola, son un montón de obispos y varios cardenales, no les puedo llevar a un local para que les despachen unas cervezas y unos pinchos!" (382). In *Hemingway*, Lola tells Uranga that in spite of being falsely arrested and accused of murder, her pain will not be tied to Pamplona, but rather to the hospital, handcuffs and snails (302), an image deriving from an unsympathetic hospital roommate who explained how to cook them and later loudly proclaims joy upon seeing Lola "the murderess" transported out of her room (188).

Society's upper crust is shown as somewhat more discriminating with their intake than are the lower classes. The parvenu Clara roundly protests the hospital coffee: "Un café. ¿Crees que aquí habrá café? [. . .] Tú debes referirte a ese líquido negro que sale de las cafeteras industriales. Yo hablo de café. ¿Tendrán en este sitio leche desnatada y sacarina? ¡Me siente fatal la grasa de la leche!" (97). Although Lola thinks it to be an excellent coffee, "[p]ara el refinado gusto de Clara, el líquido era agrio, poco denso y estaba asquerosamente templado. Para arreglar aquel *estropicio provinciano*, la joven sacó una petaca de plata labrada y añadió a su vaso un generoso chorro de coñac" (99). Lola's mother meets the renowned lawyer Gonzalo Eregui at an elegant dinner at the Palacio de Santa Ana, "un antiguo monasterio del siglo XVIII, convertido por la cadena *AC* en un hotel de lujo" (*Hemingway* 246). At the meal—"Nada de césped aliñado, nada de huevos escalfados sin más alegría que una pizca de sal: solomillo al *foie*" (247), and "en aquella cena nació una nueva amistad" (247). In *Canaima*, both Lola and the World Bank official and conference organizer David Herrera-Smith are able to indulge in the gastronomical intake of upper society during their trip to Singapore. His room is broken into at the hotel, and as a token of thanks for not pressing charges, the hotel director

> envió a la suite del norteamericano una espléndida cena al estilo cantonés [. . .] empezando por el plato de bacalao con el que había ganado el premio al mejor chef de Asia. Importaba el pescado directamente de Vancouver y lo cocinaba con una salsa Spicy Tangy. También había preparado cordero lechal con Black Pepper Sauce, una selección de variedades locales de marisco, una sopa de setas y col y una colección de miniaturas dulces. (55)

Lola, on her first-class flight to Asia, begins with champagne, and then

> Optó por la cocina oriental [. . .]. La ensalada de salmón, rociada con huevas de caviar rojo, gruesas como semillas de granada, y extrañas

> verduras crujientes, estaba deliciosa. El aceite de oliva [... era] tan exquisito que creyó que, en vez de aliñar la ensalada, la perfumaba. Le siguió una extraña carne—probablemente una variedad de ave de corral—con berenjenas asadas y brotes de soja, y un helado con galletas. (172)

Perhaps Lola sums up best the difference in food and drink consumption between different levels of society when she concludes: "los ricos sabían vivir" (172).

In addition to Clara and Rodrigo, Lola herself has her own prejudices concerning food consumption. When she awakens from having fainted upon being arrested, in *Hemingway*, she finds herself in the hospital, handcuffed to the bed, and "A mi derecha, había una mujer. No podía verla, pero sí oírla. Recuerdo bien la conversación: cómo guisar los caracoles, porque yo nunca he sido capaz de probarlos: sólo pensar que esas asquerosas babas se deslizan por mi garganta me produce náuseas" (170). Later, when Lola is being transported to a private room, her negative perceptions of this food-animal are transposed onto both this woman and the other people in the room as they are depicted in animalistic overtones in their conspiracy against her:

> "¡Qué bien!" Por la voz supe que la cocinera de babosas se había envalentonado y hablaba en voz alta. "¡Mejor así! ¡Que se la lleven! ¡Corremos grave peligro con ella aquí! Hace unos años hubo muertos en el hospital por un caso similar. ¿No lo recuerdan?" chilló, dirigiéndose a la concurrencia que escuchaba sin perder ripio. [. . .] A medida que aquellos individuos se convertían en masa sin rostro ni vergüenza, la conversación comenzó a animarse. [. . .] Incapaz de soportar aquellos dardos emponzoñados, me tapé completamente con la sábana. Los demás aplaudían mi traslado con expresiones de júbilo. Yo lloraba sin tratar de ahogar mis jadeos. (188–89)

This aversion to the consumption of snails is emphasized even stronger in the novel's last chapter—discounting the Epilogue—through both the chapter's nomenclature, "Caracoles en sus babas," and via Lola's explanation to judge Uranga that her pain will be tied not to Pamplona, but to the hospital, handcuffs and snails.

Another aversion to food that Lola has is *churros*. In *Canaima*, she comments to the bar owner Emilia that she fears a past that smells like *churros*. This, however, instead of being an unexplained negative reaction to a food enjoyed by many, owes itself to a horrible experience in her youth when she was assaulted by a pedophile, an event she explains to Jaime, evidently for the first time in their many years of marriage as he unsuccessfully interrupts her: "No sigas, Lola, me hago cargo. Perdóname, no lo sabía" (156). She continues, however, to detail this childhood tragedy as the cause for her abnormal fear of Ariel, the child molester who has promised to kill Lola unless she drops the case:

> Sé que no es racional, pero esa nota me ha devuelto a aquel portal. [. . .] Estos recuerdos llevan ahí casi cuarenta años. Tú no puedes comprenderlo, pero ese miedo, ese asco que me sube desde la boca del estómago nunca se olvida. Está ahí. Se esconde bajo la superficie, por debajo de lo cotidiano, como un poso mugriento, sigue atado con imperdibles al alma y su olor persiste aunque te frotes con estropajo. (156–57)

Lola and Iturri both presume to pass as "average folks" in the series. In fact, the first description of Iturri is "Juan Iturri era un hombre de apariencia y complexión ordinarias, más menudo que grande" (*Hemingway* 106), and "Juan Iturri se sabía un camaleón. Podía pasar completamente desapercibido sin siquiera proponérselo. [. . .] Quizás fueran [sus gafas] tan fachosas como su bigote, pero ambos elementos cumplían su misión. Disfrazado de nadie podía ir a cualquier sitio sin preocuparse de que su placa o su rostro fueran detectados" (253). Later in the same narrative, the reader learns that Iturri is "de una madre camarera y un padre desconocido" (307). In *Número primo*, Lola remarks that "Cuando nos conocimos, parecía un paisano pueblerino, escaso de gusto y presupuesto" (286). And, in *Dr. Wilson*, Lola states that "Por aquel entonces no llevaba barba y su aspecto resultaba vulgar, descuidado, rozando lo miserable. Nunca he hablado con él de esos detalles, pero tuve la sensación de que con ese atuendo pretendía pasar por uno de tantos, alguien con el que te topas pero nunca recuerdas. Supongo que la vida de un policía en una zona de terrorismo activo es complicada, y puede incluso llevarte a la paranoia" (179). Such desire of "normalcy" is certainly not evident in Iturri's drinks however; he has a weakness for cognac. In fact, eleven such associations are attributed to him in *Venganza* alone. Iturri's weakness for *churros* is evident at the Iruña bar: "Su madre había sido camarera del local hasta su jubilación, y siempre que acudía a saludarla, le obsequiaba con algún churro: ni recién hechos ni calientes, pero a él le sabían a gloria" (256–57). If this were the only occurrence of such, one might argue that Iturri's taste for the churros owes itself to nostalgia, or an attempt to recover familiar fondness from his youth. However, in *Los crímenes del número primo*, Iturri enters a bar in Pontevedra (many miles from Pamplona), and while eating a tortilla de bacalao "observó cómo la cocinera sacaba una gruesa ristra de churros de una enorme sartén y, tras escurrir el exceso de aceite, cortaba y espolvoreaba las porras con azúcar. No pudo resistirse, y se comió también media docena" (96). The website ifood.tv states that churros have "attained cult status as the national food symbol of Spain" ("Churro"). The associations of Iturri to them, then, parallel his attempting to be seen as a common citizen.[8]

While Lola, in spite of being a judge, may be viewed as ordinary as well[9] in regards to her food associations, her food and drink associations do expand as the series continues. In *Hemingway*, the only three liquids she drinks are *café* (thrice), and *café con leche* and *vino* (both once). Her coffee intake remains more than half of her liquid consumption in *Los crímenes del número primo*, but the variations are *café* (eight times), *café con nata* and *café helado* (both once). As well, she also consumes, once each, Cola Cao, menta-poleo, *agua*, Coca-Cola, and *leche* for a total drink intake of fifteen occurrences. In *Canaima*, she is associated with eleven different drinks. Coffee remains her most common drink—*café* (six times), *café con leche*, *café especial*, and *descafeinado de máquina* being the specific variations on the word—but she does consume two alcoholic drinks—*champán* and *vino*—as well as water, different juices, and hot chocolate. In *Dr. Wilson*, Lola imbibes five different types of coffee—*café* (seven times), *café con leche* (twice), *café americano*, *descafeinado*, and *café cortado*—four alcoholic drinks—*cerveza* (twice), *coñac*, Faustino del 96, and vino *de rioja*—as well as *agua* and Coca-Cola. And, finally, in *Venganza*, Lola consumes the widest variety yet of drinks: *agua*, *agua sin gas*, *café* (eleven times), *café con leche* (twice), *leche*, *leche caliente*, *té*, *té de manzanilla*, *tila*, *zumo de naranja*, coca cola light, *cerveza*, *una copa*, and *cava*. In the entire series, then, Lola is seen drinking a total of eighty-two times with thirty-one different drinks; of these, forty-eight times she drinks coffee, eleven times alcohol, and twenty-three times a non-alcoholic drink. Arguably, such qualifies as a description of a "normal" person in Spain.

Of the three characters that appear in all the novels—Lola, Jaime, and Juan Iturri—Lola clearly has both the highest number and highest variety of drinks associated with her prior to *Venganza*[10]: Lola at fifty-six and twenty-three, Jaime at nineteen and ten, and Iturri at nineteen and eight, respectively. Lola has alcohol associated with her drinking 14.3% of the time, with only six different types, the "hardest" liquor being a cognac she drinks in *Dr. Wilson*; Jaime at 31.6% of the time, with six different types, his "hard" drinks being both cognac and *ouzo*; and Iturri at 52.6% of the time, with eight different types, his "hard" drinks being cognac (his preferred drink at 33.3%), *ouzo*, and *aguardiente*. Additionally, of the fifty-two (52) different drinks mentioned in the first four novels, twenty-eight are non-alcoholic and twenty-four are alcoholic. Lola is depicted as drinking more than one-half, or twenty-four, of these drinks, of which six are alcoholic, nine are non-alcoholic other than coffee, and nine are some type of the total eleven varieties of coffee in the series. What this quantitative analysis indicates, then, is that clearly Lola is the principal character and, while no teetotaler, certainly consumes alcohol at a much lower extent than either her husband or investigative assistant.

As can be seen from the previous analysis, then, food and drink play an integral part in the Lola MacHor series of novels by Reyes Calderón, with many investigative deductions and plot twists occurring either at a local bar/café or at the Lola family dinner table. An examination of food and drink in these novels provides a vision of alimentary intake which is representative of the continuing cultural attitudes and habits of the Spanish people in a general sense. As the series develops over the first four novels, food and drink references quantitatively become more frequent, ranging from a low, in *Las lágrimas de Hemingway*, of fifty-six references to *specific* foods and drinks, or a total of eighty-one gastronomical references of all types, or approximately one in every 1,283 words, to a high of 425 references or approximately one in every 448 words referring to either food or drink, in *El último paciente del Doctor Wilson*, a novel that contains 174 references to seventy-six different and specific foods. Other, specific uses of food and drink by the author include the close association between repetitive consumption of alcoholic drinks and a personal crisis in the life of the drinker, most often a crisis involving either death or a devastating loss. The author is consistent, as well, in portraying foods stereotypical of the cultural setting, whether such be Catalonia, Greece, Russia, the U.S., or Spain. And, as might be expected by an author attempting to establish maximum verisimilitude, in all these novels varying levels and types of food and drink consumptions by different levels of society are described, be they jet-setters, parvenus, high clergy, or the common folk. In short, through a detailed analysis of food in the Lola MacHor series, it becomes readily apparent that the author both recognizes and portrays inherent sociological and cultural associations with the various foods and drinks she includes at distinct points in the works.

Notes

1 The specific foods in *Hemingway* include, in alphabetical order: *bocadillos de tortilla, caracoles, caramelo sin azúcar, caramelos de fresa, carne, césped aliñado (i.e., salad), chistorrica frita, churro, fruta, huevos escalfados, manzana asada, migas de pan, olivas, paella, pan amasado, pimientos del piquillo, solomillo al foie, verdura, verdura a la plancha* and *cagarrutas*, which, while not normally considered a food substance, in Rosario's

relating of a time in her youth when she switched olives for sheep defecation and the mother Superior actually tasted it, I am counting as such in this particular case. The specific drinks include the following: *agua, alcohol, café, café con leche, coffee, coñac, copa, descafeinado de sobre, güisqui, leche, licor, pacharán*, and *vino*.

2 The specific foods in *Número primo* include, in alphabetical order: *aceitunas, albóndigas, bizcocho de manzana, bocadillo, bollo, buñuelos, buñuelos rellenos de crema, calabacines, canela, cereales del desayuno, conejo, cruasán, churros, ensalada, espaguetis carbonara, filete, helado de chocolate, jamón serrano, limón, marisco, napolitanas, nuez moscada, pan blanco, pasta, porras, rosquillas, tomates, tortilla de bacalao*, and *tostado*. The specific drinks include: *agua, aguardiente de hierbas, algún licor, algún refresco, café, café con leche, café con nata, café helado, cervezas, Coca-Cola, Cola Cao, coñac, champán, leche, menta-poleo*, and *vino*.

3 The specific foods in *Canaima* include, in alphabetical order: *aceite de oliva, alubias, ave de corral, bacalao, bacalao a la gallega, beicon, berenjenas, bocadillos de chorizo, bombones, brotes de soja, buñuelos, buñuelos rellenos de crema, canapés, canela, carne, carne de cabra, cóctel de marisco, cordero lechal, cruasán, chocolate, churros, donuts, dulces, ensalada César, ensalada de salmón, escarola con granada, especias picantes, fécula, fideos chinos, fruta fresca, garbanzos con calamares, golosina, helado con galletas, hogazas, huevas de caviar rojo, huevos rellenos, huevos revueltos, limón, macarrones con chorizo, magdalena con pepitas de chocolate, marisco, muffins, pan romano, pasta al ajo, patatas, pavo, pescado, pisto manchego, pizza, queso, salsa Spicy Tangy, semillas de granada, sopa de setas y col, tarta de manzana, tortillas vegetales, tostadas, tostadas con mermelada, turrón, verduras a la plancha*, and *verduras crujientes*. The more generic foods include: *bufet, cocina oriental, manjares, media docena de ingredientes, pinchos, selección de delicias, tentempié, un plato precocinado*, and *viandas*.

The specific drinks include: *agua, alcohol, bebida local—una combinación de frutas de sabor amargo, café, café capuchino, café con leche, café descafeinado, cerveza, Coca-Cola, coñac, champán, chocolate caliente, güisqui, leche, licores, refresco, té, vino, zumo de naranja*, and *zumos*.

4 Besides the more common variations on both the noun and verb forms of the words *desayuno, comida, almuerzo*, and *cena*, other meal indications include: *algo de comida, cena al estilo cantonés, cena benéfica, cena de gala, comida basura*, and *postres*.

5 The specific foods in *Dr. Wilson* include, in alphabetical order: *albóndigas, almendra molida, almíbar, arroz a banda, azúcar, baklava, beicón, blinis, bocadillo, bollo, cacahuetes, cachelo, caldo, caldo de pollo, calissons, caramelo, carne cruda, caviar rojo, cebolla, chocolate, chorizo frito, dolmadakia, dulces, ensalada, entrecot con gambas, esturión, filete, fruta, gambas, gato, golosinas, hamburguesa de cangrejo, huevos fritos, huevos revueltos, jamón serrano, langosta, lentejas estofadas, madre, mantequilla, melón, mermelada, miel, migas, nueces trituradas sobre pasta filo, pa amb tomàquet,*

pan, pasta, pastel de cumpleaños, patata, pescado, pimentón picante, pinchos morunos, pipas, pizza, pulpo, queso, rollito de primavera, rollitos de arroz, salchicha, salchichón, salmón, salsa a base de alcaparras, azafrán y curry (all counting as one), *sándwiches, sepia, souvlaki, tempura, tomate, tomate rallado, torrijas, tortilla con almejas, tortilla de patata, tortilla francesa, tostadas con mantequilla, trufa, vainilla, vegetales,* and *yogur*. The more generic food references include: *alimentos, bocado, caldos, comida china, comida japonesa, guiso, suculentas dietas,* and *tentempié*. The more generic meal references—other than the more obvious *desayuno, almuerzo, comida,* and *cena*—with no follow-up to specifics include: *algo de picar, cena de clausura, cena de gala, cena ligera, comida tranquila, comida informal, desayuno bufet, festín,* and *tomemos algo de postre*.

The specific drinks include: *agua, agua con gas, aguardiente, alcohol, B 52, bebida, café, café americano, café con leche, café cortado con una generosa dosis de canela, café descafeinado, caldo, cerveza, cerveza con limón, Coca-Cola, coñac, Faustino del 96, Gentilini, ginebra, güisqui, infusión, licor, líquido ambarino, Montecristo, ouzo, qué chupar* (milk), *ron, ron añejo, té, té negro, vino de rioja, vinto tinto, vodka,* and *White Russian*.

6 The specific foods in *Venganza* include: *beicon, beicon crujiente, berza, bocadillo, bombón de chocolatina, cangrejo, chocolate, chocolate puro, chocolatina, costillas adobadas, croissant, croqueta de roquefort, desayuno continental, ensalada, ensalada César, entrecot con gambas, fideos con bambú, fruta, galletas, galletas integrales, hamburguesa, helado, huevos, huevos revueltos, macarrones con salsa boloñesa y queso, gratinado, mantequilla, panecillos, pastas de chocolate, pescadito a la plancha, piña, pizza, pollo al curry, puré, puré de patata, queso, rollito de primavera, salchichas, sándwiches de queso, sopa, ternera con setas, tortilla de bacalao y albóndigas, tortilla de patata,* and *tostadas*.

The specific drinks include: *agua, agua sin gas, alcohol, café, café con leche, café negro, cappuccino, cava, cerveza, cerveza mexicana, coca cola light, coñac, copa, Cune, L'Esprit de Courvoisier, espresso, jugo de toronja, leche, leche desnatada, licor, ron y coco, té, té de manzanilla, tila, vino, vodka, whisky, whisky norteamericano,* and *zumo de naranja*.

7 The non-specific food and drink references in *Venganza* include: *almorzar, almuerzos, beber, bebidas frías, botellín, tres botellines de distintas bebidas, cenar, comer, comida, comida tailandesa, desayunar, desayuno, desayuno medio decente, líquido ambarino, postre,* and *vaso tras vaso*.

The analogies or metaphors to food and drink in *Venganza* are as follows: "Sé que me ha pasado el arroz. Y el pollo" (79), "Hasta la zanahoria que tengo por pelo" (90), "Operación Pan de Azúcar" (91), "El cable se hundió en su cuello como el cuchillo en la mantequilla" (97), "Tienes los ojos como tomates" (105), "el tomate en su calcetín" (160), "La expresión me cayó en el estómago como una salsa picante" (274), "[Jaime] Temblaba como un flan" (323), "la Gran Manzana" (353, 394), Iturri's nose "¡Parece un pimiento!" (355), Lola's face "adquirió el color de pimiento de piquillo" (374), Jaime "tenía los ojos del color de los carobineros cocidos" (389), "la primera *señorita manzana*" (399, 400), and "Sarah cayó como fruta madura" (428).

8 While ifood.tv lists magdalenas as one of "the most popular Spanish breakfast foods" ("Most Popular"), the only mention of such in any of the novels is when Lola "se dedicó a separar vaso de café y envoltorios de magdalenas y *muffins* hasta hacer sitio" (*Canaima* 378) for the Canaima files in the trash can.

9 The author stated in a 2010 interview that "Yo creo que al lector lo que le gusta es ir poniéndose en la piel de una persona normal, alguien que es juez pero que tiene que comprar leche, o ir a levantar un cadáver pensando que tiene que recoger al niño de un cumpleaños" (Stegmeier).

10 I am including only the first four novels of the series in this comparison of the three characters since Iturri clearly increases his alcoholic consumption early in *Venganza* when Lola definitively rejects his amorous overtures. In this novel alone, Iturri drinks forty times (or approximately once every ten pages), of which twenty-nine are eleven different alcohol drinks (and six are some variation of *café*).

CHAPTER SEVEN

Reviewing the Evidence

Reyes Calderón has highlighted as her literary philosophy a desire to understand the human condition, the importance of human development over plot, and her belief that good novels will improve the reader. One of the ways in which she accomplishes such in the Lola MacHor series is through a frequent commentary—if not criticism—of the social situation in Spain of the present day. In fact, it is my argument in the preceding analyses that one of the principal themes of all five novels is the author's desire that humans understand each other better, that they have more compassion one for the other, and that they act on such understanding and compassion to make the world a better place. In the first novel of the series, *Las lágrimas de Hemingway*, for example, Lola previews the letter that ends up tarnishing her mentor's reputation by saying that "Sé que todos creemos tener derecho a juzgar a los demás, especialmente cuando se equivocan. Pero en realidad no somos quién para juzgar a nadie" (293). In *Los crímenes del número primo*, thinking once again of the repulsiveness of what she had seen and learned in Brothers, the gay bar, Lola admits that: "Me afectó [. . .] Yo no soy mejor que ellos, ¿sabes? [. . .] A veces, cuando recuerdo aquellas imágenes, pienso que he tenido suerte al caer en este ambiente, contigo y los niños . . . ¿Qué hubiera sido de mí si el destino hubiera sido otro?" (486). *El Expediente Canaima* ends with Lola asking how many innocent people have to suffer just so that one person can be benefited: "¿cuántas Marías, cuántos Parada, cuántos Herrera-Smith han de caer por cada Jimena?" (420). In *El último paciente del Doctor Wilson*, Lola's miscarriage and subsequent depression lead her to conclude that without having suffered such, she would never have understood the assassin's situation. She concludes the book with a charge to the reader that s/he her/himself does not fully understand her/his own life . . . leaving understood, then, the question: "So how do you think you can judge someone else?" And the author herself, in *Venganza*, takes away the role of social critic from the narrator and assumes such in her "Agradecimientos" in the final pages of the work by saying that comparing ourselves among ourselves is a stupid exercise, "un punto de estupidez" (445). That is, in the final analysis, Calderón creates books that are more than mere entertainment; as she herself indicated in an October 2011 interview: "Los libros enseñan con profunda humildad, algo muy necesario en una cultura de éxito arrogante como la nuestra. Los libros, si son buenos, te hacen mejores" (LESEG).

A study of the five novels of Reyes Calderón's Lola MacHor series represents an analysis of the breaking of tradition: both the main character and the author are female. Additionally, however, Lola MacHor poses yet a third break from literary tradition in that Lola is neither a police investigator nor a private detective; she is a "juez de instrucción." And, as such, she is breaking professional and gender roles when she personally conducts the investigation itself instead of handing off such to the police detectives or a *fiscal*, as would be the usual pattern in "real life." But she is intended to portray a common Spanish woman fighting the same daily battles as millions of other Spanish women, mothers, housewives, and professional women of the 21st century. As Reyes Calderón herself has commented: "[y]o creo que al lector lo que le gusta es ir poniéndose en la piel de una persona normal, alguien que es juez pero que tiene que comprar leche, o ir a levantar un cadáver pensando que tiene que recoger al niño de un cumpleaños" (Stegmeier). But, on the other hand, Lola MacHor is very much a woman who has broken through the glass ceiling of the professional world. In fact, it is abundantly clear that the author has in mind something other than a female protagonist who blindly supports or rebels against traditional masculine patriarchy or who exemplifies the feminist subversion of such. That is, Calderón's works go much beyond the easily defined ideologies of patriarchy, feminism, post-feminism, conservatism, and liberalism in an attempt to present a professional woman with a career who is much more complex than that exemplified by the commonly accepted *ángel del hogar/femme fatale* or the patriarchal/feminist dichotomies. The author converts the principal female character from the traditional background role (patriarchy), or the inverse, the fighting antagonist (feminism), into one who enters the traditional masculine arena of detective work as something more than simply another female detective; she is an examining magistrate—a first for Spanish literature. But at the same time the development of Lola MacHor parallels the typical Spanish female woman of her age who has been influenced by vestiges of traditional stereotypes very much in play in Spain during the middle to later years of the 20th century.

Some traces of conservatism that are apparent in the Lola MacHor series are the sacrificing love and affection that Lola has toward her husband, her acceptance and labor as a housewife, the large number of children she has, the accepted, stereotyped views of the woman's role in society, a strong anti-abortionist belief and certain stereotypical beliefs that she holds. At the same time, Lola demonstrates a more progressive, if not anti-patriarchal, side as well: she is a judge (one of the first females to serve in the various professional roles she has throughout the novels); she works outside of the house; she is a doubting-believer or a believing-doubter (she cannot decide which); she has problems with the Church and the clergy who allow themselves special favors, and she never takes on or accepts as her own her husband's last name. Additionally, she believes in the rights of the criminals and the accused, but she laments that there is no justice for the average person. Those psychological conflicts of Lola correspond to what opinion polls indicate about the Spanish population in general. For example, as noted in a 2009 study by Braulio Gómez Fortes and Irene Palacios Brihuega, less than one year after the publication of *Número primo*, confidence in the Church in Spain is rated at 2.9 (on a scale of 0 to 10 points), approximately the same number as say that religion is very important in their lives (Pew Research Center). Antipathy toward the Church is not documented in that report, but an October–December 2008 survey by the Spanish Centro de Investigaciones Sociológicas indicates that 22.7% of Spaniards claim that "La Iglesia y organizaciones religiosas" inspire "Ninguna confianza" (4); 51.3% state that "la Iglesia y las organizaciones religiosas de este país tienen" either "Un poder desmesurado" or "Demasiado poder" (6), and 19.8% agree that "Hay muy poco de verdad en cualquier religión" (18). Obviously, the secularization of Spanish society is quite noticeable, and doubts concerning the Church/religion are apparent in Lola's thoughts and life as well.

Admittedly, Lola presents a well-developed personality, range of emotions, and verisimilar portrayal of an advancing, post-Franco, female, adult Spanish professional; in spite of such, she remains true to many patriarchal expectations and traditional stereotypes. Corresponding to traditional conservative values, the most important thing to Lola is her family. The maternal instinct in Lola is quite evident, and motherhood is woven in the fabric of who she is personally and professionally. She is very much in love with her family, and more than anything else what she wants is to be happy. When Jaime is offered a job in Madrid, she is not willing to deny him the promotion or to remain in Pamplona working by herself (*Canaima*); therefore, she immediately finalizes her plans to request a position on the Audiencia Nacional. In *El Expediente Canaima*, she once again puts her family first, placing what she believes to be the original Canaima files into the designated trashcan in an intent to save the life of her son Javier, knowing that this puts her own career in jeopardy. Lola believes that her car being strewn with children's items, and the subsequent perception by her kidnapper of her as a mother, is what deters him from killing her in *Los crímenes del número primo*. Afraid that someone has invaded her home, Lola's defense of her home and family results in her son Javier receiving a blow from the candelabra-turned-weapon and suffering a head wound that requires "cinco puntos y muchas explicaciones" since "el médico de guardia dedujo que estaba ante un caso de malos tratos" (*Canaima* 354). The fifth child, a daughter born between *Las lágrimas de Hemingway* and *Los crímenes del número primo*, is the result of an unexpected pregnancy. At the beginning of the fourth novel, *Dr. Wilson*, Lola herself is once again unexpectedly pregnant, a pregnancy that she is determined to see through to the end, but which ends in a miscarriage. While her views of abortion as an ethical/moral issue are never specifically detailed, her conservative opinions concerning such are quite clear. In fact, she and Jaime agree that "no lo vamos a tirar a la basura" (*Dr. Wilson* 227).

It is evident that Lola quite often follows the dictates of traditionally patriarchal values of the woman as the goddess of the domestic domain. She often completes household chores: When the Nuncio appears at her house, she insists on making sandwiches for him even though he says that such is not necessary, and she prepares dinner for Iturri when he comes to her house to discuss the case (*Número primo*). She loves her home, and she says that she is just an ordinary mother.

Stereotypically, as an object of the male gaze in the patriarchal paradigm, the woman Lola is concerned with her appearance, in particular her hair. At the same time, her obsession with her personal appearance is apparent through her frequent visits to beauty salons—most notably in *Número primo* and *Dr. Wilson*—and she worries when weather changes might alter her coiffure. By the fifth novel, when she is appointed a Magistrate to the Spanish Supreme Court, she decides it is time for a complete makeover; she cuts her hair, and thereby submits even further to the patriarchal pressure of maintaining a more youthful appearance. Such is her concern for appearing to be aging that, in *Venganza*, she is reluctant to let her investigative partner Juan Iturri know that she now has to don reading glasses in order to make out the words in the newspaper. In sheer number of portrayals, however, it is the third novel of the series, *El Expediente Canaima*, where Lola seems to be suffering the most from an obsession with her physical appearance, her battle against weight-gain, and her sex appeal. Lola's sentiments toward the detective Juan Iturri go beyond simple gratitude for his exonerating her of murder in the first novel, *Las lágrimas de Hemingway*; she clearly has romantic feelings for him, even after his drug-induced attempt to force himself on her in the second novel, *Los crímenes del número primo*. While she also has feelings of lust for him, she realizes that "[s]i me acuesto contigo, sólo te utilizaré" (451), and she rejects his advances. Realizing that her feelings toward Iturri—whose indisciplina y la insociabilidad [. . .] le parecían deliciosas" (*Canaima* 283)—are not dead, she refuses to meet him alone, and instead invites him to dinner with her family, proposing that after the meal she, Iturri, and her husband discuss the case.

Once again in the fifth novel, *La venganza del asesino par*, Lola finds herself being tempted by the excitement of a youthful dalliance with Juan. These feelings are, however, only recurrences of previously felt school-girlish giddishness upon seeing him. While a tryst with Iturri would parallel the woman's role in much of traditional detective fiction, Lola's commitment to traditional values goes much deeper. Lola, then, maintains her marriage vows, professionalism, and conservative values by decidedly rejecting his advances, as well as her own carnal desires, knowing that a break with the traditional vows of a monogamous, heterosexual marriage will change her into someone she does not desire to be, and she tells Iturri, in *Venganza*, in no uncertain terms that there will be nothing other than a professional relationship between the two of them.

Stereotypically, Lola, as a woman in a man's world, is not strong in mathematics; in fact, any type of mathematical calculations confuses her, and those who work with/around her are very much aware of such. Other feminine stereotypes that correspond to her are those of the absentminded female who repeatedly misplaces her purse, umbrella, and cell phone, being a weaker, emotional being, being a poor driver, and having strong, frequent, and emotional outbursts of fear and/or crying. In fact, Lola herself probably describes it best: "Yo lloro por amor, por miedo, por odio, por dolor, por injusticia, por emoción . . . Puedo hacerlo en un cine, por un mal final [. . .]" (*Venganza* 30). Clearly, Lola fulfills the patriarchal feminine role as a crier, and there seems to be no common thematic causality for such. That her emotions have a strong impact in her life, and a strong influence over her actions, cannot be denied. As a female in a patriarchal society, she is very much an emotional being.

And, in a final nod toward traditionally patriarchal values, Lola at various times throughout the series both demonstrates and acknowledges her dependence on Jaime and her deference, or submissiveness, to males in general. Throughout the different novels, she consults, and generally follows the advice of her husband, Iturri, the Leyre Monastery sacristan Chocarro, her former law-school colleague Gabriel Uranga, and her mentor Fernando Serrano, to name only five. In spite of being the *juez de instrucción*, when she summarizes the cases Lola even demurs to the males in spite of her own abilities, professional status, and accomplishments alleging that she is not the one who solves the mysteries. Clearly, no one would mistake her for an over-assertive individual.

On a philosophical and professional level, Lola takes her responsibility as a judge seriously and obviously supports the redefining and redistribution of power from solely the masculine sphere to include women also. Lola may consult with Juan Iturri, her husband, or other males from time to time concerning various aspects of the cases, but in all of the novels (save the first, in which she is the accused) she is most often the one in control, the one who writes down the various clues and organizes the files, and she plays an important part in ultimately wrapping up the investigations in spite of her own demurring comments to the contrary. She may, in *Número primo*, think about ceding the case and, in *Venganza*, have to be forced into joining the investigation, but in both instances she comes back and proves herself equally as capable as the men. In fact, it is worth noting that her recounting of the events leading up to the assassin's taking of the priests' lives ends when both her husband and the Nuncio are left in awe, mouths agape, at her conclusions (*Número primo* 544). In *Número primo* Lola has a public stare-down with Álvarez—the policeman who wants to lead the investigation—before he finally must accede to her authority and withdraw (294–96). And, in *Dr. Wilson*, Lola confronts and overcomes both Jaime's and Iturri's initial beliefs that the manuscript she has received is more than merely the fantasy of a morbidly creative mind, clearly demonstrative of a nascent feminism.

"Feminist" can also be understood as the viewpoint of a committed movement. Lola obviously plays this role as well; in fact, Jaime states that Lola "Lleva la reivindicación feminista en los genes" (*Venganza* 258). Perhaps for that reason, and even though she recognizes that she has been named to the Supreme Court because she is a woman (*Venganza* 16, 25) and suspects such to be the case when she was named presidenta of the Sala Penal de la Audiencia Nacional (*Canaima* 98), Lola is very much in favor of a quota system (*Venganza* 16). But it is not just in the professional arena where Lola is committed to destroying the historical subordination of women; she also carries out the same in her personal life. When Lola perceives that Jaime is seeking more and more fame and power, and his quality time with the family has diminished to practically nothing, Lola forces him to move out and get his own living quarters.

Lola's commitment to feminism, while definitely more subdued than the more militant, or radical, second-wave feminism, is not just aimed toward increasing the number of women in the workplace, giving women a voice, or the destruction of those patriarchal values such as the objectification of women; rather, she goes to the point of even subverting the patriarchal "male gaze" (Mulvey) into an instrument of her own, becoming herself, then, a "female gazer." Evidently, from all textual indications, this female gaze has been present from the beginning of Lola and Jaime's relationship and continues even in the last novel of the series when Lola goes to be with him in Boston (*Venganza* 153). Further evidence of the fact that she converts the "male gaze" into a "female gaze" for her own pleasure are her multiple adventures with Iturri which, by her own admission, "representaba el feliz pasada" (*Canaima* 277).

Lola's relationship with other males involves more than just a gaze. While she is not one to resort to outright violence or abusing criminals'/suspects' rights, she does fairly frequently employ trickery and fabrications in order to ensnare them or throw them off her real intentions. Her manipulativeness and deceit are evident from the first novel of the series when Iturri is investigating the murder charges against her and meets with her to get her version of the events. In *Número primo*, she tells Father Lucas that she has no intention of using his answers to her questions against him, and then in a narrative aside admits to the reader that "mentí" (213). In *Dr. Wilson*, she is the one who comes up with the idea of her, Jaime, and Iturri pretending to be journalists in order to interview the psychiatrists at the conference in an attempt to determine which one is really Doctor Wilson (260). And in *Venganza* she repeatedly tells people that Jaime is not at her investiture on the Supreme Court due to a flight delay when, in fact, he is on his way to Boston for a three-month period (52). Her deceits, in fact, are merely a means to an end, an intentional manipulation of facts and events in order to operate most successfully in the masculine world, and they reveal that Lola is quite capable of subsuming masculine characteristics or traits when such is necessary.

Having said that Lola never resorts to the physical violence so common to the *novela negra*, it should be noted that Lola can be especially combative and fierce with matters that deal with gender-related cases. She is very much in tune with the bonding of women, and it is in these matters where she most clearly approximates the feminist cause of solidarity among women and fighting for women's rights, causes, and issues: "Algún tipo de delito, sobre todo los de naturaleza sexual, o los relacionados con el género, despertaba a la MacHor combativa, fiera y, al mismo tiempo, casi miedosa" (*Canaima* 133). She is especially bothered by criminals who escape punishment, such as Ariel, the drug lord who preys on young girls and, ultimately, is responsible for the death of Telmo's granddaughter María. But this passion also extends to the personal, to cite only one example, when Lola unsuccessfully attempts to get Ángela, in *Número primo*, to file charges against, and divorce, her abusive husband.

"Postfeminist" is another type of critical framework that rejects as too restrictive both the stereotypical, traditional values of patriarchy and the women-united-against-oppressive-males focus of feminism for one in which the woman plays an important role both in society and in the home but with marked ramifications. Lola demonstrates a tendency to both accept and reject various characteristics commonly associated with this paradigm.

Aspects of postfeminism apparent in the series include "nesting"; i.e., a voluntary escape from public life into a place where the woman wishes to be. Obviously, in the first novels of the series Lola is no latter-day domestic goddess, but as the series progresses Lola assumes more and more that role, such that by the fifth novel, *Venganza*, Lola has her own little garden. Postfeminism also reduces the separation between private and public space, with the woman bringing work home from the office. Such is, indeed, the case in the MacHor series with Lola frequently carrying work home in order to get it finished and discussing the facts of the investigation with multiple individuals who either stop over or who she invites to her home. In fact, such is true in all four novels of the series where she is a judge (in *Hemingway* she is the accused, not the investigating judge). And, clearly, Lola is a working woman struggling to balance family and career, another postfeminist characteristic noted by Pérez and Pérez.

Three commonly named aspects of postfeminism, however, Lola does not share; the exaltation of the individual over the collective (Godsland 90), the female as a materialistic individual, and violence as arising from the female. Lola's competitiveness is almost exclusively individualistic in nature; while she does, as noted previously, suffer a special twinge of compassion for crimes relating to abuse of young girls, there are no young, female professionals whom she mentors. With the exception of Jaime's commenting that Lola is in favor of the quota system, the reader fails to see her supporting women's causes in general, nor are the gains she has made in breaking the glass ceiling ever globalized as favorable toward women as a whole, other than the one comment that "Somos ya muchas las mujeres que ejercemos en este juzgado" (*Número primo* 501). Clearly, Lola is not a violent individual.

While it may be true that there are certain residual elements of a patriarchal, feminist and postfeminist mindset within the portrayals of Lola, the preceding analyses of the narratives elucidates both how Calderón denies each as her sole aesthetic and goes beyond those ideologies in creating and reflecting a new paradigmatic—or non-sexist ideological—structure. That is, Calderón seems ultimately to reject the masculine-oppressive patriarchy and the masculine-as-oppressor feminist, as well as the liberated-professional-suffering-woman postfeminist aesthetic. Relations between the sexes demonstrate more clearly Calderón's presentation of an almost gender-neutral—although certainly not libido-absent—narrative. Having said such, there is a fair amount of traditionalism still in her works. Clearly, the novels closely reflect the changing role of women in Spain at the beginning of the third millennium.

Lola, then, as a representative of a certain time period and generation of Spanish society, by necessity remains quite static chronologically. Her age does not correspond to the years that transpire in the novels; that is, throughout the five novels she ages at most nine years, depending on the date of her birth, while those represented in the works are at least twenty. In *Las lágrimas de Hemingway* Lola is forty-one years old, but in the fifth novel, *La venganza*, she is only forty-nine. Other data presented in the novels, however, affirm that the events of the novel can, at most be only three years apart (unless one accepts as veridical the narrator's use of the past tense for a future year not yet come). An analysis of the calendar places the events of *Hemingway* in 2009, and *Venganza* was published originally in 2012. This obvious discrepancy in day and years, especially when considering the normally verisimilar description of Lola's thoughts and actions, emphasizes even more clearly the author's stated purpose of always presenting Lola as a "mujer de mediana edad" (*Hemingway* 79) in her fourth decade of life with a minimum of aging. This additionally offers credibility to Calderón's interpretation of a generation of Spanish women born during the so-called "Spanish Miracle" of the 1960s who today are more or less the same age as Lola and who may be suffering the same mid-life crisis as Lola herself.

Lola goes through several changes in her career throughout the series. In part, this represents career advancement, but on the other hand these changes also arise because of Lola's frustration with the judicial system. More specifically, the sources of her frustration seems to be that she "estaba harta de gente imposible de recuperar" (*Canaima* 47), being "ofendida por el hecho de que la gente se refiere al lugar de su empleo como el Palacio de Justicia" (*Canaima* 92), and believing that justice is not meted out equally to all citizens. In fact, she is bothered by the knowledge that some criminals, in particular the drug trafficker responsible for the death of María Bravo (*Canaima* 114–15), are never brought to justice, and she is incapable of effecting change due to the legal constraints placed upon her by the rules governing the judicial system itself. She is also fed up with politicians and journalists who presume to be the moral voice of the people, and she refers to them as "vultures" (*Canaima* 125). Once again the reader sees in Lola's anguishes a reflection of the Spanish mentality; the aforementioned 2009 Eurobarometer, for example, reports that confidence in the "media" in Spain is at only 44%. In regards to politics, only 20% of Spaniards trust the national government, 21% the Spanish parliament, and only 36% the regional or local authorities (European Commission). And confidence in the judicial system is rated at only 2.73 (on a scale of 0 to 5) according to a 2009 study by Gómez Fortes and Palacios Brihuega.

Reyes Calderón, while portraying and reflecting contemporary society, realizes that history plays an important part in the creation of what Spain is today. Consequently, she employs a fairly frequent usage of both earlier and modern narrative forms and techniques in the creation of her novels. As can be seen even in the first novel of the series, the two main male characters (Jaime and Juan Iturri) do not necessarily belong wholeheartedly to the contemporary world. Iturri, in fact, uses "la antigua fórmula—'permiso'—" (*Hemingway* 258) prior to sitting in a chair to talk with Dolores and Gonzalo at the café, and the case of Jaime is stated even more explicitly: "Al conocer más a fondo a Jaime Garache en su entrevista en la cárcel, al inspector Iturri le había parecido retrotraerse a más o menos el siglo XIX" (*Hemingway* 254). Such, then, provides ample justification for a narrative examination of the author's use of dehumanization, animalization, the pathetic fallacy, and more modern techniques such as the braided narrative.

Los crímenes del número primo is the novel which contains the most varied use of animal imagery with every major character (except for Nuncio Tagliatelli) and many minor characters being described in this manner. In fact, some sixteen different characters are depicted via thirty-two animal images, two plants, and nineteen other elements in a total of seventy distinct, dehumanizing portrayals. Even the title of the novel itself dehumanizes the criminal, but it is the assassin who applies that clue to who he is as a reflection of his prime nature; i.e., his homosexuality. The assassin's "feline eyes" are further described on multiple occasions. Chocarro, the sacristan of the Leyre Monastery, twice has a dream in which he envisions the assassin as a dehumanized man with two faces, one benevolent, the other extremely malevolent. But what the faces have in common are "los ojos; son verdes y en ellos se puede leer la palabra *muerte*" (373). But a close textual analysis reveals that even the benevolent appearance of the assassin that appears in Chocarro's dreams is dehumanized through the use of the word "faz" (372, 398), a word more commonly associated with buildings, topography, or coins than with humans, and which generally carries a negative connotation. To the staff of Faustino Gorla, the assassin's lover who lives in Málaga, the suspect "es como un fantasma" (430). They have never seen him at all, and there are no pictures of him anywhere in Gorla's house; Gorla always sent the staff away or told them not to come to work when his lover was to be in town. And at the end of the novel, when Lola confronts him with the fact that his mother would not have approved of his tactics, he takes a gun, shoots himself, and "[s]e convirtió en una masa sanguinolenta que se desparramó por la habitación" (565). That is, with the exception of very brief periods—such as Lola's recapping of his biography as a novitiate at the Leyre Monastery and as an adult interested in antiquities—the assassin is always presented in dehumanized fashion: he assumes other names and professions as an adult, his feline, green eyes predominate any discussion or description of him; his being concealed in a monk's habit and/or bomb squad suit/mask at every crime scene, and even his shadowy, phantom-like presence in Málaga all work together to present a character of the basest sort far from the realm of normal humankind.

The clergy, as well, is presented via dehumanizing portrayals in *Número primo*. Pello Urrutia, the Leyre Monastery abbot, is an old man suffering from dementia who is further tangentially dehumanized when he dies upon inhaling cat hair and who, even in his younger days, is most noted for his "nariz, de por sí aguileña, [que] se incline peligrosamente hacia su boca" (13). Blas de Cañarte, the Navarra Archbishop, is the second cleric killed and mutilated in the novel. While no negative animalization is directly related to the Archbishop, his face "simulaba un sudario blanco y muerto" (127). This single, direct, negative dehumanization occurs only a few pages before his demise and, as the case with the Abbot Pello Urrutia, corresponds to an unstable cleric about to make a decision and act in a manner which will lead to his own death. On three occurrences Lucas Andueza, Blas de Cañarte's secretary, is portrayed through negative animal imagery which presents him in a negative light as a priest collaborating and supporting a bad decision to attempt to negotiate with kidnappers and unwilling to voluntarily assist in the criminal investigation. The Leyre Monastery rector, padre Ignacio, and the Maestro de Novicios, padre Francisco, are described as "aquellas cucarachas marrones" (277) by Lola because of their obfuscation and refusal to assist in the investigation, with the rector's eyes additionally being described as "ojos felinos" (259), an obvious attempt to associate his deeds, if not the character himself, with the assassin.

Contrasting with these priests is the Leyre sacristan who discovers the missing paten, host and abbot, Fermín Chocarro, and who offers tremendous help in resolving the crimes. The bull and bear imagery associated with him reflect a survival of the fittest character trait which ultimately leads to his salvation—and, in the novel's epilogue, election by the monks as their new abbot to replace Urrutia—and contrast sharply with the presentation, actions, and deaths of Urrutia and Cañarte, the two "weak" priests who wind up assassinated. Such is Lola's respect for him, her belief in his assistance to the investigation and his gift of prophetic dreams that Lola states that "por Chocarro pondría la mano en el fuego. Y no me quemaría" (*Dr. Wilson* 287).

One other cleric also voluntarily participates in the investigation and assists in the resolution of the mystery, the Nuncio Tagliatelli, who is never described via either dehumanizing or animalistic portrayals, either positive or negative. Such lack of animalization may owe itself, in part, to Lola's positive impression of him and his assistance in resolving the investigation; in fact, Lola meets with him twice in her home and discusses the case even though she knows she should not be doing so, and he is the one who suggests to Lola that she contact the artist guild president, leading her directly to the assassin himself. Additionally, by refusing to present the Nuncio—Rome's representative in Spain—in a negative light, the author is further demonstrating that it is only certain Church officials, and not the Church as an institution, with whom the assassin is angered: "él no iba contra, digamos, la base de la Iglesia; iba contra la jerarquía porque no había entendido" (personal interview with the author). While *Número primo* does have the most varied animalization and dehumanization, both quantitatively and qualitatively, the author also employs this technique in the other novels of the series.

Three of the principal characters—Lola, Jaime, and Iturri—are present in all of the novels of the series, and the imagery associated with them remains quite stable. Deviations from such, in fact, generally reveal significant changes in the character, his/her circumstance, or the relationship(s) that said character has with others. All three, with only minor variations, represent the positive side of the equation in the various investigations. The animal imagery associated with each is therefore representative of their function in the novels. Lola is repeatedly portrayed as a mule, but one who is persistent in solving the crime. Other animal imageries associated with Lola are personal in nature and do not reflect either positively or negatively on her professional career; they serve, in fact, to make her appear more similar to a normal person and not a stock character. Her snoring is legendary and is described in increasingly powerful imagery; in *Hemingway*, Jaime tells her that night "te convierte en rana" (83), later saying that she is "como un tren" (124). In *Número primo*, she herself admits, however, that "Ronco con una intensidad digna de un tren y con las formas de un perro en cello" (423). And by the end of the series, Jaime simply says that "Parece que, al dormirse, la poseyera un demonio vengativo de voz cavernosa" (*Venganza* 227). Lola, surprised and upset that she is, in her late 40s, pregnant, questions why "la naturaleza me había dotado con genes de coneja" (*Dr. Wilson* 55), especially since she is unhappy with "la zanahoria que tengo por pelo" (*Venganza* 90) and "mis patas de gallo" (*Venganza* 122). Jaime is not often portrayed via animalistic imagery; in fact, surprisingly, for the frequency in which he appears and assists in the investigation, most often it is in relationship to his total concentration on work, to the detriment of his family life, like an ox or mule. The imagery associated with Iturri, the third "good" character in all the novels, is somewhat more complex; such follows, however, from his dual roles in the narratives. As a member of the police/Interpol force, he assists in the intervention of criminals and represents a positive force for change in the society. Because of his obsession with Lola, and multiple attempts to have carnal relationships with her, however, he also at times represents a negative or, as the author herself has noted, "Iturri representa la tentación" (personal interview). Professionally, "Juan Iturri se sabía un cameleón" (*Hemingway* 253); his ability to pass undetected allows him to uncover clues to crimes not available to other uniformed policemen. Lola, in fact, says that he has the "mejor olfato que cualquier perro sabueso" (*Número primo* 293) and that his dedication to, and focus on, crime interdiction is such that he is "Como un toro brava recién salido de toriles" (*Número primo* 401). In *Venganza*, however, Iturri finally realizes that Lola will remain faithful to her marriage vows and bemoans his failure to conquer her: "¿Quién sino un estúpido teje una tela de araña y queda enredado en ella? La presa era Lola, pero yo era quien estaba atrapado" (*Venganza* 297).

Corrupt policeman and journalists are always referred to via negative animal, or dehumanizing, imagery. Ruiz, the Madrid policemen who goes to Pamplona to investigate Alejandro's murder and incarcerates Lola and Jaime on unsubstantiated charges, is a friend of the assassin's and not as strong as he would appear: He "bramó" (*Hemingway* 156) that nothing is wrong with Lola (who is suffering a heart attack), but one of the policemen immediately comments to another that Ruiz "[e]stá bufando" (157), to which another responds: "Eso intenta, pero con la voz de pito que tiene, lo que realmente hace es cacarear" (157). This emasculation of Ruiz is further emphasized by Lola, who, when writing the story, remembers only his deformed body and "su voz de flauta efeminada girando alrededor de su incipiente calvicie" (163). Inspector Álvarez is the policeman initially involved with the investigation in *Número primo*. Lola, however, has no remorse in demonstrating her dislike for him and considers him a corrupt officer: "Si el inspector Álvarez nació dotado de algo parecido a un alma, desde luego la perdió por el camino" (232). At the crime scene where the two violently murdered priests are found, Lola objects to Álvarez's use of the word "curioso" to describe the case, to which he responds that policemen are "pacientes águilas que patrullan el techo del mundo, esperando que los ratones abandonen confiadamente su madriguera y delincan" (232) and that such a case "alegran [sic] el día a cualquier investigador que se precia" (233). Obviously, Lola does not esteem him as highly as he does himself, and when she dismisses him from the case, "[s]us ojos aparecieron tan repulsivos como su boca. Sus rasgos, propios del ave rapaz que era, se afinaron hasta enmarcar la estructura de su calavera" (295). Iturri, meanwhile, is also involved in a pedophile case in which he is convinced that one of his superiors is continuously informing the suspect of the investigation's progress; he tells Lola that "continuaré abriendo manzanas . . . hasta dar con el gusano" (321). In the same novel, Clara refuses to leave the hospital to smoke due to the large "enjambre" (94) of journalists—"cantidad de buitres" (*Hemingway* 97)—outside. And while it may be Lola's arch-enemy who calls them such, obviously Lola is of the same opinion: "¡Qué bárbaro, estos tipos [los periodistas] son como los buitres!" (*Canaima* 125).

Murderers are often presented as animals, or with animal imagery. Rodrigo Robles, in *Hemingway*, has a tattoo of a snake on his groin (116). The as-yet unnamed priest-killer in *Número primo* has "ojos felinos [que] resplandecían con el metálico brillo de las luciérnagas" (15). Ariel, who had raped the 15 year-old María Bravo "no deseaba ejercer de cabeza de un ratón escuálido, encerrado en su gueto" (*Canaima* 107) and so becomes a major drug dealer/importer. Rodrigo, the murderer attempting to conduct a psychology experiment in *Dr. Wilson*, is warned by Dr. Wilson that someone carrying out such an experiment "irá poco a poco trasformándose en un animal ávido de sangre" (67), and later he confirms that Rodrigo es "un animal" (469). Rodrigo writes that Sarah Shibata, the intermediary between Rodrigo and the murderer, "Me recuerda al corderito que se dirige al matadero dando saltos de alegría por caminar junto a su amo" (*Venganza* 424). And Itoo, the actual exactor of Rodrigo's murderous plans has "ojos [. . .] fríos. Impenetrables e inquisitivos, como hielo nego" (365).

Another stylistic technique common to many of the novels, also frequently employed in 19th-century literature, is the use of the pathetic fallacy. Calderón's use of the pathetic fallacy becomes more apparent throughout the series, and its use points out to the alert reader significant points in the plot while foreshadowing important moments in the development of the novels' denouements. In, *Hemingway*, the pathetic fallacy bookends the various crimes, deaths and plot twists of the narrative and the resolution of said mysteries. *Número primo* opens with the narrator, Lola, seemingly affirming a disbelief in the pathetic fallacy. In spite of this, the author employs the aforementioned narrative technique on at least six occasions throughout the work, establishing a direct relationship between the events of the novel and contemporaneous weather conditions. That there is a strong narrative correlation between the plot and meteorological events cannot be denied. In the third novel, *Canaima*, the author continues the use of overt personifications of the weather (i.e., rain storms), this time most frequently corresponding its usage to death. *Dr. Wilson* also opens with the narrator's use of the pathetic fallacy, but this novel associates most frequently color patterns of the sky, environment, and nature to events in the novel. And in *Venganza* there are multiple and similar, overt utilizations of the pathetic fallacy. That is, Reyes Calderón's use of the pathetic fallacy serves as a means of highlighting the emotional nature of events occurring in the novels, or to nature as it reflects the emotions resulting from those events, thereby creating a more mimetic environment and characters and strengthening the reader's emotional response to such.

The author's attempts at creating a mimetic environment also play a role in the presence of overt sexism and stereotyping in the series; these reveal a mindset tied to a traditional ethos which distances the offending character from the progressive values of a more modern society and thereby present another view of Lola's both adherence and repulsion to the patriarchal, feminist, and postfeminist ideologies. She is, in effect, a conflicted personality, who rejects the patriarchal oppression of women but performs almost exclusively the stereotypical roles traditionally relegated to the woman, such as preparing the meals and watching the children. Indeed, it is not only her thoughts and subtle, if not unconscious, actions and word choices which reveal the depth of those engrained stereotypes in Spanish society but those of the other characters as well. In *Las lágrimas de Hemingway*, Clara is the stereotypical *femme fatale*, but one who is acting out of a desire for vengeance for the suffering she endured as a physically malformed child. The sexism and stereotyping in *Canaima* are more complex, generally double-edged in nature, presenting men in a positive light while backhandedly stereotyping women; the narrative includes the stereotype of criminals as primarily minorities. In *Número primo* Lola unsuccessfully attempts to use traditional sexist stereotyping to her advantage when she does not want to be the investigative judge of the priests' murders, but the chief judge—a male—will have none of it and asks: "¿Y eso qué importa? La justicia carece de género" (238). Lola, in *Dr. Wilson*, is the one who typecasts most frequently, employing even an ethnic stereotype when she says that "Hasta unos orientales le dedicaron sendas fotos" (140) of Josep María crying on the beach. *La venganza del asesino par*, however, has the highest number of sexist and/or stereotyping comments—sixteen—with at least one appearing, on average, every 28 pages, or every five chapters of the novel. While one might be inclined to think that such owes itself to the novel containing four different first-person narrators, three of whom are male, 65 percent of these, or eleven, appear in the "Primera parte," which is narrated by Lola. Additionally, 41 percent of the stereotypes, seven, are comments that Lola herself makes; quantitatively, then, Lola reveals herself to be more bound to traditional ideas—or at least more free to express such overtly—than the men.

Lola's views of women, in fact, range from negative to positive, with sexism, stereotyping, and traditional gender roles being a frequent expression of belief. She supports the traditional, sexist roles when they are to her advantage: after dinner with Iturri, she is upset because he is too drunk to drive and "Se suponía que Juan iba a llevarme a casa" (*Venganza* 110). But her sexist views are displaced from the female gender itself onto the parking garage and its "dichosas rampas, que parecían diseñadas para fastidiar a mujeres" (111). At the same time, the aforementioned traditional stereotypes are also tempered, and women are stereotyped in a positive manner. When Lola sees the condition in which Jaime has fallen, suffering from a blackmailer's threats, she notes that she wishes she could exchange positions with him: "Las mujeres encajamos mejor el dolor. Y la vergüenza" (151). And when she visits the prison where Dr. Wilson is incarcerated and sees the building named with letters of the alphabet, her sexist thoughts both praise women and denigrate men: "de quién fue la feliz idea de emplear letras para identificar sitios. [. . .] Seguro que no fue una mujer quien escogió ese sistema" (172).

Traditional sexism and stereotyping, in fact, actually work in Lola's favor on one occasion and play a major role in her becoming, in *Venganza*, a judge on the Spanish Supreme Court. She is originally chosen as a candidate simply to fill out the ballot (23), but a journalist writes a short article which becomes fodder for vociferous protests by the feminists and Basques, who raise such an outcry that Lola winds up "siendo nombrada por ser mujer y vasca (o vasca y mujer, si se prefiere)" (25).

As opposed to the narrative tropes in the Lola MacHor series, which demonstrate a profound attachment to traditional dehumanization, pathetic fallacy, and sexism/stereotypes, the narrative structure of the novels themselves increasingly demonstrate a modern, or progressive, angle. Only with *Las lágrimas de Hemingway* does the author construct a work that approximates the classical unities of plot, time, and place.

But even here, while the events of the novel occur in Pamplona, the work contains both a third-person and a first-person narrator and transpires during the entire week of the *Sanfermines* festival. With *Los crímenes del número primo*, Calderón makes several changes to the narrative structure which reveal an even more progressive mindset. The author retains a division of the work into three main sections, plus an "Epílogo," but calls each division a "Libro" and adds a "Prólogo" which serves as an introduction to the novel. While the novel basically retains a linear chronology, Lola travels in the course of her investigation fairly extensively outside of Pamplona: to the outskirts of the Navarra capital, to the Leyre Monastery, to Málaga, and to Toledo, where the novel's *denouement* occurs. Additionally, there is a subplot of the pedophile case in which Iturri in also investigating an international pedophile ring. *Canaima* corresponds to a more global environment with the "Prólogo" becoming, in essence, the first chapter of the novel and detailing Jorge Parada's murder in Caracas, chapter one relating the World Bank offices' break-in in Madrid, the FBI's collaboration in the ultimate resolution of the crime, and the remainder of the work taking place in Pamplona, Singapore, or Madrid, to where Lola moves at the end of "Libro Segundo" when she takes a job on the Tribunal Supremo. Interestingly, the topic of Lola's presentation at the World Back conference in Singapore, certain events in the main plot itself, and a fairly extensive account of an attempted extortion of Herrera-Smith foreshadow what later occurs to Lola herself. Additional foreshadowing, and simultaneous reflection back on Herrera-Smith, are Lola's positive thoughts regarding her own death (143), suicide being something she will later attempt to carry out in *Dr. Wilson*. Multiple subplots populate this narrative, with the child-rapist Ariel's threats against Lola and Telmo, and Iturri's infatuation with Lola comprising a significant amount of space. Calderón reveals even more clearly a more progressive narrative structure through her use of a parallel narrative, with alternating chapters recounting simultaneous events in Singapore and Pamplona in "Libro primero" until chapter twenty-three when the plots merge with Herrera-Smith calling and Jaime arranging for Lola to catch a flight to the Singapore conference that same day.

This parallel narrative structure becomes, in the "Primera parte" of *El ultimo paciente del Dr. Wilson*, a braided narrative detailing a psychological experiment which involves the murdering of people in different places around the globe. Obviously, the issue of globalization plays an extensive role with the theme of the panel Lola chairs at the conference in Barcelona being crime and globalization (16); Lola going to the nearby Starbucks to drink coffee in Pamplona instead of a local café (378); her receiving Google alerts and PowerPoint files (378); five of the seven deaths occurring in non-Iberian countries; the psychologist being a Catalan whose practice is in New York; a key clue appearing when Lola, Iturri and Jaime visit the Aegean island of Santorini; the appearance of the FBI and Interpol to assist in unraveling the crimes; and the actual arrest, trial, and incarceration of the suspect occurring in the U.S. *Dr. Wilson* contains several subplots which parallel or closely relate to, and foreshadow, the principle plot of the novel. Additionally, Lola's own psychological instability and attempt at suicide turn out to be a mini "psychological thriller" which anticipates the novel's end and serves as a rationale for Lola's eventual understanding of the assassin (352). And, finally, there are several instances of events that foreshadow the novel's end.

La venganza del asesino par also departs from the traditional novel structure in a myriad of manners. While the novel is for all practical purposes linear in nature, it also pertains to the subgenre of the psychological thriller with the assassin attempting to prove that the perfect crime does not exist (43). It contains multiple twists and turns in two parallel plots—one consisting of Jaime's unexplained flight to the U.S., and the other being Rodrigo's detailed recounting of murders of important people around the world from the confines of his jail cell. These two plots never merging into one represent an even more progressive narrative structure given that the investigation of both continue in a parallel and simultaneous fashion as Iturri is the only one who can resolve the attempted blackmailing of Jaime, and he refuses to assist unless Lola agrees to join in the Rodrigo investigation. Additionally, the novel contains a strong intertexual element with the various literary genres represented including letters, notes (both hand-written and typed), newspaper articles, blogs, and a SMS.

The narrative structures of Calderón Reyes's Lola MacHor series, then, parallel the characterization contained therein. Lola grows professionally throughout the novels, moving from law professor in Pamplona to Supreme Court justice in Madrid. In her journey, she becomes more affected by a globalized society but manages to retain what she considers positive, traditional traits. In a similar fashion, the novels of the series become increasing more complex, more global in theme and setting, and with an ever more progressive structure—culminating in two parallel plots. Yet, at the same time, the novels retain certain traditional aspects, techniques, and structures that help them to retain their high artistic value.

In agreement with more modern theorists, Reyes Calderón's Lola MacHor and other major characters do not generally perceive the issue of criminal culpability to be simply a matter of nature, nurture, or free will—or even that these three are mutually exclusive. In fact, many of the characters believe that the presence of a fourth element, fate or destiny, may also play a role, at times, in one's thoughts and actions. At different times throughout the novels, each of these is viewed as the motivator for criminal actions; these are variously expressed as genetic makeup, congenital characteristic, exercising one's free will, the environment, the loss of self-control due to alcoholic intake, one's personality, religious fervor, and the influence of a malevolent divinity. Lola, however, pleads for mercy for some criminals because of another causality: mental illness. Iturri, as a professional policeman, has his own beliefs concerning motives that lead people to turn to crime, condensing those motives into three basic reasons: covetousness, vengeance (and/or crime of passion), and the desire to quieten someone. Lola's early concept of criminality involving the taking of human lives corresponds remarkably to Iturri's list of motives, but she calls these motives: ambition, money, vengeance. As Lola is involved in cases of increasingly more global corruption, her views of criminal motivation evolve until, in *Dr. Wilson*, she states that in the case of serial killers, "los informes forenses señalaban influencias hereditarias y factores somáticos como coadyuvantes en la conversión del individuo en un psicópata" (134). Interestingly, the various arguments and debates provide information which foreshadows the eventual resolution of the narrative plot of *Dr. Wilson,* in which the assassin turns out to be a person who suffers from an extreme case of dissociative identity disorder. In fact, while Lola plans actions that may not be described as "criminal," even she herself is unable to explain rationally, after the fact, why she would attempt to take her own life (*Dr. Wilson* 351), other than to suggest that her actions owed themselves to a chemical imbalance following an unexpected miscarriage.

Public perception of criminality in Spain, as reported by Duffy, Wake, Burrows, and Bremner, in 2006, is that 81% of the Spanish people agree that "Nowadays there is too much tolerance. Criminals should be punished more severely" (40). An additional study on Spain's criminal law reforms carried out between 1996 and 2011 by José Luis Díez Repollés concludes that the criminal justice system in Spain has gotten increasingly harsh over the time period in question. Such sociological concerns become apparent in the series and most often correspond to a reversal of presumed innocence. Lola knows that public opinion may forever be against her for having "killed" Alejandro in *Hemingway*. The convicted face even worse treatment and are ostracized, cast away and forgotten; penal institutions as capable reformatories is a concept long out of favor. Susan, the prison guard who escorts Lola *et al.* to Dr. Raspy's office behind the walls, states that the prison should really be a hospital, but that it, in fact, is really simply a place where society can lock up the undesirables and make them disappear. That is, there is no conclusive evidence or decision presented in the MacHor series about the true reasons, catalysts, and/or causes of malevolent behaviors/personalities nor can Lola, Jaime, or Iturri agree on such either. In fact, Lola's opinions evolve from the first novel of the series, where she appears to emphasize most strongly personal responsibility, to the fifth novel, in which she appears to lean toward accepting more environmental or physiological causalities as the culprit. At the very least, throughout the series criminal motives range from ambition to vengeance, from demonic mandates to thrill seeking, and from voluntary manslaughter to lunacy-induced malfeasance. All of these, in fact, are portrayed at different points and in different manners in the MacHor series. But what distinguishes this narrator—if not author—from her peers, and from society in general, is that her narratives are not universally negative against all criminals, or supposed criminals; those crimes resulting from psychological or physiological abnormalities merit our sympathy. In this manner, the author thereby finds herself in the position of advocating for better mental therapies and treatments.

Other social commentary is expressed by the words and actions of the characters even though Reyes Calderón's social criticism most often appears more subtly in the narrative than in traditional detective fiction. In addition to the previously studied leitmotif of the "Golden Rule" found throughout the Lola MacHor series, the various novels offer additional examples of social commentary or social criticism which, while loosely related to the immediately surrounding narrative, is largely independent of such and could be easily excised from the text without any significant change in the novel itself. As an academic thriller, the world of education comes under intense scrutiny in *Hemingway*. Lola, however, has lost faith in higher education, and her additional allusion to Roman gladiator fights establishes a connection between bullfighting, the winning of a professorship, and the inhumanity of the higher education system.

Hemingway is a novel situated in Pamplona during the week of the Sanfermines festival; thus, it is no surprise that both the running of the bulls and bullfighting itself would earn additional scrutiny. Tellingly, by setting the novel in the Sanfermines festival, and having the murder occur during the *encierros* themselves, the author juxtapositions celebration and death, the traditionally sacred and evil, and the commonly known with the mysterious. This duality is accentuated by the narrator's dubitative stance toward the merits of the *encierro*, a stance that both questions the playing with death while recognizing its economic and cultural importance to both the city and its citizens.

Bullfighting itself comes under a harsher criticism; in fact, the wording and symbolism associated with the sport relegate it to a level inferior to that of a civilized society. On one hand, bullfighting is associated with the most violent aspects of Roman culture. On the other hand, the narrator simply compares bullfighting to another social gathering where much of the audience is unconcerned, and unlearned, about what is happening on stage; it has become, in essence, another idolatrous sacrifice.

Society's attitude toward death itself is also examined in *Hemingway*. In spite of society's playing with death, enjoyment in having "cheated death," and even tempting such by running through cobblestone streets in front of horned animals quite a bit larger than oneself, few individuals consider death's true ramifications, and that everyone, some day, will die. Perhaps for that reason, society tends to separate itself from the physical proof of its mortality At the same time, and as noted by Iturri, the somewhat-conservative nature of the text and main characters lead humankind to long for the certainty that death is not final, that something follows death, and that there is a higher power than the earthly.

The second novel of the series, *Número primo*, continues in this vein of the spiritual, the belief that humans search for something more than simply the physical on this earth. Lola, even while in the gay bar in Malaga, views the people awaiting the "magical hour" as actually on a quest to escape reality. Obviously such parallels the Church's position on the subject as well. Additional social commentary in *Número primo* relates to both the Church and society's support and opposition to that institution. Church secrecy and the desire to protect itself play a role in the early part of the novel. Such commentary and Lola's "acusando formalmente de encubrimiento, delito tipificado en el artículo 451 del Código penal, amén de otro delito de coacción a un testigo" (276), however, are not merely indictments of the Church for its unwillingness to cooperate with secular authorities, they are really a critical commentary about society at large, the loss of the Church's prestige within society itself, and society's propensity to rush to believe anything negative concerning the Church, if not other institutions and individuals as well.

The obvious social commentary in *Canaima* both echoes the series' leitmotif and criticizes the weaknesses of the political and judicial systems. Lola's concern for humanity in general is blatantly obvious, and her desire to help the less fortunate frequently is front and center. In fact, she has often dreamed of making a difference in society, and when she sees such efforts thwarted by the technicalities of the legal system, she is quite upset, even to the point of ranting against the intricacies of the law and how such intricacies do not correspond to reality. But it is not just the judicial system that Lola thinks is not living up to its potential; she considers the same to be true of the political system. Additionally, Lola believes that politicians cannot be fully trusted either and are really only going to do whatever is necessary in order to retain power. In fact, Lola's lack of political activism closely parallels the growing apathy of the Spanish people at large during the early years of the third millennium.

Perhaps more so in fourth novel, *Dr. Wilson*, than in any other, the reader notices intrinsic social commentary that the world is increasingly globalized. In this work, Lola no longer goes to the local café, but instead goes to Starbucks (378); she moderates a conference panel in Barcelona on crime and globalization (16), and her email is full of spam, Google alerts, and "seis reenvíos de Power Point" (378). The fifth novel, *Venganza*, is a sequel to *Dr. Wilson*, and comments on a disheartened penal system that has succumbed to the realities of privatization and the lack of true interest on the part of the public and politicians in rehabilitating the prisoners.

Another element in the novels which contains important sociological aspects is the prominent role that food plays in the Lola MacHor narratives, with many investigative deductions and plot twists occurring either at a local bar/café, at Lola's family dinner table, or at other venues involving gastronomical consumption. As the series develops throughout the first four novels, food and drink references quantitatively become more frequent. By the fourth novel, *El último paciente del Doctor Wilson*, much, if not almost all, of the narration occurs over meals. It is important to point out that the murders that Rodrigo carries out occur in several nations around the globe, and Rodrigo describes, often in detail, meals that he consumes while at these various locations. Consequently, it is no surprise that food and drink references are extremely frequent in this novel, with some 425 references, or approximately one in every 448 words, referring to either food or drink; in fact, there are 200 references to thirty-four different and specific drink items. In the entire series, then, there are 1,045 distinctive references to food and drink, with a total of 178 different foods and 63 different drinks being named. The drinks are comprised of thirty-four non-alcoholic types and twenty-nine alcoholic types, with the latter group being comprised of only nine beers or wine; thus, the occurrence of hard liquor is rather frequent. The single, most frequent type of drink is coffee, with fourteen different types and serving styles being named. Interestingly, the only time in the novels when a character repetitively consumes alcoholic drinks in one sitting is when that person is at a crisis point in her/his life; in fact, the association between such and devastating loss is unmistakable, and it occurs in each of the novels under study.

Junk food is described as normal for North Americans, and hamburgers are consumed quite frequently by the investigative team when, in *Venganza*, they are in the United States. Extensive examples of other nationalistic food and drink are portrayed in Rodrigo's travels around the globe: in France, he samples *calissons*, in Russia *blinis* and vodka, and in the Middle East *souvlaki*, *dolma*, *baklava*, and *ouzo* (*Dr. Wilson*). Lola calls a Chinese restaurant and orders "rollitos de primavera [. . . ,] fideos con bamboo [. . .] y una ternera con setas" in *Venganza* (95–96). The Russian Elena Polvoskha drinks vodka with her visitor and killer before her murder (*Venganza* 290). In *Canaima*, Lola and Jaime attend a fund-raising dinner for African women hosted by Jimena, of which she says that the meal is "los manjares que ellos sirven en los días de fiesta y bonanza" (341). Obviously Lola recognizes the inherent sociological associations with food as she decides that the best souvenirs to bring home to family and friends from Singapore are boxes of candy in the form of a dragon, and she later offers Kalif a box of Spanish chocolates when he leaves Madrid headed back to the U.S. Other, "typically Spanish" foods and drinks in the series allude to Iturri's weakness for *churros* (*Hemingway* 256–57, *Número primo* 96)—and Lola's revulsion at such (*Canaima* 124)—*rosquillas* (*Número primo* 96), *tortilla* (*Número primo* 96), *jamón serrano* (*Número primo* 414, *Dr. Wilson* 60), and Jaime's telling Lola to drink "un Cola Cao" (*Número primo* 301). Even more regional in nature are the *pinchos* typical of the Basque region (*Número primo* 382, *Canaima* 249), the Catalan *pa amb tomàquet* (*Dr. Wilson* 257), the *pisto manchego* (*Canaima* 96), and Faustino, a Rioja drink from a winery with the same name (*Dr. Wilson* 345).

But Lola is not the only one who recognizes either the sociological implications of food or the fact that certain foods can impact in a meaningful way. In fact, fortunately for Lola, it is probably the food on the car floor, in part, which causes her kidnapper to view her more as a mother than as a *juez de instrucción*, and such thereby saves her life in *Número primo* (551). Rodrigo's offering of a chocolate to Dr. Wilson is the only way that he can get the psychiatrist to speak about the trail of murders in *Venganza* (5, 62), and Jaime employs the same technique himself for the same purpose (267). And Lola, at the end of *Dr. Wilson*, goes back to Clyde, in Washington D.C., and eats the same meal that Dr. Wilson and Rodrigo tended to share in an attempt to break the nightmarish spell of terror that the memory of them continues to hold over her (475–76).

Society's upper crust is shown as somewhat more discriminating with their intake than are the lower classes. The parvenu Clara roundly protests the hospital coffee as simply "ese líquido negro que sale de las cafeteras industriales" (*Hemingway* 97). Lola's mother meets the renowned lawyer Gonzalo Eregui at an elegant dinner at the Palacio de Santa Ana, where, at the meal, "[n]ada de césped aliñado, nada de huevos escalfados sin más alegría que una pizca de sal: solomillo al *foie*" (247). In *Canaima*, both Lola and the World Bank official and conference organizer David Herrera-Smith are able to indulge in the gastronomical intake of upper society during their trip to Singapore. Perhaps Lola sums up best the difference in food and drink consumption between different levels of society when she concludes: "los ricos sabían vivir" (172).

Lola and Iturri both presume to pass as "average folks" in the series, and food and drinks related to them generally bear that out, in spite of Iturri's obvious weakness for cognac. Iturri's weakness for *churros* is evident at the Iruña bar, among other places. Lola, in spite of being a judge, may be viewed as ordinary as well in regards to her food associations, but food and drink associations to her do expand as the series continues. In *Hemingway*, the only three liquids she drinks are *café* (thrice), and *café con leche* and *vino* (both once). But, by *Venganza*, Lola consumes the widest variety yet of drinks: *agua*, *agua sin gas*, *café* (eleven times), *café con leche* (twice), *leche*, *leche caliente*, *té*, *té de manzanilla*, *tila*, *zumo de naranja*, coca cola light, *cerveza*, *una copa*, and *cava*. Having said such, however, in the entire series Lola is seen drinking a total of eighty-two times with thirty-one different drinks; of these, forty-eight times she drinks coffee, eleven times alcohol, and twenty-three times a non-alcoholic drink. Arguably, such qualifies as a description of a "normal" person in Spain.

As can be seen, then, food and drink play an integral part in the Lola MacHor series of novels by Reyes Calderón, and an examination of food and drink in these novels provides a vision of alimentary intake which is representative of the continuing cultural attitudes and habits of the Spanish people in a general sense. As might be expected by an author attempting to establish maximum verisimilitude, in all these novels varying levels and types of food and drink consumptions by different levels of society are described, be they jet-setters, parvenus, high clergy, or the common folk. In short, through a detailed analysis of food in the Lola MacHor series, it becomes readily apparent that the author both recognizes and portrays inherent sociological and cultural associations with the various foods and drinks she includes at distinct points in the works.

Reyes Calderón's Lola MacHor series offers a unique view into the society of present-day Spain, in particular, adult women in Spain who grew up under the Franco dictatorship and thus generally failed to enjoy many liberties available to younger generations. Instead those women were relegated almost always to the more traditional roles of wife, mother, or prostitute. The cultural and social transition accelerated after the death of Franco in 1975, however, and Spanish women and society have been adopting less traditionally acceptable roles in society. Due to, perhaps, her own experiences in breaking the glass ceiling—the author was the first female Dean of the Facultad de Ciencias Económicas y Empresariales en la Universidad de Navarra—Reyes Calderón is better prepared and more capable of presenting in a convincing manner a judge who performs a myriad of aspects of a "more human," more verisimilar, woman with a "normal" career climbing through the various professional levels of university professor (*Las lágrimas de Hemingway*) to President of the Sala Penal de la Audiencia Penal in Madrid (*El último paciente del Doctor Wilson*). Lola MacHor is not portrayed as a stereotypical feminist ideologue (oppressed or rebellious), a post-feminist, a static character or other type of caricature. She is a working mother growing old with several children, feeling herself pulled by family and professional responsibilities, by her own personal history, and by a desire to be loved and to escape the devastations of growing old. When all is said and done, Lola is—in the Spain of today where there are a plethora of ideas thought, expressed, and promoted—an opportune model for Spanish women in a rapidly changing culture at the beginning of the third millennium.

In spite of the fact that detective fiction has been the most popular genre utilized by Spanish authors over the last thirty or so years, the female detective has appeared in such works on relatively rare occasions. Less frequent are Spanish female authors of detective fiction who employ a female detective as their main character. With the creation of her Basque character, Lola MacHor, Reyes Calderón is able to design a normal woman who confronts abnormal situations and remains true to herself. Through such, Reyes Calderón aptly portrays both how far Spanish women have come since the days/restrictions of the Franco dictatorship but yet how remnants of conservative thought still pervade their mindset. She thus uses the most popular of genres to make a myriad of cultural observations concerning her native country and the women of "her generation." That is, via the main character Lola MacHor, Calderón is conducting a cultural studies experiment/explanation of modern-day Spain and commenting on the pervading conservative/feminist dichotomy as it transpires in Spanish social commentary and moralizing.

CHAPTER EIGHT

Interview with Reyes Calderón

10 mayo 2012

Questions by the author of this monograph are indicated by "JO"; responses by the novelist Reyes Calderón are indicated by "RC." An ellipsis without brackets indicates pauses in the novelist's comments. A bracketed ellipsis indicates that a portion of the conversation has been deleted by this author; these deletions are generally single or repeated words or "false starts" to an answer which were left unfinished or altered mid-stream by the novelist. Thus, the deletions are merely to improve the flow of the answers for reading purposes. No change in meaning has resulted from any deletion.

JO: ¿Por qué empezó a escribir ficción—no tenía bastante que hacer con las investigaciones académicas?

RC: Sí. Yo escribo antes de hacer investigaciones; es decir, yo escribo desde pequeña. Lo del bien o mal, eso ya es un adjetivo, ¿no? [. . .] El primer relato que recuerdo fue cuando mi padre me llevó por primera vez a los toros, y el espectáculo taurino es impresionante. Yo era pequeña, pues tendría once, doce años, y me impresionó muchísimo. Y cuando llegué a casa, quería expresar lo que sentía pero no era capaz de decirlo con palabras. Y cogí un papel y lo escribí.

JO: ¿El evento?

RC: No, escribí los sentimientos que tenía. Cada vez que me ocurría algo importante, me era más fácil hacerlo con una pluma y un papel que hablarlo. Y luego a los trece años gané un concurso de cuentos que me presenté, y me lo dieron bajo condición de que hiciera un curso de ortografía porque yo en aquel tiempo era muy deficiente: un rato bes, un rato uves, un rato haches, un rato no había haches. Yo andaba mirando a ver a qué escondía la be y la uve. Entonces me dieron el premio, pero mi madre se comprometió a que hiciera [. . .] Me tuvieron todo un verano largo haciendo un dictado diario a que aprendiera las haches en su sitio. Y luego seguí escribiendo. Y lo que pasa es dedicada a las matemáticas me dijeron que era incompatible, que eran las cosas de la educación española; que si por ciencias o por letras, pero no había más. Quiero decir, la escritura me venía de antes.

JO: Es decir, ¿no era una autora innata?

RC: Bueno, yo soy creyente. Creo que existe un Dios que nos creó, y nosotros tenemos . . . somos imagen suya. Pues todos tenemos una veta de creadoras. Ahora, cada uno tiene la suya: hay quien pinta, hay quien hace unos pasteles estupendos. Yo creo que . . . yo pinto fatal y mis pasteles no son estupendos. Entonces creo que lo más probable es que me dedique a escritura, ¿no? Y luego lo que pasa es que yo seguí escribiendo pero no publicaba hasta que ya un día pensé que, "¿Por qué tenía que hacerles caso a quienes decían que en ciencias no podía escribir?" Y publiqué la novela que tenía escrita, que era *Ego te absuelvo*. Y luego ya seguí.

JO: ¿Por qué la novela, si empezó con un cuento?

RC: A mí me gustó. No sé. Yo creo que soy una mujer de contrastes. Me encanta el agua muy fría y el café ardiendo. Entonces, a mí [. . .] lo que me gusta [es] aprender, y por eso estudié después economía; estudié filosofía, es la condición humana. La economía cada vez es más técnica, más fría, menos . . . no es para personas, es para agentes—qué llamamos nosotros agentes económicas. Pero esos agentes no tienen sentimientos; no tienen alma. Pero yo me daba cuenta que cuando, por ejemplo, cuando el Barça ganaba la Liga, aumentaba el consumo porque la gente se siente satisfecha, hasta más confiada en sí misma, y consume más. Bueno, hay una variable psicológica que despreciamos siempre, ¿no? Entonces para entenderla, yo necesitaba entender al hombre. Y yo soy de matemáticas. Y pregunté quién sabía de hombres, y me dijeron que los filósofos. De filosofía para saber, no porque quisiera ser filósofo, porque nunca he tenido ningún interés, sino para entender al hombre, y cada vez me reforzaba más en que el hombre es incapaz del agua fría y del café ardiendo, de ser un ángel o ser un demonio. Habitualmente estamos en el medio pero podemos escorarnos, supongo, como los ciclos económicos de bonanza y ciclos de una crisis terrible, ¿no? Y se refuerza.

También aquí en España suelen poner las noticias de televisión—no sé si es bueno o malo pero las ponen, ¿no?—que un señor ha matado, ha salido con un rifle, por ejemplo, en Estados Unidos, y ha disparado a siete. Aquí es que no tenemos rifles, pero si los tuviéramos, pasaría igual, ¿no? Y preguntan a los vecinos, y dicen, "Ah, pues era un vecino estupendo y era muy amable." Recuerdo una señora que contestó: "Y reciclaba la basura." Y ellos decían, "¿Cómo es posible que una persona con esos valores de reciclar mate a siete personas?" Bueno, es que en la condición humana nos cabe todo. Entonces a mí me interesaba mucho entenderme a mí misma, probablemente, y entender a los que me rodean y la mejor manera era quizás sea . . . por eso el diseño del personaje. Es un personaje totalmente corriente, una persona del montón, una jueza con—una jueza, no me gusta la palabra "jueza"—pero una juez con una vida normal, una familia, un trabajo, y la normalidad se contrasta con flashes terribles, ¿no? La combinación de eso era como el agua fría y el café ardiendo, ¿no? La intriga te permite hablar de esas cosas aparte de que te da un recurso estupendo para que el lector vaya contigo o tú vayas con él. Y yo sólo poniendo . . . suelo decir que escribo como el cuento de "Hansel y Gretel": yo voy poniendo miguitas [. . .] de pistas. Él que quiere seguirlas, las sigue, y él que no, se encuentra el asesino al final. Pero si quieres, puedes ir comiendo y siguiendo las pistas. Y esa manera hace que, por ejemplo, el lector cuando te llama, o te manda un email, no habla de la juez Lola MacHor, habla de Lolilla, que es el apelativo cariñoso de su marido. Yo creo que eso es un poco la idea que se puede sentir identificada porque es una vida normal, en la mayor parte. El personaje no es un superhéroe ni un supervillano; [. . .] muestra sus debilidades, y al mismo tiempo supera sus propias debilidades.

JO: ¿Ha escrito alguna vez poesía o teatro, o siempre ha sido narrativa?

RC: He escrito poesía, pero sí, la hacía mal.

JO: ¿Por qué la novela detectivesca ya que la primera novela que usted escribió—o libro—fue una historia; porqué no la novela histórica, por ejemplo?

RC: Era también de intriga; nunca me he separado de la intriga.

JO: ¿Cómo llegó a la novela detectivesca?

RC: En realidad era suspense y por lo tanto investigación. Luego ya empezaron los policías. Entonces ya se convirtió en una novela de detectives. No sé. Yo creo que en economía la . . . por ejemplo el factor azar que yo . . . Creo . . . Estudio bastante la teoría del caos, que a mí me encanta la teoría del caos. Me parece dentro de su orden, encontrar ese orden dentro del caos. Pero hasta la propia matemática tiene una perturbación en la esquina, ¿no? Y eso es lo que, la perturbación de una ecuación matemática, es la que te da sentido, o no, a lo anterior. Es muy pequeñita, pero es la que produce todos nuestros cambios, ¿no? Igual que una pequeña cantidad de una enzima que nos falta produce una depresión, y es pequeñísima esa perturbación. Yo quería insistir en que pequeñas cosas cambian el rumbo, y esas pequeñas cosas no las conocemos. No las esperamos; no las preveemos, ¿no? Ese es el suspense. Eso mismo hago en las novelas. Coger un pequeño factor, ir viendo hacia donde nos conduce. Obviamente para el lector yo lo tengo previsto de antes, ¿no? Obviamente, pero, no, para el lector no [es previsto]. Entonces él se involucra porque hay distintos escenarios que se pueden abrir. No puedes ir sintonizando con unos y otros. Al mismo tiempo, el suspense te da este tipo de entornos, te da para hablar de lo que quieras. Cualquier tema que tengas en la cabeza cabe: la violencia de género, el estado de la cuestión respecto a los jueces en determinado sitio, las prisiones, puedes hablar de lo que quieras. Si hablas de una novela más intimista, tienes que ponerlo siempre en boca del relator y le estropeas si le pones algunas cosas en la boca. Así puedes decir lo que te parezca.

JO: Sé que niega usted que sus novelas sean "novela negra"—y francamente estoy de acuerdo—pero ya que la crítica continúa diciendo/llamando sus novelas "novela negra" y usted lo rechaza, ¿cuál es su definición de la novela negra? ¿Cómo se distinguen?

RC: Depende de qué novela negra hablamos. O sea, la novela negra norteamericana es de un tipo; la novela negra que se lee en España es de otro. En España se lee mucha novela nórdica, fría, donde lo que importan son los hechos, y las descripciones son sobre las escenas criminales o sobre las maldades del asesino en cuestión. A mí, pues, yo por supuesto lo relato, pero yo hago novela de personajes. A mí lo que más me importa no es la escena sino cómo afecta esa escena a los personajes. Yo particularmente nunca me cebo ni me regodeo en la sangre; no, no creo que haga falta. En esta última novela, hay una descripción de una autopsia, cuando lo leas verás cuánto pesa un cerebro humano, por ejemplo, y cómo se extrae el cerebro. En ningún momento uno tiene ganas de vomitar porque lo que estoy contando es qué es lo que está pensando el que está viendo aquello y no aquello en sí mismo. No me importa nada la escena. Por eso creo yo que la novela es más mediterránea. O sea, la novela negra es una novela de hechos, y es una novela de hechos criminales, pero lineales. A mí no me interesa nada la línea recta. Me interesa que el personaje vive, sube y baja, y por eso sería una historia de personas. Por eso digo que le va más la palabra o una historia de suspense o—claro, lo que utilizamos es una palabra norteamericana—el "thriller"; una historia de aventuras es lo que le va más. El lector vive la aventura muy distinta que uno vive la novela negra que se mantiene al margen. Yo creo que en mi caso viven los personajes.

JO: ¿Escribe con un esquema previo; es decir, tiene en mente el final de la novela al empezarla o escribe "a lo que salga," como dijo Unamuno?

RC: No, yo no. [. . .] En eso ejerzo de matemático. Yo primero las pinto. Tengo unos folios cuádruples; los utilizo así. Entonces, tengo uno por personaje. Los dibujo. El otro día estaba con un director de cine, y me decía que lo mismo hacía con las escenas, pero al revés. Los iba pegando en la pared e iba viendo las secuencias de las escenas antes de filmarlas. Yo dibujo . . . Cada folio tiene un personaje, y voy contando qué es lo que ocurre hacia abajo. Y luego voy uniendo con flechas donde se producen las conexiones entre los personajes porque es posible que las aceitunas que salen en *El número primo* en la página 36, que luego se las comen todos los curas en la página 198, el lector las tiene en mente. Pero si no las tienes tú, tienes que tener una línea que trance y comprobar que no hay . . . Si no, se producen bastantes imprecisiones, y creo que las imprecisiones molestan mucho al lector. Son faltas de calidad. Y como son novelas, que las tramas son complejas, si no las dibujo, no. Entonces, primero leo, mucha documentación; después dibujo. Y luego me pongo a escribir. Luego escribo a mano, las versiones que hagan falta.

JO: ¿No escribe en ordenador al principio? ¿Empieza en papel?

RC: Empiezo en papel, sí. En cuadernos. Y luego ya cuando tengo más claro . . . Es verdad que a veces aunque tú tengas un esquema muy cerrado, el personaje secundario pide paso, y se lo das, y tienes que poner líneas de otros colores.

JO: ¿Conserva usted los papeles o una vez escrita la novela los tira?

RC: No, conservo todo. Tengo unos baúles llenos de papeles. No sé para qué, pero los guardo.

JO: En enero de 2011, la Universidad de Navarra publicó el artículo "24 Horas con Reyes Calderón." ¿Podría hablar un poco de eso, de si su día típico ha cambiado desde entonces? Específicamente, estoy preguntando acerca de su manera/rito/técnica de escribir. ¿Suele trabajar en las novelas por la noche cuando se han acostado ya los niños? ¿Una vez que empieza una obra, vuelve a leer lo ya escrito o siempre sigue adelante?

RC: No, hago . . . sigo más o menos el mismo esquema. Viajo bastante y para mí los aviones, los trenes y demás, es cómo me aíslo completamente. Es como si estuviera en la mesa de mi despacho. No sé por qué motivo porque me hacen incómodos los aviones, y los trenes menos. Pero aprovecho . . . tengo mucha capacidad para concentrarme. Eso es un don. No tengo nada de meritorio ahí. Trabajo por la noche cuando me encierro y . . . Ahora, es cierto que cada vez cuando estoy maquinando algo lo tengo siempre en la cabeza en cuanto . . . Cuando estoy aquí, estoy dando clase o atendiendo el Rectorado o lo que esté preparando pero esto está todo el tiempo bullendo.

JO: ¿No suele tener bloqueos de escritor?

RC: Normalmente no. No, porque estoy . . . Estoy, o sea tengo tanta ansia de que llegue la noche para . . . solamente cuando estoy al final de la, a lo mejor, de la versión número veinte de una tal me canso, ¿no? Pero, hombre, es muy cansado; yo creo, que dirían un 10% de inspiración y un 90% de transpiración. Por lo menos en mi caso es así. Me cuesta muchísimo trabajo, mucho tal . . . pero ahora estaba estudiando por ejemplo un . . . estaba preparando una novela sobre un despacho de abogados muy pequeñito, especializado en derecho laboral. Entonces tuve que irme a una feria del libro en Valladolid que eran . . . fui por un día y el día siguiente eran cuatro horas de tren y cuatro horas de tren, ocho horas. Me llevé anales de los casos de derecho laboral en España de los mayores despachos, en total, dos volúmenes así. Y yo decía, "¡Dios mío! ¿Cómo lo voy a hacer?" Pero era la única manera de meterse porque yo no me he dedicado al derecho laboral, y me tragué los dos tomos de . . . Bueno, había cosas divertidas y otras que eran un rollo de despide improcedente con base no-sé-qué. Bueno, eso forma parte del trabajo. [. . .] Eso lo hago en los trenes, en los aviones; me llevo un libro, y lo empiezo, y lo acabo. Utilizo a lo mejor 5% de la información que obtengo, pero me ambienta. Me permite que la cabeza se vaya, y ya cuando vuelvo por la noche pues tengo el escenario metido, ¿no?

JO: ¿Cuál es su inspiración? ¿Cómo decide qué crímenes va a investigar en cada novela? O, ¿se relacionan con el trabajo académico que hace?

RC: Bueno, en algunos casos [hay] relaciones, pero también mayormente me dedico a la anticorrupción, y eso era un caso que había estudiado. Estuve en la . . . O sea, lo que hago sí que hago porque tampoco ni por presupuesto ni por tiempo puedo permitírmelo. No es . . . salvo casos excepcionales, que necesito un escenario y voy a ese escenario, y aprovecho las vacaciones para visitarlo y demás. Normalmente lo que hago es utilizar los escenarios donde voy a los congresos míos. Entonces, me levanto temprano por la mañana alrededor de las cinco de la mañana cuando amanece. Nadie te atraca. Vamos, en Nueva York no me atreví, pero en el resto de las ciudades más pequeñitas los que atracan están dormidos, y los demás no se han despertado, y entonces a esa hora se puede visitar las ciudades con más . . . Entonces como los congresos suelen empezar a las nueve o las diez de la mañana, pues yo de cinco a diez me pateo los sitios. Luego, pues, procuro buscar un restaurante que me guste para . . . Bueno, eso, aprovecho la cuestión académica, y así reduzco costes de transacción.

Respecto a qué crímenes, yo normalmente no busco un crimen. [. . .] Yo, lo que quiero es transmitir una cosa, una idea, y monto un crimen alrededor. [. . .] Por ejemplo, en *Los crímenes del número primo*, me ocurrió una cosa que puede ocurrir donde sea, pero a veces se me enciende una chispa y cuando tengo esa chispa hasta que monto una novela alrededor no . . . En una iglesia de aquí fui, pues, un domingo, y a la salida me encontré al párroco, al sacerdote, todo cabizbajo, y le dije "¿qué le pasa, don Fulano?" Y me contó que un chaval de 17 años que iba a catequesis allí, que era de la parroquia y tal, que había ido a comulgar, y le había visto que salía muy nervioso, muy de prisa con la forma en la mano, fuera de la iglesia. Y salía así corriendo. Y fue detrás de él, y se encontró que había un coche fuera, con los cristales pintados, y la ventanilla un poco bajada, y salía un billete de cincuenta euros. Y lo que estaban haciendo era una transacción. Entonces, él estaba horrorizado porque no había sido capaz de transmitir a ese chico que llevaba tantos años en la parroquia que allí eso no, que una forma no era una cosa sino que era una persona. Y él estaba horrorizado porque nadie había sido capaz de transmitirlo. Bueno, eso en Pamplona, y dices, "¿Cómo puede existir en Pamplona?" Pues eso era en Pamplona. Y entonces me dijo, "Es que no sé cómo podemos transmitir a la gente que esto no es un rito, que la gente tiene . . . cree que hay una persona. Y, claro, las personas no se venden. Y mucho menos por 50 euros," decía él, "pero bueno, no se venden, ¿no? Eso ya es lo de menos." Y le dije, "Don Fulano, pues mire, si quiere, puedo escribir una novela." Y me miró con cara de . . . Pero yo empecé a darle vueltas. Y luego yo tenía también un amigo homosexual que me decía que no entendía porque la Iglesia Católica los despreciaba. Y yo, yo le dije, "Pues, yo creo que no es una cuestión de desprecio; es una cuestión de que quizás no conozcas bien, ¿no?" Entonces se juntaron esas dos cosas, y dije—bueno, empecé a dar vueltas—cómo podía yo ayudar al sacerdote aquel y al mismo tiempo intentar contestar a esta persona que es amigo y que hasta cierto punto podía entender los plantamientos, ¿no? Y entonces empecé a dar vueltas al tema hasta que diseñé *Los números primos*. Entonces los números primos no tenían ninguna importancia. El crimen, por supuesto, pero bueno, este hombre va vengándose quien cree que le ha hecho, al final, terminar cogiéndose un SIDA; va vengándose de la autoridad. Pero él atrae al Abad de Leyre, secuestrando lo más valioso que tenían en Leyre, que no eran sus grandes sino que era la persona que cuidan. Y de hecho, él, cuando lo encuentran al final, tiene una lucecita en el sagrario. Es decir, él no iba contra, digamos, la base de la Iglesia, iba contra la jerarquía porque no había entendido. Eso me permitió hablar—me permitía, es decir—hablar de la homosexualidad desde todos los frentes. De hecho, no he tenido ninguna crítica por parte de nadie. A los obispos, les ha gustado, pero también a otros colectivos, al colectivo gay y demás. Era una novela arriesgada, más viviendo en una sociedad tan conservadora como ésta. Pero yo pensaba diseñar los personajes así con una sensibilidad. O sea, efectivamente hay unas escenas duras pero hay una parte de la homosexualidad que es de un tipo, otra parte es de otro, otra parte es . . . o sea, había que contemplar todo el fenómeno y luego retirarse y dejar mostrar y no demostrar nada. Pero sí que queda la idea clara, me parece a mí. De hecho, es un libro que se vendió muchísimo. Y hay gente que te escribe a las tres de la mañana donde uno no piensa lo que escribe y luego dice todo de una vez con la idea de que . . . aquella del cura, ¿no? Esto no, hay una persona, ¿no? Y por eso, este hombre jamás trató de hacer daño; no vendió para una misa negra; ni hizo . . . no. Era un secuestro. Nadie fuera de la religión entiende cómo un secuestro, pero ¿sí es pan? Bueno, esa idea . . . Y las novelas las suelo construir así. No busco un crimen. De alguna manera, me captan a mí algo, algo que me preocupa. Pues, yo he tenido algún alumno verdaderamente inteligente, esquizofrénico, pero de una inteligencia . . . pero que tenía un problema mental que le pasaba un poco como al doctor Wilson. ¿Cómo hablar, cómo intentar transmitir que todos estamos un poco cuerdos, pero no todo, o un poco locos, simultáneamente [. . .]. Entonces, quiero hablar de algo, y monto una novela alrededor, no al revés. O sea, no voy a un juzgado a buscar un caso. Es un poco al revés.

JO: ¿Por qué una mujer? ¿Por qué Lola? Ya que las novelas detectivescas suelen tener un personaje masculino como protagonista.

RC: Hay un autor muy bueno en España que tiene una jueza [. . .]. Esa jueza—he estado leyendo un libro suyo que escribe fenomenal—la jueza tenía un amigo que . . . la jueza iba a levantar un cadáver. En ese caso era jueza, y la llamaban jueza—a mí no me gusta la palabra "jueza" porque indica que hay jueces y juezas. Y a mí me parece que la normalización del lenguaje hace . . . esa normalización de la vida que no hay estudiantes y estudiantas, es que hay estudiantes. Nos da igual el género. Si ponemos jueza, estamos intentando decir que hay pocas mujeres que no, no; hay ya muchas jueces. Entonces, somos iguales. Es una profesión, no tiene género. Pero, bueno, él habla de jueza. Y esta señora, empieza la novela, y va a levantar un cadáver. Da orden de que se levante, y se bebe dos güisquis.

JO: ¿Y no tres?

RC: El güisqui no es una bebida de mujeres; no es lo que haría habitualmente una mujer. [. . .] Estadísticamente [las mujeres] no bebemos el güisqui; no es lo que más nos gusta en España. Y luego, ella llama a un amante que tiene, como si fuera un hombre, y le dice, "Quedamos en la habitación del hotel de diez a doce." Eso no lo haría nunca una mujer: poner horas a una aventura. Es que no, no. Aquella mujer era un hombre con faldas. Entonces, dije, "Ya está. No me gusta; me encanta cómo escribe, pero esta jueza no, no me gusta nada." Entonces fue cuando empecé a diseñar el personaje. Yo tengo muchas amigas que [. . .] son en fiscales, presidentes de tribunal, jueces que tienen una vida normal, y que van al supermercado. Están a régimen, y por tanto no beben dos güisquis porque el güisqui engorda mucho. En fin, entonces traté de diseñar una mujer normal que se enfrentaba cosas no normales. Pero que yo pudiera sintonizar con ella y por tanto el resto de las mujeres pudieran sintonizar con ella, y al revés, ¿no? Y poco a poco, tardé mucho en diseñar el personaje. Me costó perfilarla pero . . . bueno, esos son retazos efectivamente de mucha gente que conoce de eso.

JO: ¿Y la importancia de Iturri? Porque a veces Lola tiene, casi tiene una crisis psicológica en que ella admite, confiesa, que ella no ha hecho nada. Y que ha sido Jaime, o Chocarro, o Iturri quien ha resuelto los crímenes.

RC: Esa es una cuestión casi local. La juez es de Bilbao. En Navarra, la capital no es Madrid; es Bilbao. De Bilbao son los que han tenido la ciudad grande, los que han sabido vivir, los que . . . como dicen, se cuenta un chiste que [. . .] dice que Jesucristo fue tan humilde que pudiendo haber nacido en Bilbao, nació en Belén. Eso es toda una tradición, y siempre ha habido un poco de pique entre el de Bilbao y el navarro. El de Bilbao era más liberal, más de izquierdas, republicano, más está que venía de Inglaterra. El navarro es más de la tierra; es menos exhibicionista, carlista, religioso. Entonces, el tener una jueza, o una juez, bilbaina, y un investigador le daba un poco más de gracia dentro del triángulo. [. . .] Luego es una madre de familia, más liberal que su marido que es muy navarro, e Iturri que está un poco en el medio, ¿no? Allí hay unos detalles que . . . hay dos cosas que quizás se perciban menos. No son todo . . . Hay mucho lenguaje taurino detrás. Hay muchas metáforas; hay unas referencias a la vida de la capital, Bilbao, con respecto a la vida tradicional de la España carlista. El carlismo en Navarra es muy arraigado, ¿no? O sea, si vas por el mundo hace diez o doce años había cualquier misionero del mundo. Había uno navarro, o sea era . . . siempre hemos exportado de aquí todo tipo de misioneros a todo el mundo, ¿no? Mientras que ahora, pues, la apertura a la modernidad, al vicio. Era puerto, también, de entrada, y aquí ha habido siempre esa reticencia.

JO: Al final de *Los crímenes del número primo*, dice la narradora que "Llaman color infierno al rojo intenso, carmesí, ramillete de pasiones encendidas por ardientes deseos. Se equivocan: el color del diablo es verde; un verde frío y aséptico, vengativo" (569), todo eso. Sin embargo, en varias de las novelas parece que enfatiza la narrativa que los ojos de Juan Iturri son verdes. ¿Es mera coincidencia, o cree que hay algo de diablo en Iturri?

RC: No. O sea, el verde sí es un color mucho más frío. En ese final, a mí siempre me ha llamado la atención. A ver cómo me lo explico [. . .]. A mí me llamó mucho la atención, y se lo pregunté a los curas que tenemos allí en una facultad de Teología, que es fácil preguntar, de "¿Por qué en la Biblia Jesucristo da tanta importancia a la mentira? ¿Por qué dicen que el demonio es el padre de la mentira? Podría haber dicho que es el padre de la lujuria, del asesinato; a mí me parecía que había cosas mucho peores que la mentira. Total, una mentirijilla no es tampoco para tanto. Pero no. Siempre es el padre de la mentira." Y me decían, "No, no. Es que detrás de la mentira, la consecuencia de la mentira, son todos lo demás. El diablo es mentiroso; se muestra como mentiroso. Nunca muestra la sangre como sangre [. . .] Siempre camufla las tentaciones como necesidades, y había que ponerle un color a la mentira. Por supuesto, la mentira no es negra ni es blanca porque la estrategia digamos del mal es mezclar un poco de mentira con un poco de verdad porque si no, no le creeríamos nunca. Y al intentar poner un color, salió el verde.

Al mismo tiempo, el verde es el color de la tentación de Juan Iturri. Digamos, uno sabe que se mete, qué es meterte en el agujero. Es importante que sepas qué es el agujero; luego, si te quieres meter, te metes. Pero tienes que saber qué es un agujero, ¿no? En el caso de MacHor la tentación es Iturri. [. . .] Pero [dejarse llevar] sería una mentira a sí misma, sería una mentira a su marido, sería una mentira a esa vida que ella ha querido construir, ¿no? Entonces hay una cierta conexión dentro de que son paralelas, ¿no? No es que Iturri sea el . . .

JO: ¿Entonces no es decir exactamente que Iturri es malo sino que es la tentación?

RC: Es la tentación. Es una tentación de la misma manera con que se presenta el diablo. Lo que pasa es que él . . . Él no es la tentación; es la tentación para MacHor porque él se mantiene aparte hasta que, en ese caso, está fuera de sí porque han . . . le han, ya, bueno, vamos, le ha dado este producto, y digamos que ya no tiene el dominio sobre sí mismo. Si no, probablemente esa escena no hubiera ocurrido. La editorial me insistía, "Tienes que acabar esa escena." Yo digo: "No, no; es que no me estropeéis los personajes de esa escena. Esa escena queda donde queda, y no hay más. Porque estáis confundiendo" . . . Eso quizás sea otra de las diferencias con otras de las novelas de detectives aquí en España. Me hizo mucha gracia porque me dijeron que si necesitaba que alguien me ayudara con ése, que me ponían. Y le digo, "Hombre, teniendo nueve hijos, me da la sensación de que no." Pero es que estropeamos la barrera social entre un juez y un policía en España. No es tan alta como en Estados Unidos, pero es bastante alta. No es nada fácil que esa barrera se corte aunque sea un inspector. No es habitual, para empezar, ¿no? Y luego ya están las cuestiones morales o personales, o . . .

JO: ¿Son también simbólicos los nombres; es decir, Juan, de Navarra, Lola, irlandesa, MacHor? Pero, ¿tienen algo simbólico?

RC: MacHor es un apellido irlandés. Lo que hice fue coger dos apellidos habituales en Bilbao y poner un trozo de cada uno y juntarlo. Ahora, le puse Lola como contraste. Lola es un nombre típicamente español. Ella tiene rasgos no españoles, y además vive en Bilbao—que es una tierra donde uno puede decir que cada vez se llevan más los nombres de aquella zona, pues Necane, Erasneo, cosas así. Y ella se llama Lola, netamente española viniendo de una ciudad . . . Es un poco la vuelta a los contrastes, ¿no?

Iturri es un apellido navarro. Chocarro, también. Son apellidos navarros. Son apellidos de la tierra, ¿no? Chocarro, además es el apellido de un buen amigo navarro, grandón, un personaje muy entrañable. Garache es un apellido de la zona, de distintas zonas del Baztán, de zonas navarras. Como éstos eran navarros. Y se llama Jaime, eso es porque . . . Lola porque es un típico nombre. Pero mis abuelos se llamaban Lola y Jaime, y yo decía—bueno dije—si le pongo a ella Lola ya para que no se enfade en el cielo le pongo Jaime.

JO: ¿Considera usted el raciocinio importante? Es decir, ¿quiere que el lector vaya tratando de "descubrir" el criminal y el por qué?

RC: Sí, sí. Yo creo que es . . . Yo vuelvo a insistir; yo demuestro las matemáticas pero aquí sólo muestro. Le pongo delante el problema, y tiene que posicionarse la mejor manera, bueno, tiene, si quiere, posicionarse. La mejor manera de hacerlo es que se meta en el asunto, que siga él. Entonces, al final tendrá una opinión sobre ese tema, sobre cualquiera de los muchos temas. Y la mejor manera es que se meta en la intriga, y por eso el suspense te da mucho juego para hablar de lo que quieras.

JO: ¿A qué otros autores considera usted importantes como influencia en su propio desarrollo como autora?

RC: Yo tengo que reconocer que leo poca novela negra porque cada vez disfruto poquísimo porque leo de otra manera. [. . .] Yo prefiero leer a los clásicos, soy bastante ecléctica según me da . . . Por ejemplo, *Almas grises*, de Claudel, que lo leí; lo terminé hace poco, y me encantó. Pues me paso a Murakami, la novela más de intriga. Leo norteamericana; me gusta bastante más que la nórdica. A mí la nórdica me . . . les he comprendido bien . . . He estado este año en Estocolmo en la entrega de los Nobel, mirando escenas para una novela, y los he comprendido perfectamente. La cantidad de tiempo que tienen que estar en casa por el frío cambia la personalidad de un escritor, la del escritor y del relator, pero a mí me gustan menos. Prefiero el oriental, el norteamericano, y por supuesto lo latinoamericano. Borges me fascina. Lo leo; lo releo, y lo vuelvo a leer. Para mí es filosofía más que cualquier . . . más que literatura. Por supuesto, Delibes. Pero luego me gustan los japoneses, los coreanos; me gusta esa sensibilidad con independencia de que no es mediterránea. No tienen nada que ver pero me permiten contrastar, para diseñar los personajes.

JO: Por curiosidad, ¿Giménez Bartlett?

RC: La conozco personalmente; me parece una mujer muy valiosa. La leo pero no la releo . . .

JO: ¿No la considera una influencia muy importante?

RC: No. Para mí, lo importante es lo que releo. Dicen que es ineficiente leer dos veces el mismo libro. Pues yo he leído a veces ocho o diez veces el mismo, y siempre encuentro algo nuevo. Hay un libro que no tiene nada que ver con esto, pero siempre me impresiona mucho. Cuando estoy un poco baja de ánimos, me lo leo . . . que se llama *La luz apacible*, que es la vida de Santo Tomás de Aquino [. . .]. Pues, Santo Tomás de Aquino parece un pensador ahí metido en una biblioteca, pensando. Pero tuvo una vida bastante azarosa, pero siempre mantenía la paz. Y era . . . ésa es la palabra . . . son libros que hablan sobre la pacibilidad: *La luz apacible*. Está perfectamente puesto el título. Y yo, cuando necesito paz, pues lo leo. Y me lo conozco. Vamos, a todo el mundo que se lo he prestado, pues da paz. Murakami da . . . a mí, para mí leer a Murakami, por ejemplo, es leer creatividad si definimos creatividad como buscar soluciones nuevas a problemas viejos. Siempre te da una solución nueva a un problema viejo porque te lo enfoca en una manera tan rara, para un español, que me llama mucho la atención. O la sensibilidad que tiene Ogawa, por ejemplo, en *La fórmula preferida del profesor*, como ve cual es el concepto de persona que nosotros hemos perdido en Occidente. Está allí la coreana esta, *Por favor, cuida de mamá*. Luego, por ejemplo, cambio, y me leo a los rusos; me gusta bastante el contraste. He leído . . . Acabo de terminar hace un poco, y el libro es antiguo ¿eh? pero no lo he leído hasta ahora, y es la . . . *El invitado del Papa*, se llama. Está escrito por un ortodoxo ruso nacionalizado en Francia, que cuenta a veces un poco [. . .]. El prelado ortodoxo ruso se fue a ver a Juan Pablo I, y se le murió en los brazos. Eso es real; es una historia real. Y a las dos semanas se murió el Papa que duró un mes. Nunca se supo qué pasó allí, ¿no? Entonces este hombre monta una novela sobre quien mató, quien envenenó, al prelado ortodoxo que era de la KGB. Entonces es una novela que habla sobre la vida vaticana, sobre la vida . . . La compara un poco con la vida interna del partido en la Rusia ya no pos-comunista, y te da también flashes muy distintos a los que estás acostumbrado. Y la novela negra te da flashes que yo, a veces . . . ya los conozco; entonces prefiero leer otras cosas. Y pues, y por supuesto vuelvo a Delibes, a *Los santos inocentes*; me fascina. El primer Nobel nuestro, el primero, *La familia de Pascual Duarte*. Vargas Llosa, algunos, bueno . . . Pues, hay mucha gente ahora que escribe fenomenal . . .

JO: Ha dicho alguna vez que las novelas, si son buenas, te hacen mejores. ¿Cree, entonces, que sus novelas tienen un elemento didáctico, una moraleja?
RC: Creo que la primera parte es cierta, que si las novelas son buenas, te hacen mejores. Yo me conformaría con que la gente sería más contenta. La alegría es algo que nos falta cada vez más en Occidente.

JO: Y eso; ¿qué significa: "ser mejor," "más contento"?
RC: Bueno, la alegría es un signo de felicidad, ¿no? La alegría es un signo de felicidad y . . . Bueno, creo que nos hace pensar en cosas que si no, no pensaríamos. Y como las cosas son bastante fuertes, tomar posiciones sobre cosas que no te gustan . . . por ejemplo, hay varios niños en varias novelas al maltrato a las mujeres, ¿no? Al maltrato en general, a los niños y a las mujeres . . . porque yo las ideas que vemos en televisión respeto a lo que vemos en los juzgados no estamos hablando de lo mismo, ¿no? Es quizás ver otras variantes sean distintas, ¿no? Me gustaría pero no sé si eso se consigue o no.

JO: ¿Cree que Lola resolverá algún día sus dudas sobre la religión o será siempre su marido el más religioso, el que tiene más fe aunque él es científico, lo cual es un poco curioso, ¿no?

RC: No. Yo he encontrado que los que tienen fe más seria son los científicos, curiosamente. Hay uno que se pasó no sé cuantas horas hablándome de las apóptosis, que es el suicidio de las células. Y estaba fascinado en cómo alguien había pensado hasta en eso, digamos, la complejidad les lleva hacia arriba. Rodeado de tanta maldad es lógico que uno tenga dudas, de si verdaderamente estamos hechos a imagen de Dios porque . . . Quizá en esta última novela [. . .] resuelve allí no sus dudas de fe pero sí dudas respecto a sí mismo, ¿no? A su posición en el mundo. Yo no sé si hay que esperar a . . . No sé . . . que al final la fe no es tenerla por kilos sino que sea más de calidad o menos y eso irá llegando con el tiempo, ¿no? Pues, no nos dan tiempo.

JO: ¿Y habrá, entonces, más en la serie?

RC: De momento los vamos a dejar descansar un poquito porque son cinco entregas ya. Yo ya tengo otras dos novelas terminadas de otros personajes.

JO: ¿Son novelas históricas?

RC: No, no. Son novelas. Hay una novela de intrigas sobre un . . . que trabajo, ésa me ha costado, llevo siete años escribiéndola. La he dejado cogida; la he vuelto a empezar. Me ha costado muchísimo. Trabajo con un exorcista bastante tiempo. No es una novela de miedo; es una novela de suspense pero hay un personaje que es el demonio, y eso me ha costado muchísimo.

JO: ¿Hay algo más que le gustaría comunicarles a sus lectores o a los críticos?

RC: Bueno, es que en realidad no escribo para los críticos. Leo las críticas en la medida que me ponen . . . que me critican. Porque, por dos motivos, primero porque suelen tener algo de razón; entonces, así aprendo para la siguiente. Espero que mi mejor novela sea la última, no la primera. En poesía, es muy probable que tu primera poesía sea la mejor. Y yo creo que en novela hay que ir avanzando, y siempre mejorando. Entonces para eso están muy bien los críticos. En eso es interesante por independencia que si hablan de ti. Pues, es estupendo que hablen de ti, pero yo escribo para la gente normal que lee, ¿no? Y me hace mucho más ilusión decir que he prestado la novela a mi cuñado, y después mi cuñado se la dio a mi hermana. El número de veces que tus novelas se prestan es, para mí, el éxito de un escritor porque sólo prestas las novelas que te gustan. Claro, mejor venderlas, obviamente, pero después de venderlas, prestarlas.

Yo creo que el crítico tiene por profesión diseccionar una obra. Es como el forense, y el forense va viendo lo que no está bien, pero deja quizá al lado lo que . . . O sea, no ve la persona; ve un cuerpo en trozos. Y a mí me interesa más el conjunto, ¿no? Creo que cuando te dicen, "Este libro, ¿de qué va?" Tú lo que cuentas; lo acabo de hacer yo ahora mismo con el libro de la . . . Cuento el argumento, pero en realidad el argumento no tiene ninguna trascendencia; lo que tiene son los personajes que han quedado en el lector. Entonces, yo creo que los críticos por profesión y por forma de educación tienen que ir más a hacer disección que duda.

JO: Ha dicho que quiere que su mejor novela sea la última. ¿Es decir que le gusta más *La venganza del asesino par* que *El número primo*?

RC: A *El número primo* le tengo mucho cariño porque fue una novela muy arriesgada, y digo de ésta: me echan de España, me echan de la Iglesia, me echan de casa . . . Mi madre que me dijo que me había mandado a un colegio de monjas, ¿cómo era posible que supiera yo esos tacos? Estaba muy horrorizada mi madre con los temas; eran temas fuertes. Esa me encantó escribirla pero sí que . . . yo sí que veo que voy . . . yo aprendo muchísimo con cada novela. Aprendo sobre los temas pero me los trabajo mucho. Los vivo; los huelo. Para mí, el olor es importantísimo muchísimo. Necesito oler los sitios. Si no los veo y no los huelo, no, no, no, no estoy en ellos. Pero aprendo mucho de muchas cosas. Estudio psiquiatría, patología criminal. He estudiado criminología, pero también he estudiado los casos de los abogados, la psicología. Todo eso me hace aprender, y si no aprendiera es difícil escribir más, ¿no? Pero, sí, que espero que . . . y no por una cuestión de dominar una técnica sino porque sea capaz de comprender mejor al hombre. O la mujer, en este caso. Pero los hombres me resultan mucho más complejos que las mujeres.

La siguiente novela está escrita en tres voces: La primera habla MacHor en primera persona. La segunda, habla Jaime, en primera persona, y después habla Iturri. De manera que todos pueden hablar de lo que opinan del resto que hasta ahora no lo había podido hacer, ¿no? Entonces, me ha tocado meterme no sólo en el papel sino en serie escribir en primera persona, sino escribir en cómo veía Iturri a MacHor, ¿no? Claro, ese perfil no estaba dentro de mi mente, ¿no? Entonces cuando se lo he ido dando a gente de ese perfil me decía, "Esto es lenguaje femenino. Nosotros no pensamos así. Nosotros cuando vemos a una mujer vemos esto, esto otro." Y también me ha hecho aprender mucho de esa visión masculina que siendo yo una mujer, teniendo esta jueza—en este caso con "a"—pues me perdía, ¿no? Eso también me ha divertido. Y con la siguiente . . . Yo en realidad escribo para conocerme a mí misma; o sea, no me entiendo en absoluto. Tampoco tengo mucho interés en entenderme. Si me entendiera mucho, ya me habría muerto. Pero entenderme a mí, entender a los de alrededor . . . poder . . . no perderme la potencia que tienen todos que tienen alrededor que vamos, van de prisa, que me la pierdo. Y eso . . . pues, luego en cada novela me voy fijando en más cosas que no . . . Ayer, estaba con un director de cine a ver si conseguimos que esto se ponga en la pantalla a la juez, y le decía, "Bueno"—un director de cine muy apremiado de España, y le decía—"¿Qué es lo que te ha llamado la atención de éstas?" Y el director de cine, es como lo opuesto a mí físicamente, de aspecto, de todo, de vida, de todo, pero nos llevamos francamente bien, y me decía eso, "La sensibilidad de una mujer ordinaria, en el mejor sentido de la palabra, vive una vida ordinaria, en un sitio pequeño, en un . . . cualquiera de mi abuela, de mi madre, mi tía, mi hija, ante situaciones que nos superan a todos y cómo es capaz de ir superando el reto que tenía sin perder su propia identidad." Yo creo que sin perder lo que somos y aprovechando para entender el . . . sin perder tu identidad, si eres capaz de mirar al resto, tu identidad mejora. Y eso mismo, si tú lo consigues transmitir en los libros los demás, miren a los demás. Si los miráramos a los ojos, no nos mataríamos.

JO: ¿Le habría gustado estudiar psicología?

RC: Sí, la psicología es una ciencia fascinante, tan imperfecta como la economía. Todo el mundo de la mente es fascinante, tanto desde el punto de vista patológico como desde el punto de vista no patológico. La ventaja es que como puedes no matricularte y aprender, pues alguna vez también me dejan ir a la clase cuando puedo; asisto a los cursos a que puedo, que es muy distinto escucharlo al profesor, pero, bueno, siempre están los libros.

Appendix A: Main Characters

Las lágrimas de Hemingway
Dolores (Lola) MacHor, aspiring law-school professor
Jaime Garache, Lola's husband; psychologist
Juan Iturri, Pamplona police investigator
Niccola Mocciaro, Lola's law-school mentor
Alejandro, Lola's law-school colleague; son of Niccola
Clara, Alejandro's brother
Miguelón Ruiz, Madrid police office
Gabriel Uranga, Lola's law-school colleague; Pamplona judge
Rodrigo Robles, another law-school professor; colleague of Niccola

Los crímenes del número primo
Dolores (Lola) MacHor, judge
Jaime Garache, Lola's husband; research scientist
Juan Iturri, Interpol agent
Pello Urrutia, Leyre Monastery abbot
Blas de Cañarte, Pamplona Archbishop
Lucas de Andueza, Blas de Cañarte's personal secretary
Fermín Chocarro, Leyre Monastery sacristan
Gabriel Uranga, Pamplona judge; Lola's superior
Monseñor Tagliatelli; Spanish Nuncio
Javier Mugarra Garciandía, assassin

El Expediente Canaima
Dolores (Lola) MacHor, judge
Jaime Garache, Lola's husband; research scientist
Juan Iturri, Interpol agent
David Herrera-Smith, Head of the World Bank's Office of Institutional Integrity
Lorenzo Moss, Spanish Secretary of State of the Economy
Kalif Über, FBI agent
Roque Castaño, tax auditor
Ramón Cerda, president of the Buccaro business group

Jimena Wittman, Ramón Cerda's wife
Norberto (Ariel) Rosales, drug dealer, child molester
Telmo Bravo, old man; María Bravo's grandfather

El último paciente del Dr. Wilson
Dolores (Lola) MacHor, judge
Jaime Garache, Lola's husband; research scientist
Juan Iturri, Interpol agent
Rodrigo, wealthy man who desires to know if a sane person can kill and remain sane
Dr. Wilson, psychiatrist who agrees to oversee Rodrigo's experiment
Marc Ross i Roví, Spanish/Catalan psychiatrist with a practice in New York
Kimio Shibata, wealthy owner of a home in the Aegean Sea
Sarah Shibata, Kimio's wife; patient of Marc Ross i Roví
Ignacio Vicens; Kimio's architect; introduces Lola to the Shibata couple
Joe Lombardo, police officer in Washington D.C.

La venganza del asesino par
Dolores (Lola) MacHor, judge
Jaime Garache, Lola's husband; research scientist
Juan Iturri, Interpol agent
Marc Ross i Roví, imprisoned Spanish psychiatrist
Dr. Wilson, alter-ego of Marc Ross i Roví
Rodrigo, alter-ego of Marc Ross i Roví
Kimio Shibata, wealthy owner of a home in New York
Sarah Shibata, Kimio's wife; former patient of Marc Ross i Roví
Itoo, Sarah Shibata's personal bodyguard
Joe Lombardo, police officer in Washington, D.C.
Dr. Raspy, prison psychiatrist
Dr. Hernández, Dr. Raspy's assistant

Appendix B: Plot Summaries

The following, basic plot summaries of the novels will provide the necessary context in which to understand the critical arguments.

Las lágrimas de Hemingway **(2005)**

Alejandro Mocciaro, who has recently won a *cátedra* in law at the University of Valladolid, dies after being gored during the running of the bulls in Pamplona. Lola MacHor, a colleague and competitor for the *cátedra*, and her husband Jaime Garache are maliciously impugned in Alejandro's death by Miguelón Ruiz, a Madrid police officer and would-be lover of Clara, Alejandro's sister. The stress of the arrest causes Lola's heart condition to flare up again, and she is chained to the hospital bed to avoid any potential flight risk.

Prior to the current story line, Alejandro's father, Niccola, had served as Lola's academic and professional mentor and become a close friend of both Lola and Jaime. When Lola failed to win the *cátedra*, Niccola discouraged her from appealing, and it is only a short time later when he unexpectedly dies. After his death, Lola, Clara and Alejandro are summoned to Pamplona during the San Fermines festival—during which time Alejandro dies—for the reading of his will. Because of Miguelón's precipitous arrest of Lola and Jaime, however, Pamplona police officer Juan Iturri conducts a secret investigation of his own into Alejandro's death. In the course of that investigation, Iturri discovers that the executor of Niccola's will has been given special instructions to hand-deliver a bound copy of various Sherlock Holme's works to Lola along with a strange, and seemingly false, statement. With this in mind, and through Lola's discovery of the death-bed, tell-all confession by Niccola which he had placed in the books' binding, both Lola and Jaime are declared innocent and another ambitious law school professor is found culpable.

Los crímenes del número primo **(2008)**

Lola Machor—now a judge on the *Tribunal Superior de Justicia de Navarra*—unexpectedly finds herself in charge of the investigation of the kidnapping and murder of both the Leyre Monastery abbot and the Pamplona archbishop. Upon beginning the investigation, she soon learns that the Pamplona Archbishopric has received a package with what is supposed to be the severed finger of one of the clerics. Following her initial investigations at the remote crime scene and at the Leyre Monastery, she goes to the archbishopric and discovers that Interpol agent Juan Iturri is on the premises and already well aware of the situation—the archbishop had called him for advice and assistance shortly before being murdered. Lola recruits Iturri to join the investigation, and a few days later, while a large group of priests and the Spanish Nuncio are assembled for the funeral service, the assassin plants a bomb in the archbishopric bedroom where the nuncio is to stay. At Iturri's insistence, Lola and Iturri go to Malaga to investigate a possible connection between the death of a renowned fashion designer, Faustino Gorla, and the priests' assassinations. Because of a near-fatal attempt on Iturri's life in Malaga, Lola is forced to leave him there and return to Pamplona to continue the investigation on her own. She herself is soon kidnapped but receives enough information during the encounter to be able to determine after the abductor abandons her who the assassin must be. This individual, however, had been declared officially dead nine years earlier. In spite of that, discussions with the Nuncio lead to another avenue in finding the assassin and the case soon concludes when Lola confronts him with the facts of her investigation.

El Expediente Canaima **(2009)**

The third novel of the series relates the attempted extortion of David Herrera-Smith, a high-ranking World Bank official, who is in possession of the file containing the details of a Word Bank-sponsored road project in Canaima, Venezuela. Herrera-Smith, unable to determine from the file exactly why he is being extorted, calls Lola MacHor—who is scheduled to make a presentation on fraud in his session at the World Bank conference in Singapore—to get her advice and move forward her plans to fly to Asia. Lola, meanwhile, has received a threatening note from Ariel, a local drug dealer in Pamplona who has raped 15 year-old María Bravo. María's grandfather, Telmo, goes to Ariel's nightclub and threatens him, and in return he himself nearly dies from the beating he receives at Ariel's hands.

Lola returns to Spain from the Singapore conference and, after moving to Madrid to begin working on the *Audiencia Nacional*, decides to investigate further the Canaima case. A tax auditor friend of Jaime, Roque Castaño, agrees to investigate and discovers proof of international racketeering. When Lola subsequently learns that the car she has seen following her around town belongs to the FBI, she promptly calls

Kalif Über, her FBI escort in Singapore, and remonstrates him for collusion in the Venezuela affair, the various associated murders, and an attempt on her own life. He successfully defends himself and the FBI, explaining that the Americans have read the Canaima file—which Lola has locked up in a bank safe box—and are also interested in solving the case. Shortly thereafter, with his and Iturri's assistance, the guilty meet their just reward.

***El último paciente del Doctor Wilson* (2010)**

Lola speaks at a globalization conference in Barcelona and, while there, receives a package indicating that the sender of the papers fears that he will be Rodrigo's next victim. Rodrigo, as detailed in the narrative enclosed in the package, is a wealthy egomaniac who has decided to prove that a sane person can commit multiple murders and retain his sanity. Something immediately convinces Lola that she is dealing with a real case, but both her husband, Jaime, and friend/Interpol agent, Juan Iturri, believe otherwise and urge her to ignore her premonitions. Lola persists, however, until she finally convinces Iturri to make a phone call to the forensics doctor in France who conducted the autopsy on the first victim. The results of that call, and subsequent conversations with police in other localities around the world where Rodrigo details his killings, lead Iturri to conclude as well that the narrative Lola has received describes actual murders.

Additional investigations by Lola, Iturri, and Jaime—following a temporary mental setback on the part of Lola—eventually lead them to a home in the Aegean Sea owned by the Shibata couple. While on a weekend visit there, they become convinced that the psychiatrist they have identified as the chief suspect, and to whom they talked at a conference in Portugal, does hold the keys to finding Rodrigo. Sarah Shibata, in fact, has resorted to his office on multiple occasions, but when she calls him on their behalf, he refuses to elaborate. Back in Pamplona the next week, Lola receives an anonymous email which she interprets as a coded message that Rodrigo and the psychiatrist will be meeting at a Washington D.C. restaurant in approximately forty-eight hours. Lola, Iturri, and Jaime immediately make plans to fly to the U.S., and with the help of Joe Lombardo and other police officers, the assassin is arrested and sentenced to prison.

***La venganza del asesino par* (2012)**

On the same day as Lola's investiture on the Spanish *Tribunal Supremo*, she receives a package from Joe Lombardo indicating that the assassin from the previous novel in the series has written Lola a letter saying that "blood will flow again." Even though Rodrigo is incarcerated, Lola remains tremendously frightened of him and refuses to join Iturri in investigating the mysterious deaths of two of the world's richest people in Argentina and the U.S., about which Rodrigo claims to hold privileged information. Meanwhile, Lola's husband Jaime has inexplicably gone to Boston for a three-month stay. Convinced by her superior, the court judge Fernando Serrano, Lola decides to fly to Boston and confront Jaime. Prior to leaving, however, television news reports indicate that one of the richest men in Japan has suddenly died, but the reports fail to explain certain anomalies of which Joe and Iturri are aware and which closely correspond to Rodrigo's statements. At this point, Iturri decides to fly to the U.S. with Lola and further attempt to convince her to join the investigation and go visit Rodrigo, as he has requested.

Once in the U.S., Lola visits Jaime, and he explains that his sudden departure was his attempt to escape an attempted extortion by the pharmaceutical company for which he is conducting experimental drug research. Lola, unable to imagine a solution to Jaime's problem, calls Iturri for help, but he refuses to assist unless Lola agrees to go with Iturri and Joe to visit Rodrigo in prison. Furious, she finally acquiesces. During a conversation with Rodrigo, he gives the name of the next victim. Joe immediately calls his superiors, and they are who discover the body of the Russian magnate dead in her own living room.

When Lola, Iturri, and Joe visit the crime scene, they discover the connection between the various victims and the name of the fifth victim yet to be murdered. Their attempts to avoid this death, however, yield surprising results as well as the identity of both the assassin and the intermediary between the assassin and the incarcerated Rodrigo.

Works Cited

Agencia EFE. "Reyes Calderón afirma que en esta sociedad 'cada vez importa menos la muerte del otro.'" 8 septiembre 2010. 13 January 2012. Web.

Aranda Ocaña, Monica. *Prison Conditions in Spain.* Rome: Antigone Edizioni, 2013. 4 October 2014. Web.

Berk, Laura. *Infants, Children, and Adolescents.* 7th ed. Boston: Allyn & Bacon, 2012.

Bieder, Maryellen. "Cultural Capital: The Play of Language, Gender, and Nationality in Carme Riera." *Catalan Review* 14.1–2 (2000): 53–74.

Calderón Cuadrado, Reyes. *Los crímenes del número primo.* Barcelona: RBA Libros, 2008.

——. *El Expediente Canaima.* Barcelona: RBA Libros, 2009.

——. *Las lágrimas de Hemingway.* 2nd ed. Valladolid: Editorial DIFÁCIL, 2005.

——. "Lola Machor. Autodescripción." *Reyes Calderón Web Oficial.* N.d. 2 October 2014. Web.

——. *El último paciente del Doctor Wilson.* Barcelona: Editorial Planeta, 2010.

——. *La venganza del asesino par.* Barcelona: Editorial Planeta, 2012.

Carlson, Elof. "Scientific Origins of Eugenics." *Eugenics Archive.* N.d. 27 June 2014. Web.

Centro de Investigaciones Sociológicos. *Religión (II) ISSP.* October–December 2008. 31 July 2014. Web.

Cercas, Javier Rueda. "Lo leo todo negro." *Aceprensa.* 4 febrero 2010. 1 October 2014. Web.

Chamberlin, Vernon. "Las imágenes animalistas y el color rojo en *La barraca.*" *Duquesne Hispanic Review* 6 (1968): 23–36.

"Churro." *ifood.tv.* 10 June 2010. 18 August 2014. Web.

Committee on the Rights of the Child. *United Nations Convention on the Rights of the Child.* 25 February 2014. 1 August 2014. Web.

Cook, Judith A. Cook, and Mary Margaret Fonow. "Knowledge and Women's Interests: Issues of Epistemology and Methodology in Feminist Sociological Research." *Sociological Inquiry* 56.1 (1986): 2–29.

Council of Bar and Law Societies of Europe (CCBE). 21 December 2012. 23 February 2013. Web.

Crow. John A. *Spain: The Root and the Flower.* 3rd ed. Berkeley and Los Angeles: U of California P, 1985.

"Current Religious Climate in Spain." *Free Will Baptist International Missions*. 2006. 1 August 2014. Web.

Díez Repollés, José Luis. "Rigorismo y reforma penal. Cuatro legislaturas homogéneas (1996–2011). Parte II." *Boletín Criminológico*. 143 (2013): 1–5. 4 October 2014. Web.

Duffy, Bobby, Rhonda Wake, Tamara Burrows, and Pamel Bremner. *Closing the Gaps: Crime and Public Perceptions*. N.p.: Ipsos MORI Social Research Institute, 2008. 4 November 2014. Web.

Ekberg Fredell, Asa, and Drude Dahlerup. "Cracking the Glass Ceiling: The Representation of Women and Men in Political and Public Decision Making in the Council of Europe's Member States." *Stockholms Universitet*. 2006. 23 February 2013. Web.

Encarnación. Omar G. *Spanish Politics: Democracy after Dictatorship*. Cambridge, UK: Polity Press, 2008.

European Commission. *Eurobarometer 72. Public Opinion in the European Union. Vol. 2*. Brussels: TNS Opinion & Social, 2009. 13 February 2012. Web.

Faludi, Susan. "Postfeminism." *Routledge International Encyclopedia of Women*. Eds. Cheris Kramarae and Dale Spender. Vol. 3. New York: Routledge, 2000. 1646–48.

Farrington, Pat. "Interviews with Ana María Matute and Carme Riera." *Journal of Iberian and Latin American Studies* 6.1 (2000): 75–89.

Fernández Rodríguez, Carolina. *La Bella Durmiente a través de la historia*. Oviedo: Universidad de Oviedo, 1998.

Fischer, David Hackett. "The Braided Narrative: Substance and Form in Social History." *The Literature of Fact: Selected Papers from the English Institute*. Ed. Angus Fletcher. New York: Columbia UP, 1976. 109–34.

Glenn, Kathleen M. "Voice, Marginality, and Seduction in the Short Fiction of Carme Riera." *Recovering Spain's feminist tradition*. Ed. Lisa Vollendorf. New York: Modern Language Association of America, 2001. 374–89.

——. "Voz, marginalidad y seducción en la narrativa breve de Carme Riera." *Literatura y feminismo en España, S. XV–XXV*. Ed. Lisa Vollendorf. Barcelona: Icaria Editorial, 2005. 339–52.

Godsland, Shelley. "From Feminism to Postfeminism in Women's Detective Fiction from Spain: The Case of Maria-Antònia Oliver and Alicia Giménez-Bartlett." *Letras Femeninas* 28.1 (2002): 84–99.

Gómez Fortes, Braulio and Irene Palacios Brihuega. "Testing the Quality of Democracy: The Case of Spain." *European Political Science*. 11 (December 2012): 492–508.

Gowers, Emily. *The Loaded Table: Representations of Food in Roman Literature*. Oxford: Oxford UP, 1993 [Reprinted 2003].

Groff, Philip and Laura McRae. "The Nature–Nurture Debate in Thirteenth-Century France." Paper presented at the annual meeting of the American Psychological Association, Chicago. August 1998. 24 June 2014. Web.

Hackney Blackwell, Amy, and Ryan Hackney. *The Everything Irish History and Heritage Book.* Avon, MA: Adams Media, 2004.

The Herb Society. "The Herb Society of America's Essential Facts for Rosemary: Rosmarinus officinalis." *The Herb Society of America.* 2009. 4 October 2014. Web.

Hill, Gerald, and Kathleen Hill. "Crime of Passion." *The People's Law Dictionary.* N.d. 16 September 2014. Web.

Holmlund, Chris. "Postfeminism from A to G." *Cinema Journal* 44.2 (2005): 116–21.

Hutcheon, Linda. "Postmodern Paratextuality and History." *Texte-revue de critique et de theorie litteraire.* 5 (1996): 301–12.

International Association of Women Judges. 2011. 23 February 2013. Web.

Janerka, Malgorzata. "Las relaciones de poder en la novela policiaca española después de 1975 a la luz de la definición de poder de Michel Foucault." *Itinerarios* 7 (2008): 111–29.

Klein, Kathleen Gregory. *The Woman Detective: Gender and Genre.* 2nd ed. Champaign: Illini Books, 1995.

Knutson, David. "Still Crazy After All These Years." *Hispanic and Luso-Brazilian Detective Fiction: Essays on the Género Negro Tradition.* Eds. René W. Craig-Odders, Jacky Collins, and Glen S. Close. Jefferson, NC and London: McFarland, 2006: 46–59.

Korsmeyer, Caroline. "Feminist Aesthetics." *Stanford Encyclopedia of Philosophy.* Ed. Edward N. Zalta. 7 May 2004. 19 July 2007. Web.

Lafuente, Javier. "Más juezas que jueces." *El País* 22 abril 2008. 8 March 2013. Web.

Landeira, Ricardo. *El género policiaco en la literatura española del siglo XIX.* Alicante: Universidad de Alicante, 2001. *Publicaciones Universidad de Alicante.* 2010. 20 February 2013. Web.

Lehan, Richard. *Realism and Naturalism: The Novel in an Age of Transition.* Madison, WI: U of Wisconsin P, 2005.

Lemmo, Nora. "Crisis de la mediana edad. Estrategias para la segunda mitad de la vida." *Universo Mujer.com.* 21 October 2011. 16 December 2011. Web.

LESEG. "Los libros muestran belleza y apunta a la Belleza." *Biblioteca de la Universidad de Navarra.* 25 octubre 2011. 13 February 2012. Web.

Ley Orgánica 2/1979, de 3 de octubre, del Tribunal Constitucional. 22 February 2013. Web.

López-Sáez, Mercedes, J. Francisco Morales, and Ana Lisbona. "Evolution of Gender Stereotypes in Spain: Traits and Roles." *The Spanish Journal of Psychology* 11.2 (2008): 609–17.

Lyne, Nick. "Overcrowding Leaves Spain's Prisons on the Brink." *IberoSphere* 9 June 2010. 1 August 2014. Web.

Martínez, Miguel. "Ejecutan en public a una mujer acusada de adulterio en Afganistán." *Menéame.net.* 26 April, 2013. 11 July 2014. Web.

McLeod, Saul. "Nature vs Nurture in Psychology." *SimplyPsychology.* 2007. 27 June 2014. Web.

Medina, Jeremy. "The Artistry of Blasco Ibáñez's *Flor de Mayo*." *Hispania* 65.2 (1982): 200–11.

"Most Popular Spanish Breakfast Foods." *ifood.tv*. 18 August 2014. Web.

Mulvey, Laura. "Visual Pleasure and Narrative Cinema." *Media and Cultural Studies: Key Works*. Eds. Meenakshi Gigi Durham and Douglas Kellner. Malden, MA, Oxford, UK and Victoria, Australia: Blackwell Publishing, 2006. 2–52.

Ororpesa, Salvador. "Prólogo." *La mujer en la novela policial: Evolución de la protagonista femenina en cinco autoras hispanas*. Myung N. Choi. Bloomington: Palibrio: 2012. 7–9.

Ortiz García, Carmen. "Comida e identidad: Cocina nacional y cocinas regionales." *Alimentación y cultura: Actas del Congreso Internacional, 1998*. Madrid: Museo Nacional de Antropología, 1999, 301–24.

Oswald, Kalen R. "Detecting 1979 Barcelona: The Cases versus the Context in *El misterio de la cripta embrujada*, *Los mares del Sur*, and *A la vejez navajazos*." *Crime Scene Spain: Essays on Post-Franco Crime Fiction*. Eds. René W. Craig-Odders, and Jacky Collins. Jefferson, NC, and London: McFarland & Company, 2009. 11–33.

"Pathetic Fallacy." *A Handbook to Literature*. 6th ed. C. Hugh Holman and William Harmon, eds. New York: Macmillan Publishing Co, 1992. 347–48.

Pérez, Genaro J. *Ortodoxia y heterodoxia de la novela policiaca hispana: Variaciones sobre el género negro*. Newark, DE: Juan de la Cuesta, 2002.

Pérez, Genaro J., and Janet I. Pérez. "Postfeminism in Hispanic Literatures: An Introduction." *Monographic Review/Revista Monográfica* 23 (2007): 7–46.

Pew Research Center. "During Benedict's Papacy, Religious Observance Among Catholics in Europe Remained Low but Stable." 5 March 2013. 31 July 2014. Web.

Piepmeier, Alison. *Postfeminism vs. the Third Wave*. 17 March 2006. 19 July 2007. Web.

Pike, Ruth. "Penal Servitude in Early Modern Spain." *The Library of Iberian Resources Online*. N.d. 1 August 2014. Web.

Rakow, Lana F. "Feminist Approaches to Popular Culture: Giving Patriarchy its Due." *Cultural Theory and Popular Culture: A Reader*. Ed. John Storey. 2nd ed. Athens: The U of Georgia P, 1998. 275–91.

Reddy, Maureen T. *Sisters in Crime: Feminism and the Crime Novel*. New York: Continuum, 1988.

Reynolds, Laura. "The Meaning Behind Cypress Trees." *GardenGuides.com*. N.d. 4 October 2014. Web.

Riera, Carme. *El verano del inglés*. Madrid: Alfaguara, 2006.

Rubio, Jesús. "Reyes Calderón y el esfuerzo por (con)sentir." *Diario de Navarra* 19 noviembre 2010: 60. 1 October 2014. Web.

Rutledge, Tracy. *The Spanish Female Detective: A Study of Petra Delicado and the Evolution of a Professional Sleuth*. Diss. Texas Tech U. 2006.

Sanfermines.net. 30 July 2014. Web.

Schoenberg, Thomas J. and Lawrence J. Trudeau. "Food in Literature – Introduction." *Twentieth-Century Literary Criticism.* Ed. Thomas J. Schoenberg and Lawrence J. Trudeau. Vol. 114. Gale Cengage, 2006. *eNotes.com.* 9 March 2012. Web.

School of Humanities and Social Sciences. "La decana de la Facultad de Económicas señala que existen 'luces y sombras' en la situación de la mujer actual." *Universidad de Navarra.* 28 abril 2010. 13 February 2014. Web.

Secretaría General de Instituciones Penitenciarias. N.d. 23 February 2012. Web.

Stegmeier, Ion. "Reyes Calderón vuelve a la intriga con la juez MacHor y el inspector Iturri." *Diario de Navarra* 8 septiembre 2010. 13 February 2012. Web.

Storey, John. *An Introduction to Cultural Theory and Popular Culture.* 2nd ed. Athens: The U of Georgia P, 1998.

Tasker, Yvonne and Diane Negra, ed. "In Focus: Postfeminism and Contemporary Media Studies." *Cinema Journal* 44.2 (2005): 107–10.

Tribunal Constitucional de España. N.d. 11 July 2014. Web.

Ugarte, Michael. "Madrid." *Iberian Cities.* Ed. Joan Ramon Resina. New York: Routledge, 2001. 93–121.

"24 Horas con Reyes Calderón." *Universidad de Navarra.* 29 enero 2011. 13 February 2012. Web.

Index